INVISIBLE FOUNDERS

INVISIBLE FOUNDERS

How Two Centuries of African American Families
Transformed a Plantation into a College

Lynn Rainville

berghahn
NEW YORK · OXFORD
www.berghahnbooks.com

First published in 2019 by

Berghahn Books

www.berghahnbooks.com

© 2019, 2022 Lynn Rainville
First paperback edition published in 2022

Library of Congress Cataloging-in-Publication Data

Names: Rainville, Lynn, author.
Title: Invisible Founders: How Two Centuries of African American Families
    Transformed a Plantation into a College / Lynn Rainville.
Description: New York: Berghahn Books, 2019. | Includes bibliographical
    references and index.
Identifiers: LCCN 2019008851 (print) | LCCN 2019011095 (ebook) |
    ISBN 9781789202328 (ebook) | ISBN 9781789202311 (hardback: alk. paper)
Subjects: LCSH: Sweet Briar College--History. | African Americans—
    Virginia—Sweet Briar—History. | Slaves—Virginia—Sweet Briar—History.
    | Women's colleges—Virginia—Sweet Briar—History.
Classification: LCC LD7251.S92 (ebook) | LCC LD7251.S92 R34 2019 (print) |
    DDC 378.755/496—dc23
LC record available at https://lccn.loc.gov/2019008851

British Library Cataloguing in Publication Data

A catalogue record for this book is available from the British Library

ISBN 978-1-78920-231-1 hardback
ISBN 978-1-80073-444-9 paperback
ISBN 978-1-78920-232-8 ebook

Contents

❧ Illustrations

Figure 0.1. A groundskeeper standing in front of Sweet Briar House (the former plantation mansion). A promotional postcard for the college, circa 1906. Sweet Briar College Library Archives.

✺ Preface

The first time I saw this hand-colored photograph, the only thing that registered was the color pink. In most photographs, Sweet Briar House, referred to as the Administration Building on the card, is yellow. The image is undated but was likely a promotional postcard from 1906, the year Sweet Briar College opened to educate "white women." I wondered whether the house had indeed been painted pink to honor the school colors (pink and green) or whether the artist was taking liberties.

It was only when I looked more closely that I noticed a person looking out from behind one of the boxwood hedges: a black man, wearing red pants and a bright yellow top. In front of a nearby hedge is a wheelbarrow, indicating that this man may be the groundskeeper. Was he posed as part of the original image, or—given the length of time it took to set up and expose an early twentieth-century shot—did he wander into the frame without the photographer's knowledge? Or is this image doctored by an artist who added the man and his wheelbarrow to promote a nostalgic image of an historic plantation? Although we'll never know the answers to these questions, the postcard struck me as a potent visual metaphor for African American heritage at Sweet Briar: hidden in plain sight, and usually ignored and uncredited.

Invisible Founders is the record of a history unknown not only to Americans born in the North like me, but even to the Southerners on whose land it unfolded. Although the lives of the white plantation owners and college founders are recorded in minute detail, the more than one thousand African and Native Americans who have lived and worked at Sweet Briar over the past two centuries appear only as footnotes.

The book is based on my literal and metaphorical excavations at Sweet Briar College, a historic jewel nestled within three thousand acres of Virginia pastures and forests, with the plantation house and a slave cabin still standing at the center of campus. As an archaeologist, I have surveyed large swaths of the rural campus, uncovering the ruins of everyday life from past centuries and studying the artifacts recovered from on-campus excavations. As a public historian, I have endeavored to share my archival and ethnographic research with a wide audience through online databases, social media, and public lectures. In the process, I uncovered the untold stories of one of the only institutions of higher education that grew out of an antebellum plantation.

Over the past eighteen years, I have sought to steer the college toward, and lead it through, the difficult process of confronting Sweet Briar's racist past. In collaboration with local descendants, like-minded colleagues, and cohorts of undergraduate students, I have worked to bring to light the slavery-era roots that the college attempted to suppress for a century. The slave cemetery, long used as part of a riding path, was rededicated in 2003 with an official ceremony and a community ritual led by descendants of those who rest there. We have begun to acknowledge individual African Americans who made significant contributions to the plantation and college: the invisible founders.

It is my hope that this work will draw attention not only to those who contributed in the past but also to those who continue to make the college what it is today. After researching several dozen family lineages for this book, I estimate that about 30 percent of nonwhite hourly wage earners at Sweet Briar are descended from the local antebellum slave community. Most can trace generations of family members who have worked at Sweet Briar, either as employees or as slaves. The idyllic campus of today was built by the labor of their ancestors, and their stories follow the arc of American history. Drawing from census records, wills, photographs, archaeological evidence, oral interviews with descendants, and other documents, *Invisible Founders* collects, for the first time, the stories of these hitherto overlooked slaves, servants, and college employees. I begin each chapter with an example of an obituary, letter, or legal document—one of the countless examples I reviewed while writing this book—and proceed to contextualize each document, since no single source can tell a complete story. The narrative arc of the book follows the same process of reviewing multiple lines of evidence to tell the rest of the story.

This book illuminates the contributions of African Americans to the success of a thriving plantation while highlighting the everyday struggles of black Americans during slavery and the Jim Crow era. It reveals how African American labor enabled the plantation's transformation into a private women's college and tells the story of how a college founded by and for white women did not integrate its student body until more than a decade after *Brown v. Board of Education*. In the process, *Invisible Founders* challenges our ideas of what a college "founder" is, restoring African American narratives to their deserved and central place in the story of a single institution—one that serves as a microcosm of the American South.

✿ Acknowledgments

I arrived at Sweet Briar College in the fall of 2001 having recently completed a PhD that focused on Mesopotamian households. I knew very little about Southern history and even less about the everyday lives of enslaved families. Through a series of unexpected circumstances, I accepted a position teaching anthropology and archaeology at a women's college that was originally an antebellum plantation. I was interested in integrating local history into my classes. With that goal in mind, I began to explore my new surroundings, which included the former "big house" (plantation mansion), a preserved slave cabin, and a cemetery used by enslaved families. During my explorations, I was very fortunate to meet and learn from dozens of college employees. Later, I realized that many of them were descended from the enslaved community at Sweet Briar.

I am also grateful to several of my colleagues who shared my interest in studying Sweet Briar's complicated past, especially Dr. Judith Evans-Grubbs (then a professor of classics), Dr. Rebecca Ambers (then an assistant professor of environmental science), and Dr. Christian Carr (then the director of the museum and gallery). College librarians have also helped me locate historic photographs and papers, over the past eighteen years, including Katie Glaeser, Liz Kent Léon, and Lisa Johnston. Local historians assisted me with this research, including Octavia Starbucks (director of the Amherst County Museum and Historical Society), Sandi Esposito (community historian), and Joe Stinnett (former newspaper editor and local historian). Several regional partners assisted in this research: Carla Whitfield (then superintendent of Booker T. Washington National Monument) and John Whitfield (professional genealogist) led an oral history workshop with staff members; Bob Vernon (local historian) contributed countless hours to uncover overlooked courthouse documents; Sam Towler (local historian and legal assistant) answered questions about central Virginian slave owners; and Jack LaViolette worked as a research assistant.

After I taught for seven years at Sweet Briar, President Betsy Muhlenfeld appointed me as director of the Tusculum Institute, dedicated to the study and promotion of historic preservation and local history. This appointment, in 2008, gave me more time to dedicate to this project. Over the next several years, dozens of descendants of the enslaved community provided me with insights and guidance in this research. Most of these individuals are mentioned in this book, but I wanted to recognize some of the people who went out of their way to work with me on researching and sharing their family histories, including Jasper "Eddie" Fletcher, Bethany Pace, Annette Anderson, Barbara Rose Page, Audrey Lopez, Dorothy Sales, Shirley Reid, and Barbara Reid. In particular, Crystal Rosson (the great-granddaughter of Sterling Jones) has been an invaluable research partner since 2010, when she first contacted me about her work to uncover more information about her family tree. I also enjoyed working with the descendants of a nineteenth-century couple, James and Lavinia Fletcher, who held three of their Fletcher family reunions at Sweet Briar College, in 2008, 2010, and 2015.

In the fall of 2017, I was honored to present this research alongside several descendants at an annual event sponsored by the international consortium Universities Studying Slavery. That year, the University of Virginia sponsored the event, and I joined Dr. Annette Anderson, Bethany Pace, and Crystal Rosson, who presented on the Fletcher and Jones family connections to Sweet Briar.

I am indebted to several funding agencies for supporting my research between 2001 and 2018. These institutions include the Virginia Foundation for the Humanities (recently renamed Virginia Humanities), the National Trust for Historic Preservation, the Roller-Bottimore Foundation, the Deupree Family Foundation, and a handful of internal Sweet Briar College grants. I am also grateful to the National Endowment for the Humanities for a Digital Humanities Start-Up Grant that laid the groundwork for my study of the gravestones of many of the individuals discussed in this book. As always, Kathleen Placidi, the grants officer at Sweet Briar, was instrumental in my success at raising funds to support this research.

I am very grateful to the Virginia Humanities (2016–2017) and the Virginia Center for Creative Arts (two weeks in 2016 and 2018) for offering me residencies to work on this book.

I extremely grateful to a handful of friends and colleagues who read a draft of this manuscript: Dr. Karol Lawson provided her insight into Sweet Briar history; Ellen Bowyer read through the manuscript and improved the style and content; Dr. Jeffrey Hantman reviewed my discussion of native Virginian Indians; and two anonymous reviewers improved the book with their valuable input. Minal Hajratwala offered an invaluable writer's workshop and subsequently helped me organize some of the historic accounts and oral histories into more coherent narratives. Carolyn Cades provided significant editing assistance in the last stages of this project.

My father read and commented on an earlier draft, adding his feedback to this book as he has for each of my four previous ones. I am fortunate to have very supportive parents, a spouse, and two children who patiently withstood the countless hours when I was more focused on the past than the present.

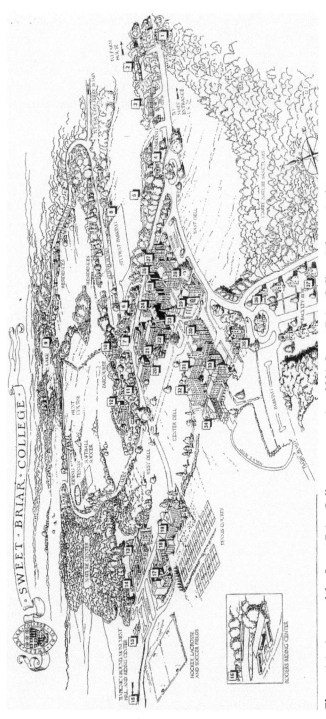

Figure 1.1. A map of the Sweet Briar College campus, circa 2001. Sweet Briar College Library Archives.

INVISIBLE WORKERS

There is no greater agony than bearing an untold story inside you.
— Zora Neal Hurston

Like many institutions, Sweet Briar College has its fair share of "founder narratives." The stories the Sweet Briar community knows and shares is one of the most important elements in crafting an identity for Sweet Briar College—past, present, and future. For a century, many of these stories have been curated by a relatively small group of people within the Sweet Briar community; most of the documented protagonists have been related to Indiana Fletcher Williams and her immediate family. But if you peel back the layers of memories and myths, you find that many other voices have been left out of these ideologically driven stories. When I first arrived at Sweet Briar, the standard campus tour presented this simplified version of college history. The tour guide would proudly point out that Indiana inherited Sweetbrier Plantation from her father, Elijah Fletcher, and used her business acumen to save $100,000 and manage thousands of acres. Then the guide would mention the tragic fact that Indiana lost both her daughter and her husband within the span of four years. As she worked through her grief, she decided to create an institution of higher education for women to exist "in perpetuity." As the student guide concluded her historic overview, she would point out that the president of Sweet Briar College still lives in the old plantation house.

At the end of the tour, the guide would pass out brightly colored brochures designed to highlight this sanitized version of events. During my first week as an adjunct professor at Sweet Briar College, I came across a geographic corollary to this story: the map shown in Figure 1.1. In this version, student parking spaces were highlighted in different colors. Above and beyond the permissible parking areas, the features on the map were part of a more widely used guide that indicated significant sites on campus. This map emphasized Sweet Briar's bucolic and historic campus, the century-old Ralph Adams Cram buildings, the abundant and diverse trees, the scenic dells and open fields, dozens of miles of hiking trails, and countless repurposed agricultural features (historic hay barns, horse stables, old wheat fields, etc.) that were designed to meet the needs of the equestrian, nature-loving students who paid tens of thousands of dollars to attend this private Virginia college. One of the most symbolically important sites, the Monument Hill cemetery, where the white founding family was buried, was located just off the map. Despite its geographic distance from the central sites on the map, it was included on the far left with the tagline "To Picnic Ground, Monument Hill, and Riding Center." The last site received its own hand-drawn inset.

Noticeably absent from this map were any sites related to African Americans and their history and contributions to the college. When I arrived at Sweet Briar in 2001, I knew very little about Southern history or the multitude of features commonly found on an antebellum plantation. Not until I began to explore the outdoor laboratory I would soon be using in my archaeology classes did I became adept at peeling away the many layers of this rich landscape and asking pertinent questions. A careful study of the built environment revealed the elements of Sweet Briar's history that were commonly missing on maps and in tours.

One of the first sites I studied in depth was the slave cemetery. Coincidentally, when I arrived at the college, a recently retired staff member was looking for someone to investigate his hunch about the location of an antebellum burial ground for the enslaved population at the former Sweetbrier Plantation.[1] Following up on this oral history, I eventually studied three dozen other slave cemeteries in central Virginia to contextualize the patterning of the burial ground at Sweet Briar.[2] Over the next two years, I worked with an administrator to locate the site, delineate its boundaries and map the graves, and find descendants who could provide information about the individuals buried within this sacred site. On the 2001 map shown previously (Figure 1.1), the slave cemetery is not identified by name, although a careful study of the geographical spot on the map reveals three lone trees. Perhaps the mapmaker had heard the unconfirmed rumors that there was a graveyard in that vicinity and tried to indicate this in a subtle way.

Another critical site was omitted from this 2001 map. While indicating the old "big house" (#12, labeled Sweet Briar House) and the former overseer's house (#11, labeled Mary Clark Rogers Garden Cottage), the third structure in what is actually a trio of buildings was not represented at all. There, behind the antebellum big house, stands the only surviving antebellum home for enslaved laborers. As with most Southern plantations, some of these cabins were built in proximity to the owner's home so that enslaved people could be easily summoned to work in the mansion and carefully supervised at all other times. At Sweet Briar, the surviving slave cabin stands immediately adjacent to an old sunken roadbed that once connected these living quarters to the burial ground of the enslaved families.

Locating and researching these sites became a focus of my research for almost two decades. After teaching archaeology and anthropology courses for seven years, Sweet Briar College President Betsy Muhlenfeld offered me the opportunity to direct an institute for public history in 2008. We called it the Tusculum Institute in recognition of another site that was critical for understanding Sweet Briar's history and that of the enslaved families: the plantation where Indiana Fletcher Williams's mother, Maria Antoinette Crawford, was born and raised. Once located about eight miles north of Sweetbrier Plantation, the college purchased this mid-eighteenth-century structure with the intention of rebuilding it on campus and repurposing it for classrooms and faculty offices. As my research progressed, I realized that the enslaved African American community had been forcibly split between Sweetbrier and Tusculum. To understand this group fully, I would need to study the history of both plantations.

By failing to research and highlight the existence of these antebellum sites, Sweet Briar College was missing an important opportunity to engage its students and community members in a dialogue about its racialized landscape. My efforts to (re)locate these places and host events and rituals in and around them have been a critical step in engaging the nearby community and more distantly dispersed descendants of the enslaved population. The college campus can be imagined as a large museum, with exhibitions that range from historic landscapes to old buildings, from artifactual mementos to sacred spaces. Curating the significant sites on our grounds, especially when the land was once an antebellum plantation and home to enslaved laborers, requires attention and care. Vivian Nun Halloran challenges museum personnel to answer the following question: "Can public displays of artifacts and works of art related to slavery contribute to a sense of community-wide reconciliation instead of reinforcing the impulse to assign blame?"[3] A similar question could be posed to colleges and universities that are built in spaces once determined by slavery: How can institutions of higher education integrate the study of their on-campus, antebellum sites into their curricula while engaging descendants and the local community? I intend to illustrate some methods of deciphering these archaeological landscapes and of learning more about their meaning from descendant communities.

The National Trust for Historic Preservation (NTHP) highlighted this perspective with its "sites of conscience" initiative, recognizing that outdoor spaces and the built environment evoke powerful emotions. To demonstrate the importance of preserving a diverse segment of historic places, the NTHP promoted spaces where brave individuals took a stand for their beliefs. These powerful places include sites associated with the civil right movement, World War II Japanese American internment camps in California, and slave markets in the American South.[4] These include mundane and quotidian spaces such as a schoolyard once segregated by race or a secondary entrance for "nonwhites" on a local business. Also included are dilapidated 150-year-old buildings, spread across the rural landscape. These were the institutions and homes created by freed African Americans in the tumultuous period after the Civil War, as the South fought to regain admittance to the Union, representation in Congress, and its economic vitality. Such sites reveal the struggles and successes of the formerly enslaved as they built new lives for themselves. Sometimes we can use these places as pins in a geographical map of antebellum social and familial ties, which survived and thrived after the end of slavery.

The founder of the Texas Freedom Colonies Project, Andrea Roberts, has argued for an even stronger connection between historic preservation and social justice. She explains that the field of preservation is "a distinct set of theories and a way of looking at the world that acknowledges agency and power." As such, preservation practitioners can wield their skills and pitch arguments in a range of ways, from conservative to cutting edge or from passive to forward thinking. She hopes preservationists will seek "to authentically engage with social justice [by addressing] both the institutions that perpetuate identity-based inequities and [by resisting] such systems." She ends her commentary with suggestions about how to convert historic preservation into "social justice practice." I have incorporated many of these approaches into my study of slavery at Sweet Briar. Roberts recommends embracing experts outside the academy; listening to "women of color and others living at 'intersections'" to better understand the discrimination these groups have faced; recognizing links between the global and the local; acknowledging "the relationship between environmental protection, minority land dispossession, sacred commons, and resource extraction"; making yourself accessible to social justice advocates; and embracing "difficult and dark heritage." Finally, she recognizes that, for some communities, the preservation of structures, a traditional historic preservation approach, is not the end goal. Preservation may also focus on "community survival, empowerment, and identity."[5]

At Sweet Briar, one of the most important examples of a place that expands the traditional historic narrative is the small wooden structure that stands just behind the plantation house. Although the "slave cabin" wasn't indicated on the 2001 map, either by number or in the sketch itself, the structure was given a name: the Farm Tool Museum. In the 1980s and 1990s, the founder of Sweet Briar Museum, Ann Marshall Whitley (a Sweet Briar alumna from the class of 1947), had used this centrally located site to display several hundred agricultural artifacts. Some were from Sweet Briar Plantation, while many others had been purchased at local antique stores in an effort to more comprehensively illustrate Amherst County's rich farming tradition.

On my first visit to this one-room structure, I struggled to squeeze between hundreds of artifacts including plows, hatchets, a rocking chair, a horse blanket, and even an iron forge jammed into the corner. Later, after a newly appointed museum director, Karol Lawson, and a student intern, Sarah O'Brien (class of 2013), cataloged more than three hundred artifacts, we learned that only one was an antebellum artifact, and even it had a dubious provenance: a pair of "slave bracelets" that hung over the mantle.[6] There was no explanation provided other than an old typed label that hung underneath the pewter-colored circlets. When I saw the tag, I immediately assumed "bracelet" was a euphemism for shackle. The two strands of metal had been curved into mismatching circles. The larger "bracelet" had a clasp that resembled the head of a lizard or snake, an oddly decorative feature for such a reprehensible piece of equipment. Indeed, the bracelets were too delicate to serve as shackles and lacked the necessary appendage to connect the chain that would have restricted the movement of the hands or feet of an enslaved person. As strange as it appeared, they really were bracelets, though a person with no money was unlikely to have owned such a precious item. We never solved the mystery of whose bracelets they were or how they had come to be placed in an agricultural exhibit.

After a decade of evaluating the structure and its history, I proposed a new use for the cabin: a small museum dedicated to African American heritage at Sweet Briar. I applied for funding from the Virginia Foundation for the Humanities, pulled together a committee of on- and off-campus experts, and, with input from descendants, designed a series of illustrated panels for the museum walls. Interestingly, several offices on campus were still reluctant to call it a slave cabin. Today, the structure goes by several names in formal maps and college literature, with descriptions ranging from its original function, "slave cabin," to the more euphemistic "nineteenth-century cabin," to what the old-timers still call the Farm Tool Museum, to sometimes, simply, "cabin."

In addition to installing the exhibition, I wanted this structure to be relevant to visitors on and off campus. Toward this end, I hosted two singular events at the cabin. The first was a sleepover led by the heritage preservationist Joseph McGill, the founder of the Slave Dwelling Project, who has dedicated his career to sleeping overnight in historic slave dwellings to ensure their preservation. McGill designs his sleepovers to highlight the lives of the enslaved families who lived in these cramped cabins, and travels the country spending the night in these fast disappearing structures. For almost a century, no one had slept in the cabin at Sweet Briar. But if you had visited it one cold night in October 2012, you would have been surprised to see lights and hear voices coming from its interior. That night, eight of us joined him, including Crystal Rosson—the great-granddaughter of the cabin's last resident, Sterling Jones (Figure 1.2).

As we settled in for the evening, I passed around a photograph of Sterling Jones and several of his children. The picture was taken a year after he and his family had moved out of the cabin. I shared some stories about Sterling and his multiple decades of service to the college. Then, Toni Battle, a social justice activist and researcher, led the nine

Figure 1.2. The next morning after sleeping in the Sweet Briar slave cabin. *Left to right:* Joseph McGill, Crystal Rosson, and Toni Renee Battle. Photograph by Lynn Rainville, 7 October 2012.

of us in a ritual. On top of the fireplace, she had created an ancestor shrine, which contained some artifacts of personal importance along with photographs of her family and one of the Joneses. We stood in a circle and called out words of a blessing in three languages: a Native American language, a West African language, and Hebrew. As we called out "aho, ashe, amen," Battle dipped her fingers into a bowl of water and blessed each name. She guided us first to call out the names of enslaved individuals at Sweet Briar and then to share the names of our own ancestors.

After the ritual, we shared stories and reactions to learning more about Sweet Briar's invisible history and that of other enslaved communities. McGill spends some of his time as a Civil War reenactor, wearing the uniform of an all-black unit from Massachusetts. Battle, too, has spent years researching her relatives, and shared some of her insights into the past lives of black families. Rosson, overcome with emotion, was quiet for most of the evening. She, too, was an expert in her family history, and now she was sleeping in her ancestors' home.

Moved by the powerful ritual of the sleepover, I decided to try a daytime event that could be accessible to more people. Later that fall, I invited a nationally known food historian to campus to break bread with the Sweet Briar community. To connect us with the history, Leni Sorensen led us in making the meal, using only nineteenth-century tools and techniques. Originally, we had planned to cook in the hearth within the former slave cabin, but the flue hadn't been cleaned in years, so we opted for a safer option: outdoor cooking with a generous amount of sand thrown down to protect the grass.

We started early in the morning and were surprised to be joined by students from a nearby technical college, the Buckingham County Career and Technical Center culinary arts program. These aspiring chefs chopped, diced, and quickly learned there are few safety features on boiling-hot cast iron pots. Other participants helped mix the batter for the corn bread and laid spoon-shaped dollops onto a hot griddle. Around noon, Sorensen gave a brief lecture on historic cookbooks and the ingredients that were available to African American cooks in the nineteenth century. It took more than two hours to prepare a relatively simple meal of corn pone, collard greens, sweet potato, and chicken.

The slave cabin stands several dozen yards from the Sweet Briar College Museum. Despite its small size, Sweet Briar has a first-rate museum. For decades, museum directors, aided by a curatorial assistant and students, have regularly curated exhibitions about a wide range of college-related topics. Because of public interest and the availability of artifacts, many of these topics have focused on the lives of Indiana and her family members. A smaller number of exhibitions have addressed Sweet Briar's decision to integrate the student population. With more funding and staff support, the museum would be able to produce more exhibitions about African and Native American history at Sweet Briar, although this would require some creativity because of the paucity of antebellum and prehistoric artifacts that have been preserved.

The preserved 1840s cabin presented a clear opportunity for interpretation, preservation, and the installation of an exhibition. It was far more complicated to decide how to locate and commemorate the dozens of other sites that were not well preserved and/or not yet rediscovered. For example, old letters mention the existence of gardens that were tended by enslaved families; the horticultural evidence for these small-scale efforts to provide additional food is long gone. Elijah Fletcher also mentioned multiple barns, each of which served as a site where enslaved people worked. The "historic" barns that remain standing today at the college date to the twentieth century. The search for other antebellum clues and ruins is ongoing, and I have spent years looking for further material evidence of the enslaved antebellum community and their postwar descendants.

When I first arrived on campus in 2001, I reviewed the artifacts unearthed by several of my colleagues—Amber Bennett, Claudia Chang, and Perry Tourtellotte—during on-campus excavations in the 1980s and 1990s. This work was part of classroom exercises, and final reports were never written. Without such summaries, it is difficult to determine whether the unearthed small pieces of pottery and metal were used by enslaved laborers, white workers, or even by the Fletchers themselves. Determining the ethnicity of an individual or group from the artifacts they used is often difficult. A decade later, with support from a National Endowment for the Humanities grant, I hired an archaeologist to work with students to excavate a mysterious settlement deep in the woods. Ravaged by time, the only remaining features were one- and two-stone-high foundations. They were challenging to interpret because they ranged in size from small enough to be an outhouse or storage shed to larger, irregular homes or perhaps communal buildings. In the absence of other historic records or remembrances, it was impossible to prove the ethnicity of the past inhabitants. The ruins suggested that the community was poor and preindustrial. Even with a rough date of the early nineteenth century, it was not possible to determine conclusively whether this was a group of Indians, freed blacks, enslaved families, or even white immigrants. Future large-scale excavations on campus—particularly around the standing slave cabin—as well as aboveground surveys, could shed light on as yet undiscovered antebellum structures.

To supplement the excavations of the settlement, I consulted oral histories and photographs to try to recover the history of these overlooked landscapes. As was often the case in researching this book, some of my best leads came from conversations with living descendants or quotes from elders who had long since passed. One of the most interesting accounts in the latter category comes from Nannie Cashwell Christian, an African American woman born two decades after slavery had ended who cooked for Indiana. She recalled that there were four rows of antebellum cabins on the property before the college was built. Correlating her geographical references with modern-day features, I discovered that one row was located on what is currently Elijah Road (between the old Boxwood Inn, currently the Alumnae Relations and Development Office, and the faculty home called Red Top); one was on a no longer extant road that led directly from the big house toward the slave cemetery; another row was more distant, near a now-defunct horse stable; and the last row of cabins was across the present highway, near another plantation called Mt. San Angelo. It is difficult to determine who lived in each of these structures, but one was home to the same George Sales[7] who, back in the 1930s, had been lauded for having "a good ear for melody and a knack for picking up tunes," playing multiple instruments, and entertaining dancers since "plantation days."[8] Sales was born during Reconstruction, in 1874, on or near Sweet Briar Plantation. He and his wife, Martha, married around 1890 and lived near campus for decades.[9] During much of that time, Sales was a teamster and eventually became the stable boss at Sweet Briar. In 1918, he registered for the Selective Service System, but it is unclear whether he ever experienced combat.[10] He and Martha had four children, including a set of twins. Together, this married couple worked for Sweet Briar for decades.

After reading Nannie Cashwell Christian's description of these old cabins, I went in search of photographic evidence. While only a handful of college photographers set out to deliberately photograph African and Native American employees, there were hundreds of photographs taken of the beautiful landscape. Surely, somewhere in these snapshots, there would be an unintentional record of some of these homes, several of which were still standing in the 1930s. After many hours of searching, I found several tantalizing clues. The first was a blurry roofline located just outside the ornamental boxwood hedges that surrounded Sweet Briar House, found in the backgrounds of May Day photographs of Sweet Briar students in white gowns dancing through the glade. To-day, that location is a flattened hockey field, but once it would have been conveniently situated near the Fletcher homestead. I could just barely see the roof of the structure in the photographs but was unable to ascertain the size or style of the building.

One day in September 2015, I sat in the alumnae office, waiting for a meeting to begin. As a faculty member, I had rarely entered this build-ing. While waiting, I glanced through the memorabilia that covered the walls and bookcases, and noticed a small watercolor depicting a wooden structure. I immediately recognized the roofline. To confirm my assessment, I turned it over and read the identification "Sweet Briar slave cabin," painted in the hand of a student from the class of 1939. Here was visual confirmation of at least one of the cabins that had once stood in close proximity to Sweet Briar House. On later visits to the college archives, I continued to search the extensive but uncat-alogued collection of old campus photographs. Eventually, I found a few more clues about the homes of black workers. In one 1940s shot, a student stood alongside her horse. Two wooden homes were visi-ble in the background. They had roughly constructed porches, leaning chimneys, and no panes in the open-air windows. No residents could be seen.

In a second photo, dated around 1913, a young African American woman stood in front of a similar three-room home holding a chubby and grumpy baby (Figure 1.3). Four older children stood at her side, holding two kittens. It wasn't clear that she was the mother; she may

Figure 1.3. Unidentified siblings standing in front of their home on the Sweet Briar College campus, circa 1913. Sweet Briar College Library Archives.

have been the oldest sibling, taking care of her brothers and sisters while her parents worked. While it is difficult to pin down the location of this home, the image was pasted into a scrapbook of college photos compiled by a Sweet Briar instructor, so it stands to reason that the home was on or near the campus. This particular house is in better repair than the homes shown near the stables. There are herbs drying on the shaded porch, glass in the windows, a baby carriage, a shingled roof, well-maintained brick supports (to level the home and prevent flooding), and a dog standing off to the side.

My forensic sleuthing for photograph documentation continues, but I have some clues regarding where to look next if faculty or students pursue on-campus excavations in the future. My next challenge is how best to share these initial pieces of information with descendants, the university community, and Amherst County residents. I have created Tumblr blogs, a Pinterest board, and a website, which have enabled me to reach dozens of descendants and community members who have added to our understanding of African American families at Sweet Briar. Many of their insights, family lore, and preserved family papers serve as the foundation for the story lines in this book.

In the future, I hope to link some of this genealogical and geographical information to sites such as Ancestry.com and FamilySearch.org, often the first sources of information for contemporary descendants. This would involve researching and creating family trees for dozens and dozens of families, and may be one of the next stages of community outreach if there is continued support for this work at Sweet Briar. Meanwhile, I continue to spread the word about this research through Facebook groups and listservs in an effort to reach as many descendants as possible. Some of these families probably have photographs, Bibles, and oral stories that would enhance our understanding of their relatives' contributions to building and running Sweet Briar.

Since 2001, I have attempted to summarize the oral and historical information about some of these historic sites through brochures, maps, signs, tours, and illustrated essays. As an archaeologist, I was most comfortable analyzing the material culture associated with Sweet Briar's nineteenth-century history. But, time and time again, I turned to ethnographic techniques to elicit stories from members of the community. After years of collecting these oral memories, I realized that hundreds of unwritten biographies needed to be collected to fully understand the origins and growth of Sweetbrier Plantation and its successor, Sweet Briar College. Fortunately, my efforts to collect these biographies have corresponded with a rapidly increasing interest in black history and genealogy.

As evidenced by Henry Louis Gates Jr.'s popular documentary television series *Finding Your Roots* (2012–), genealogy is a compelling topic, and more and more authors are using family stories as the basis for writing captivating anthropologically and historically grounded books. One of the earliest examples of this genre was Alex Haley's best-selling book *Roots* (1976) and the subsequent nationwide interest in the accompanying television miniseries. Although Haley took some artistic liberties with his family's story, the broad outlines of the narrative demonstrated the crucial role of African Americans in US history. More recently, scholars such as Lawrence P. Jackson have outlined the complex archival trail required to trace the lives of freed African Americans after the Civil War. Jackson is one of a small but growing group of scholars who combine their professional training with their family histories to reveal the struggles of these Afro-Virginians.[11]

A celebrity example of this type of successful genealogical sleuthing illustrates the importance of these discoveries at both the private and public level. Inspired by her status as First Lady of the United States, professional genealogists began to research Michelle Obama's ancestry. They learned that Obama's great-great-great-grandmother was born enslaved in 1844 on a South Carolina plantation. Described by her owner as simply "the negro girl Melvinia," she was sold away from her family in 1852 and sent to Georgia, where a white man raped her. Their biracial son, Dolphus Shields, spent his adult years in Alabama, where he and his mother rejoined friends and relatives who had been separated during slavery.[12] As Rachel Swarns explained in the *New York Times*, "The discovery of this unexpected family tie between the nation's most prominent black woman and a white, silver-haired grandmother from the Atlanta suburbs underscores the entangled histories and racial intermingling that continue to bind countless American families more than 140 years after the Civil War."

As with many of the Sweet Briar families, Obama had heard rumors of her ancestry but did not have any solid leads. For many families, the trauma of slavery was so painful and shameful that it was rarely discussed. Just as genealogical information can be passed down from generation to generation, the conspicuous erasure of data can also continue. Some relatives, both white and black, may be curious to learn more, while others remain reluctant. One of Shields's descendants observed, "I don't think there's going to be a Kumbaya moment here." That same individual spoke on the condition of anonymity, "fearful that the ancestral ties to slavery might besmirch the family name."[13] Obama's genealogical tree isn't the only one containing secrets. At Sweet Briar, I uncovered evidence of interracial marriages (a century or more before it was legal in Virginia), illegitimate children, adopted children, and half-siblings left off family trees. But I also gained remarkable insight into the strength of family bonds, the determination of black parents to provide an education for their children, and some interesting revelations about Sweet Briar's mythical founding stories.

When we integrate the often-siloed fields of genealogy and history, we are able to recover more information about the lives of African Americans in Virginia. By reviewing only aggregate data such as the percentage of enslaved people per state or the number of slaves listed in a plantation owner's will, we overlook the humanity and complexities of the families who lived through generations of slavery. Their struggles to retain their agency during this period, and their exceptional efforts to gain political, social, and educational rights in the decades after emancipation, are the heart of the story. And efforts to tell these stories result in rich accounts of black culture.[14] Sam White, a black man born free in Prince Edward County, lived through the American Revolution and the Civil War, while his own circumstances ranged from slavery to freedom, from penury to becoming a revered member of the Farmville Baptist Church, and from landlessness to purchasing acreage as a founding member of the Israel Hill community.[15] The moving story of the multigenerational black and white Hairston families reveals the impact of slavery, Reconstruction, Jim Crow, and the civil rights movement on interconnected individuals in Virginia and North Carolina.[16]

These compelling narratives demonstrate that black lives of the past do matter, even if textbooks routinely erase these individuals, substituting names with terms like "slave" or "freedman." Accurate histories detail the everyday lives of parents who struggled to keep their families together despite Virginia statutes intended to limit the autonomy of African American men, women, and children. The institution of slavery disrupted families, even in the case of children who were born in the late nineteenth century, decades after the end of the Civil War. When these individuals died in the 1930s and 1940s, their survivors were often unable to identify the "father/mother of the deceased" on state-mandated death certificates. Through careful study of archival documents, federal records, and ethnographic interviews, the complexity and dignity of these lives can be restored.

While focusing on the hidden histories of the built environment at Sweet Briar, I had been working alongside dozens of individuals who were directly descended from the enslaved community. One day's interactions serve to illustrate this complicated connection between the present and the past. In 2015, I planned a multiday retreat to Sweet Briar College to make some progress on this manuscript, arranging a three-night stay at the college's Florence Elston Inn. This indulgence allowed me to walk the campus paths at night and see the sunrise over the big house, perceiving the landscape continuously as all the past black and white inhabitants did on a daily basis, but as I had rarely experienced during my fifteen years of employment at Sweet Briar. I had moved in with the "subjects" of my ethnohistoric research for ninety-six hours. I scouted out good places to sit and work in the library, found the "F 232's" (the Dewey decimal equivalent of Amherst's local history library), and set up shop.

First, I checked into the on-campus inn. Built in the 1980s, many of the rooms retained their Laura Ashley–themed furnishings; my room looked as if a floral bouquet had exploded and imprinted itself on every cushion, bed sheet, and couch in sight. This would be my research base. Not five minutes after checking in, I heard from behind me, "Welcome, sugar." A thin, sprightly African American woman in her sixties was walking past. Normally, I am more discreet about my research interests, but you can imagine my sense of serendipity, having just arrived to undertake a major research trip about African Americans who have worked at Sweet Briar.

"Hi." I hazarded an obvious question: "Do you work here?"

"Indeed, I do. I'm Barbara."

"Do you mind if I ask your surname?" I asked hesitantly, aware of the intrusion.

"Dixon."

Scrambling through my mental Rolodex, I reviewed photographs and records associated with the Dixon family. Nothing was coming immediately to mind, so I asked the unavoidable follow-up: "What was your maiden name?"

"Reid, honey," she obliged.

"Any relation to Shirley Reid?"

"She's kin, but not directly."

"What was your father's name?" I might as well extend my probing to identify her relatives.

"John. John Reid. He worked for the college too."

We established she had worked for the college for thirty-six years, with a break of a dozen years to live in Richmond "with a male friend," and then returned to Sweet Briar, where she had worked for the past six years. She expressed relief that the college had stayed open after the spring of 2015 debacle when administrators had tried to close the school, adding, "Sweet Briar has always been good to me."

To save myself time later (I already knew I'd be jumping on Ancestry. com as soon as I got to my room to find out how her family tree intersected those I already knew and from how many generations she was removed from slavery), I asked her mother's name.

"Alice, born in 1912."

I had to let her get back to work, but I had established the building blocks needed to sketch out a brief family tree. During our brief exchange, Barbara Reid Dixon told me her dad had worked as a Sweet Briar groundskeeper, and her mother as a launderer. Sure enough, I plugged in John Reid, Amherst County, Virginia, and quickly got a hit. He was born in 1908 and is listed on the 1940 US Federal Census as a "laborer" on a "farm." John Reid Jr., age thirty, reported having five years of formal education and was listed as "employed for pay." Alice Reid, age twenty-seven, had seven years of schooling but was not employed, probably because they had an infant son, Herman, born the year prior. I surmised that Barbara, the woman I had just met, must have been born after 1940 and thus was not yet in the available census records.

As was often the case in this rural community, parents and children lived in close proximity. Just two houses away from John and Alice Reid lived John Reid Sr. (born 1882), Barbara's grandfather, who listed his employment as "campus labor" and specified "college" under "industry" in the 1940 Census. As there is no other college in Amherst, he too must have worked at Sweet Briar. He and his wife had slightly fewer years of schooling, four and five, respectively. Two of their adult children lived with them: an unmarried daughter, Bettie, age thirty-three, and a son, Joseph, age twenty-one. Bettie worked as a "presser" for a laundry. Again, this was likely the college laundry, where her daughter-in-law also worked.

I wasn't eager to interrogate Barbara again but needed to determine who John Reid Sr.'s parents were. I wondered if they had been enslaved, and, if so, had they lived at Sweet Briar? Finding data on African Americans born before 1865 remains a challenge. My best bet was to find John Sr.'s marriage license and hope he listed his parents' names in the blanks for "father" and "mother." Eventually, I learned that the twenty-three-year-old had married Willie Pettyjohn (born 1885) on 15 February 1899. Willie was the daughter of Native American parents, Smoot and Betty Pettyjohn, whose burials I had found years earlier on a trip to document a Monacan graveyard on nearby Bear Mountain. John Sr. listed his parents as Darius and Sarah Reid. When I searched for them in the census, I saw several variants for "Darius" including "Reas."

I decided to work my way through the available detailed census records. In the 1930 Census, I found Barbara's grandfather easily; he and his wife, Willie, were living in Elon, ten miles away from Sweet Briar, along with their children, who ranged in age from twenty-two (John Jr., Barbara's father) to fourteen (their son Millwood). John Sr.'s nearest neighbor was Lewis Reid, born in 1885. The census doesn't track familial relationships across households, but the close proximity, shared surname, and nearness in age suggests Lewis was one of John Sr.'s brothers. Lewis was a blacksmith, a skill often passed down from father to son, which made me wonder whether their father might have been his instructor. Lewis's wife, Bessie, was a launderer at Sweet Briar.

I scanned the rest of the page, which listed other neighbors, to see if John Sr. and Lewis's parents might have been living nearby. They weren't, but I saw a familiar name: Givens Rose, listed as father-in-law to Early Johnson. By this time, Givens was a remarkable 102 years old and widowed. Another neighbor was Frederic Smith, the brother of Daisy Williams's former playmate Signora Hollins. The only remaining African American in this group of households was a Norman J. Mitchell. He was thirty-seven years old, was divorced, and lived alone, so there were no kinship affiliations to explore. He listed his occupation as restaurant keeper, which in 1930 almost certainly meant he operated a segregated restaurant for blacks only. This left me with questions: How did employment off campus compare to work at Sweet Briar? Was there less racial discrimination among the educated faculty and students? Or was there little difference in the cultural climate between a school "steeped in Southern traditions" and their Jim Crow era neighbors in a small central Virginia town?

The rest of the neighbors were white, with a wide range of occupations: life insurance agent, firefighter, farmer, railroad mechanic, carpenter, and woodcutter. This raised other questions: What, if any, was the relationship between the white and black families in this rural community? Were any of these white families descended from slaveholders? These questions are, of course, beyond the scope of this book, let alone my three-day writing retreat. I returned to my primary question: Was one of Barbara's great-grandparents enslaved at Sweet Briar? Another step backward in time led me to the 1860s court records for marriages among recently freed African Americans to see if I could locate Barbara's great-great-grandparents. But here I ran into a brick wall. When I searched Elijah Fletcher's 1852 and 1860 estate lists, no leads panned out for a Darius or a Smoot, the two most unusual names I could search for; the presence of several Sarahs and Bettys was hardly conclusive. When I returned to the inn, I would have to ask Barbara if she knew where her great-great-grandparents were born.

On the same day I met Barbara Reid, I had spoken casually with several other African American employees. David Carter had made me an omelet at breakfast. I asked if I could pose a strange question: What was his last name, and who were his parents? It seemed I had walked past his father's gravestone in the Christian Aid Society Cemetery the night before. His parents, Edward and Shirley Carter, had attended Saint Mark Baptist Church, whose historic black churchyard included a gravestone for a "Mary Crawford" who died on 27 October 1916 at age 104. The use of the Crawford surname for a woman born in 1812 suggests that Mary may have been enslaved at Tusculum. As for David's parents, his mother, Shirley Sandidge Carter, is still living and worked at Sweet Briar for thirty-five years before retiring. Her mother, Lucy Sandidge, was a cook at the on-campus Boxwood Inn. Three generations of Sweet Briar employees, and I hadn't even had breakfast yet.

After breakfast, I walked over to the campus post office to mail a letter. There, I was helped by Jimmy Rose, a longtime Sweet Briar College employee. I've known Jimmy for years, and he is used to my genealogical questions, so I started with a hard one: "Have you ever heard of Givens Rose, a former Amherst resident who lived to be over one hundred?" Jimmy had not, but he said his uncle Roosevelt Rose, age eighty-six, was the oldest living relative he knew. Roosevelt's parents were Henry and Corinne Rose, born in 1909 and 1910. One of their other sons, James Henry Rose (Jimmy's father), worked for decades as a custodian for the Sweet Briar College Library. Jimmy's sister, Gloria Smith, also works for the college and is currently the administrative assistant in the student life office.

While I was writing down Roosevelt's contact information, Stacey Carter stopped by to pick up packages to deliver to their on-campus locations. Oddly enough, while David Carter was dishing out my omelet and outlining his family's service to Sweet Briar, he had forgotten to mention that his son also worked for the college. This added one more generation of college employees to the Carter family. Moreover, David's wife, Denise (Stacey's mom), had a brother who worked at Sweet Briar, Joe Pendleton.

Coincidentally, as I headed back to my room at the inn to write, Joe Pendleton drove past. In addition to his job as a custodian, he is a talented painter whose dreamlike compositions capture the DNA of past lives and memories. In the fall of 2002, his work was featured in an on-campus gallery show titled *The Journey*. These evocative paintings feature elements of past worlds, including slave ships and recently arrived Africans on American shores. His work reminded me of a comment made by Menene Gras Balaguer about the work of Chiharu Shiota:

> Everything in the world is imbued with the traces that the people who have been in contact with them, or touched them, have left behind. Silence becomes a noise that we have to learn to listen to, because it seals the absence of people who have disappeared in the present, who were once in contact with one object or another. . . . What is deposited in the objects is constitutive of memory—it begins with a point and becomes a line, and then a thing—which we represent in words and articulate through language.[17]

My brief tour of Sweet Briar College and its contemporary and historic people and places was just the start of an inventory of intersections between the past and the present. The woman vacuuming a dormitory corridor and the man trimming a boxwood hedge along the sinuous roads had roots that went back further in time than those of most other college employees and students.

Notes

Epigraph: Hurston, *Dust Tracks on a Road*, 176.
1. Elijah Fletcher called the plantation Sweetbrier; his daughter changed the name after his death to Sweet Briar. Thus, Sweet Briar Plantation is used for the period after ca. 1860.
2. Rainville, *Hidden History*, 107–110.
3. Halloran, *Exhibiting Slavery*, 14.
4. M. Page, "Sites of Conscience."
5. Roberts, "When Does It Become Social Justice?"
6. Lawson, "'I have lately bought me a Plantation.'"
7. Not to be confused with George W. Sales (born 1927), who married Dorothy Jones Jordan.
8. Long, "Our Colored Folks," 9.
9. The 1910 US Federal Census indicates "20 years" of marriage.
10. George Sales's Selective Service draft record, 1918.
11. Jackson, *My Father's Name*.
12. Swarns and Kantor, "In First Lady's Roots, a Complex Path from Slavery."
13. Swarns, "Meet Your Cousin, the First Lady."

14. E.g., Dunn, *A Tale of Two Plantations* (one of the "two" is Mount Airy in Tidewater, Virginia) and Walsh, *From Calabar to Carter's Grove* (about another enslaved community on a Tidewater Virginian plantation).
15. Ely, *Israel on the Appomattox*.
16. Wiencek, *The Hairstons*.
17. Balaguer, *The Hand Lines*, 17.

RUN away from the Subfcriber, in *Amherft* County, the 10th of *July*, a Mulatto Woman Slave named SALL, though commonly goes by the Name of *Sally Grey*; fhe is of a middle Size, well fhaped, *Virginia* born, and about 25 Years old; had on, when fhe went away, a brown Linen Jacket and Petticoat, and I cannot learn that fhe carried any other Clothes with her. She is of a numerous Family of Mulattoes, formerly belonging to a Gentleman of the Name of *Howard*, in *York* County, from whence I purchafed her a few Years ago, and where probably fhe may attempt to go again, or perhaps into *Cumberland*, or *Amelia*, where I am informed many of her Kindred live. I fhall efteem it a particular Favour of thofe Gentlemen who have any of her Relations in their Poffeffion, to have her apprehended, if fhe is difcovered lurking about their Plantations; and I will give a handfome Reward, befides what the Law allows, to any Perfon who will deliver her to me.

(6)   GABRIEL PENN.

Figure 2.1. Runaway advertisement for Sally Grey posted by Gabriel Penn in the 25 August 1774 issue of William Rind's *Virginia Gazette*.

2

FAMILY ORIGINS, 1685–1810

The enslaved families who worked at Sweetbrier Plantation were among a multigenerational group of laborers who had been forced to accompany their owners as they journeyed east to west from the Atlantic Seaboard settlements to the western regions of Virginia. During these migrations, a twenty-five-year-old woman, Sally Grey, ran away from an Amherst plantation in an effort to return east to rejoin her family. Sally, a "Mulatto Woman Slave," was probably born in York County on a plantation owned by "a Gentlemen of the Name of Howard," who also owned several members of her extended family. When we unpack the advertisement that her owner, Gabriel Penn, published in the *Virginia Gazette*, we learn that this individual was probably related to some of the African American families who lived at Sweetbrier and Tusculum (Figure 2.1).[1]

As British colonists in what would become the United States began to craft declarations of independence, Sally took a desperate step to flee the Glebe, the plantation where she had been enslaved. When enslaved individuals ran away, slave owners such as Penn often offered "handsome rewards" for anyone who located and returned their lost property. From Penn's description, Sally's family had clearly already been separated multiple times, resulting in extended family in York, Cumberland, and Amelia countries. York is located near the Atlantic Ocean in the Virginia Tidewater, where Virginia's first English families settled in the seventeenth century. The distribution of Sally's family members highlights the impact that these land grabs had on enslaved families: from the Eastern Seaboard, over a hundred miles (and several days' walk) inland to Cumberland and Amelia counties, and then to Sally's final residence in Amherst County. Over the generations, "second sons" of white elites journeyed westward to claim new lands taken from native peoples who had lived on that land for tens of thousands of years. In Sally's early twenties, possibly after she had selected a partner and started a family, Penn purchased "Sall" and took her 150 west miles to Amherst County. When she left, wearing a "brown Linen Jacket and Petticoat," she wasn't running away; she was attempting to return home. It isn't clear if she survived the journey.

Sally would have known that if she were captured, as a result of numerous eighteenth-century laws, she would face a punishment of twenty lashes "without further order or warrant" from the apprehending constable according to a 1705 "Act concerning Servants and Slaves."[2] An even stricter version of the law was passed in October 1748.[3] And in October 1765, responding to complaints by slaveholders, legislators passed an edict ordering any "taker up" of a fugitive to "immediately carry" the enslaved person before a justice of the peace, and, after ascertaining the surname of the owner, "the taker up shall immediately carry such runaway to his or her owner."[4] In the advertisement, Penn states he was unable to ascertain whether Sally brought any extra clothes (or, presumably, belongings). This young woman was on the run during the heat of the summer, with long days and only ten hours of darkness,[5] carrying very few—if any—provisions; and any person of color, free or enslaved, was subject to the eighteenth-century version of Search and Seizure, in which the seizure was of a bodily nature.

While runaway slave notices are valuable pieces of genealogical information about enslaved individuals, they rarely reveal the outcome. Was Sally recaptured, or mistakenly killed by a slave patrol in the attempt to apprehend her? Was she successful in reuniting with her family? The only way she could have remained free after her escape would have been to eschew her own family (in which case, she would have been hunted and unable to live in freedom) and escape to a sympathetic white family, most likely living in the North, or to blend into a free black community. Both scenarios are unlikely. And since slave owners didn't post public thanks to the individuals who caught enslaved runaways, the only conclusive proof would be to locate Sally's name on a slave list, receipt, or farm ledger dated after August 1774, which I was unable to do.

Following independence, Southern legislators sought to restrict the rights of African Americans more rigorously than was the case under British rule. In Richmond, Virginia's newly established House of Delegates passed several laws that directly and indirectly affected enslaved families. While we do not know the fate of Sally Grey, we can research the stories of the other enslaved families in Amherst at a nearby plantation, Tusculum, two decades later.

On the second Sunday of November 1792, one or more of the enslaved African American women living on the Tusculum plantation would have been called to the bedside of their mistress, Sophia Penn Crawford. That day, the mother of the Sweet Briar College founder was born. Sophia and her husband, William Sidney Crawford, named their infant daughter Maria Antoinette, presumably in honor of the Queen of the French who—as the rural residents of New Glasgow, Virginia, may yet not have heard—had been deposed, and the French monarchy abolished, two months earlier.

For the enslaved community, absolute rule was much closer to home: in the grand mansions from which white slave owners reigned over them in Amherst County. Maria Antoinette was the third white baby born at Tusculum within five years. She would usher in a miniature baby boom, as ten more white children were born by 1812. That triggered a corresponding boom in the number of nursemaids, cooks, cleaners, and plantation workers who would be bought and bred by their white owners over the same two decades.

The enslaved midwife and maids attending to Sophia Crawford had cause to worry with each birth. As these children grew up, each would inherit Tusculum "property," which included African American women, men, and children. Just seven years earlier, when Sophia had married William Crawford, she would have uprooted at least one member of her father's household. As the third of ten children born to Gabriel and Sarah Penn, a prosperous Virginian family who owned a nearby plantation called the Glebe, Sophia would have been gifted her favorite human possession to serve as lady's maid after marriage. The two plantations were so close that among the dozens of enslaved people who labored at the Glebe were several who started relationships and families with people at Tusculum, a twenty-minute walk through wooded hills.

Tracing their lives is made complex by the fragmentary nature of records of slaves. Without birth or death certificates, journals, or other evidence to document their lives, we must rely on their enslavers' records. So, we know little of the women who attended Maria Antoinette's birth, save that one may have been an enslaved woman named Nancy, classified as "very old" in an 1815 list of Crawford slaves. This designation suggests she may have been old enough to have traveled with William's great-grandparents—David Crawford II (1662–1762) and his wife, Elizabeth Smith (ca. 1673–1767)—as they left the eastern Virginia county where they were married and journeyed one hundred miles west to the Piedmont region, which encompassed Tusculum.

The Crawfords had a century-old history of westward migrations. The first traveler was John Crawford (1593–1676), a widower and most likely a younger son with little or no inheritance, who left Scotland around 1643. With his only son, David I (1625–1710), he set out for the colonies to obtain land in the seemingly limitless expanse of the Americas. The Crawfords were typical of early Virginian planters, buying up large tracts of land from British investors, many of whom never set foot in the New World. The typical post-1634 immigrants to Virginia were "rather ordinary, middling sorts of Englishmen" searching for the promise of riches.[6] John and David Crawford settled in the inland port of Jamestown, founded by British merchants decades earlier. The first British arrivals had traveled along the banks of the James River, unilaterally claiming lands long held by native peoples. David built on their initial holdings, soon owning land in James City, Hanover, and New Kent counties. Along the way, he married Jane (maiden name uncertain), and their son, David II, was born in New Kent.

As an adult, David II eventually moved westward, expanding his father's realm and claiming still more lands granted by the British Crown to any white man who was willing to till the acreage. These ever-growing agricultural pursuits required large amounts of backbreaking labor. As their holdings and wealth increased, the Crawfords increasingly turned to enslaved workers to clear the lands, plant and harvest the crops, cook and clean for their growing family, and, of course, deliver the babies. Nancy's mother may have helped deliver and care for some of David II and Elizabeth's five children (born between 1697 and 1707). To house the family, David II purchased seven acres at the foot of the Blue Ridge Mountains in Amherst County and began building a two-story house with beaded weatherboard siding, two red brick chimneys, and a fancy entry porch with decorative caps on top of tapered posts that support a neoclassical pediment that contains a frieze with an unusual, undulating scalloped lower edge.[7] This frontier home, later given the name Tusculum, faced west toward the Blue Ridge Mountains.

By the 1750s, the fourth-generation Crawford family was one of the largest slave-holding families in Amherst, Virginia. Other than the size of their human and land holdings, they epitomized a common adaptation to the agricultural riches found in Virginia: the use of slave labor camps situated on newly established plantations. The enslaved laborers, farmers, field hands, masons, blacksmiths, and domestic servants who stayed at Tusculum would have had grueling sunup to sundown days. Many had traveled with the Crawfords from Hanover County to Amherst, a one-hundred-mile journey that separated them from the families and social networks they had left behind. When David II died a decade later, in 1762, their efforts to rebuild a community in their new home would have been threatened again, as they were dispersed among the five Crawford children, including David III (1697–1766), and numerous grandchildren, including David IV (1734–1802). Meanwhile, David II would be memorialized as a gentleman. As one family historian opined, "David Crawford belonged to that slave-holding aristocracy of the Old Dominion which so closely resembled the feudal nobility of earlier times."[8]

The paper trail for seventeenth- and early eighteenth-century black Virginians is sparse. But just as the name Crawford points to the family's English and Scottish lineage (combining the Old English for "crow" with "ford"), we can study the names of enslaved individuals to try to trace their countries of origin. The names of people owned by the colonial era Crawfords suggest at least two geographical points of origin: West Africa and the Caribbean.

The first documented Africans to arrive in Virginia were roughly two dozen individuals who had been kidnapped and chained for a treacherous multi-month voyage, arriving on the shores of the British colony in 1619.[9] These early arrivals would have joined a larger workforce made up of white European indentured servants. In the first century after their arrival, some Africans could earn their freedom after a period of indenture.[10] But a series of laws gradually constricted the lives of people of color in the American colonies. By the mid-seventeenth century, Virginia enacted laws to place Africans in lifelong servitude and doom the children of enslaved women to the same fate. The 1662 declaration of the Virginia General Assembly concluded, "All children borne in this country shall be held bond or free only according to the condition of the mother."[11] The differentiation between white and black servants only increased over the next several decades as the life expectancy of African immigrants and their children increased. For the enslavers, the lifelong labor of Africans was a better investment than the seven-year period of indenture associated with Europeans.[12] By the time the General Assembly passed the official "slave code" in 1705, the custom of forcing people of color to serve their masters for life was already well established. As their children were automatically enslaved, the historian Phillip Morgan estimates that "a majority of Virginia slaves were native-born as early as the second or third decade of the eighteenth century."[13]

Still, the importation of slaves continued: from 1708 to 1750, more than thirty-eight thousand enslaved men, women, and children entered the Colony of Virginia.[14] Among these were probably Warwick and Armistead, two enslaved men owned by David IV (1734–1802) whose names suggested a recent African ancestry. By 1775, on the eve of the American Revolution, the Crawfords were dispersed throughout counties that were more than 50 percent black.[15] The white majority had become a mathematical minority in several central Virginian counties.[16] White Virginians continued to acquire Africans until after independence, when an October 1778 General Assembly act prohibited the "farther importation of slaves into this commonwealth . . . by sea or land, nor shall any slaves so imported be sold or bought by any person whatsoever."[17] During the eighteenth century, enslaved families in Amherst County had clear connections to African groups. A 1771 advertisement placed by a slave owner named Edmund Wilcox described a runaway man as "an African Negro Fellow who cannot speak English." For anyone who abducted and returned the "middle age" man, Wilcox offered a reward of forty shillings.[18]

The Transatlantic slave trade in the mid-eighteenth century included not only Africa but also the West Indies. Enslaved individuals born in the West Indies were brought by boat to the port of New Orleans or the Carolinas, and then traded inland to the fast-growing plantations of Virginia. Again, the naming practices of enslaved individuals can provide a clue about these places of origin. One woman owned by David IV used the name Parene, a name common in St. Croix and other Caribbean Islands. Another Amherst resident, an enslaved woman named Sealy Rose, was born around 1793 in Saint Thomas Parish, Jamaica. Sealy, also known as Cecillia, was owned by John Rock Grosett.[19] A Nelson County planter purchased her, and she started a family with a James Rose, son of Lucy Rose.[20] James died before emancipation. After the Civil War, Sealy settled in Nelson County with her son Aaron Rose, born in 1820.

Another source of enslaved labor for the Crawfords was native peoples. The first documented evidence that the Crawfords owned slaves dates to 1685 when David I sued a Roger Jones for "harboring three Indian servants" of his in the Tidewater region. The trio—a boy, a girl, and a woman—may have been members of the Powhatan/Nansemond tribe.[21] More than a decade earlier, in 1672, the Virginia General Assembly had passed an act that enabled slave owners to pursue and even kill a "Negro, mulatto, Indian slave, or servant for life" if they attempted to run away.[22] It was Pamunkey Indians who killed David I in his eighty-fifth year at his home on the Assasquin plantation in New Kent County.

In Amherst, European-American settlers crossed paths with the native residents of this land by at least 1730. That year, Dr. William Cabell encountered a group of Virginian Indians while he was surveying land.[23] Sometime earlier, perhaps in the 1710s or 1720s, "Trader Hughes" and his Algonquian wife, Nikiti, opened a trading station at the junction of two Indian paths—most likely the Saponi-Saura trail that went from Charlottesville to Salem—in the vicinity of modern-day Amherst County.[24] Many of these native pathways were incorporated into the routes of white settlers.[25] By the end of the eighteenth century, many of the native peoples had been pushed farther west or partially assimilated into either white or black society. Yet, as late as the 1780s, two or three Indian villages remained near the city of Lynchburg, near Lynch's Ferry.

Native names appear on Crawford documents as late as the 1800s, suggesting more than a century-long continuity. For example, a man named "Mingo" was listed on the 1810 estate settlement of David IV's "property." A corruption of a word used by the Delaware tribe to mean "treacherous or stealthy," the term Mingo was used to refer to groups of Native Americans who migrated west to Ohio. He may or may not have been directly related to those groups; perhaps his white owners assigned him the name. Likewise, when David IV's son, William, died in 1816, an enslaved woman on his estate was referred to as "Aggy (yello)." Again, this does not reveal her original name but was rather a European-American term for a Native American.

Whether of Native or African origin, the enslaved families listed in David II's 1762 will and that of his son, David III, who died in 1766, were part of a growing number of slaves building the newly founded plantations in an area that European-Americans called Albemarle County. It had been named in 1744 after the second Earl of Albemarle, a governor of the Colony of Virginia, on land inhabited by a Siouan-speaking tribe called the Saponi. European-Americans overtook the area, attracted by its "salubrious atmosphere, its beautiful scenery, its varied landscape, its pure water, its temperate climate, its productive valleys, its abundant forests, its mineral hills, its towering mountains, and its rapid streams."[26] In 1761, Albemarle County's southern half was designated as Amherst County, named after a British soldier who had served at the 1758 Battle of Ticonderoga during the French and Indian War. In 1807, Amherst County split again, and Nelson County was formed out of the northern portion. That division holds to the current day.

Throughout this period, several dozen white families bought land, often land grants from the British Crown directly, and established farmsteads. The larger operations included rows of tobacco and wheat fields that required dozens of field hands. Most of these early homesteaders relied on the labor of enslaved field hands. Meanwhile, enslaved cooks, maids, wet nurses, midwives, and housekeepers lived and worked in the "big house." The owners of these farms traveled intermittently to the county center, in a community originally called Five Oaks, to conduct financial business and legal proceedings at the county courthouse. Scottish immigrants who settled there named their town New Glasgow. The Episcopal Church built a home it called the Glebe to house its rector. Along the Piney and Tye rivers, Rev. Robert Rose patented more than twenty three thousand acres in 1744 and built a house he called Geddes, from which he served a large area known as St. Anne's Parish. He established St. Mark's Church in Amherst County, just down the road from Geddes, bringing enslaved African field laborers and house servants.[27]

Numerous other homes in the region were built by enslaved workers and their white owners in the second half of the eighteenth century, including Mountain View (by the Spencers in the early 1700s), Red Hill along the Pedlar River (by Charles Ellis in the 1750s), Winton (by Col. Josiah Cabell in the 1760s), and the Brick House (by David Shepard Garland in the early 1800s). The fate of African Americans living in New Glasgow was intertwined with that of their kin further afield at plantations such as Thomas Crews's Locust Ridge, which would later be renamed Sweetbrier (eventually Sweet Briar).[28]

David II directed the construction of his timber-frame house in Amherst in the last decade of his life, using the popular federal style to accentuate an otherwise plain, one-room-wide structure. The builders, quite likely white shipwrights given their technique, carved Roman numerals into notched pieces of wood to assist laborers in piecing together the boards in the correct positions. The floors, walls, and ceilings were wooden; the hearths, chimneys, and decorative façade that wrapped around the English basement at the ground level were made from locally made bricks. Some of the eighteen people enslaved by David probably dug out the iron-rich clay from nearby burrow pits, setting aside some bricks for heating and thereby strengthening in kilns and others for drying in the sun and for use as fill.[29]

The floor plan was relatively simple: a long entrance hall branching off into two main rooms probably used as a living room and a dining room. The kitchen was in a separate structure, due in part to the hazards of hearth cooking and fires in wooden buildings, and to establish "a clearer separation between those who served and those who were served," as was the custom of the time.[30] The bedrooms were upstairs. During the winter months, some of the enslaved women who lived here were required to tend to the fires in each room, adding multiple trips up and down the stairs to check on the status of each fireplace and carry heavy loads of wood when the flames dwindled.

For the black families at the Crawford plantation, the grueling days and nights of hard work did not end with the building's construction. They labored on and faced the constant fear of separation. Working for a white man and woman in their nineties probably produced emotional anguish daily, not knowing whether it would be David or Elizabeth's last day. As they knew, the death of the patriarch set in motion a se-ries of consequences that would divide their families. After David II's death in 1762, his will, which also expressed the hope that he would "receive free pardon for all of [his] sins," allocated his eighteen slaves among his children and his elderly wife. He expected his widow to re-main in residence at their home, so to provide her with help, he left her five people: Will, Ben, Bob, Pompey, and Tye. The last two were a cou-ple; the other three men were probably facing a separation from their families. Assuming his centenarian wife would not long outlive him, David II also established a series of contingencies that passed on his property, both human and material, from his wife to his son David III. In each stipulation of David's will, two to six "negroes" were given to each of his four children or, in the case of his daughters, their husbands.

This domino effect tore apart several families. The two men and two women who were given to David II's fifty-nine-year-old daugh-ter, Mary Crawford Rhodes, were destined for future separations upon Mary's death just thirteen years later. The "six negroes" who had been in his son John's "possession a considerable time" would remain with him, David II stipulated, suggesting that, years earlier, these six people had been forced to leave kin and friends behind. In December 1761, as David II wrote the instructions for his will, he did not realize John had recently passed away at his home in South Carolina. So the fate of those six people then hinged on the terms of John's will. David III inherited ten people, several of whom were married pairs, but this did not guarantee them any stability. Pompey and Tye—who had passed from David II to Elizabeth and then on to David III—upon his death were "to be sold, to pay part of my debts."[31] The highest price for en-slaved men during that time was paid by planters heading farther west to clear new lands. Pompey and Tye were probably sold farther west, either individually or together, leaving behind their children, siblings, and perhaps parents.

David III's will also dispersed another four enslaved people whom he had inherited from his father just four years earlier. Cupit and Phillis would stay with his widow; Anaky was given to his son, David IV; and Jack was given to a more distant paternal relative. Whatever friendly or marital bonds may have existed among these four enslaved individuals were torn yet again as the various heirs settled hundreds of miles apart. One enslaved woman who lived at the Crawford plantation while David II was alive, Hanah, is not listed at all in David III's will, suggest-ing that she was sold or died over the course of the four-year gap. Else-where, David III listed Robin "in lieu of" Cupit, suggesting that Cupit may have fallen ill, died, or run away and thus needed to be replaced unexpectedly.[32] After the series of deaths and divisions that wracked the Crawford family and the people they enslaved, it was David II's seven-year-old grandson, William Sidney Crawford (1760–1815), who eventually inherited the Amherst County plantation and, almost certainly, several descendants of the enslaved families his grandfather had brought from eastern Virginia.

The next decade saw British subjects in Virginia and the other colonies take up arms against the Crown for "liberty or death," fighting against a tyrannical oppressor while maintaining their right to hold other people in bondage. In 1776, Amherst soldiers mustered under Samuel Jordan Cabell, a College of William & Mary student. And, in 1779, David IV joined the traitorous American cause and fought against the British for nine months. The fighting would continue after his return home until the 1783 Treaty of Paris that ended the conflict and confirmed the colonies separation from Great Britain. For his loyalty and service, David IV was promoted to the rank of captain, and after the war ended, he returned to Amherst, where he served as the sheriff.[33]

By the time the American Revolution was fought and won, Amherst County (larger in size than today, encompassing what is now Nelson County) was home to more than eight thousand free and enslaved residents. Whites still outnumbered blacks by a slim margin, 53 percent to 47 percent. Most were farmers or worked in support industries such as blacksmithing or milling. Others were engaged in the riverine trade, which had just been made more profitable and reliable thanks to two Amherst County brothers. Anthony and Benjamin Rucker launched the first James River Bateau during the Revolutionary War, with a 1775 design that streamlined boats to improve the speed and efficiency of transporting tobacco and other crops via Richmond east to larger markets.[34]

At the Crawford home, everyday life in the 1770s would have been similar to dozens of other large-scale farms in Amherst. African American men, women, and children cared for the 204-acre plantation, and all its inhabitants.[35] Their annual plantings would have included tobacco, wheat, and rye. They managed packs of cattle and sheep; flocks of chickens, ducks, and geese; droves of hogs; and herds of draft horses. During the colonial era, many farms functioned as miniature villages, with the capacity to plant, grow, harvest, and sometimes process (through mills and tobacco barns) the abundant crops. On-site processing may have included nail and brick production; the collection and spinning of flax, wool, and hemp; and the grinding of wheat and corn. These tasks required a human and built infrastructure.

William S. Crawford reached his colonial era "majority" in 1781, at age twenty-one. When he reached legal adulthood, he came into control of Tusculum. In preparation for a lifetime of gentleman farming and political service, he attended the College of New Jersey (the name was changed to Princeton University in 1896). It was he, most likely, who suggested a fancy name for his new home. When he returned to Virginia in 1782, after he completed his study of the law, he copied the name of the college president's home, Tusculum, for the family homestead. The New Jersey home had been named after an ancient Roman city famous for its fancy villas, including the home of Cicero.

As befitted his social and economic position in the growing Virginian planter elites, William searched for a suitable marriage partner. In 1785, he married Sophia Penn, the daughter of his neighbor Gabriel Penn, owner of the prosperous plantation the Glebe. Gabriel purchased the parish house just after the end of the American Revolution. He served as a colonel in the Revolutionary War, bought large swaths of property in and around Amherst, represented the community as a delegate during the 1776 Williamsburg convention, and served as a church warden for the Lexington Parish from 1779 to 1784; between 1780 and his death, in 1798, he lived at the Glebe.[36] Five years after he bought the Glebe, in October 1785, Penn, along with his white neighbors—Hugh Rose, Samuel Meredith, John Wyatt, Charles Rose, and Samuel Jordan Cabell—established the town of Cabellsburg on fifty acres of land at a place "known by the name of New-Glasgow."[37]

Sophia's family background was similar to William's. Both came from multigenerational Virginians who emigrated from Great Britain in the seventeenth century. Men like the Penns and Crawfords served together on multiple civic-oriented committees and political groups, and often attended the same churches. Both grew up in a culture of owners and slaves, wielding large amounts of control over their communities, enslaved and free. During Sophia's childhood, in the late eighteenth century, central Virginia's European and African population increased dramatically, while the native population began to dwindle. During these turbulent sociopolitical times, federal and state politicians began to grapple with the implications of a growing enslaved population.

First, in what appeared to be a step in the right direction to free all Americans, the Virginian legislator Thomas Jefferson drafted language in 1778 that ended the importation of slaves into Virginia "by sea or land." Moreover, it said, "no persons shall, henceforth, be slaves within this commonwealth, except such as were so on the first day of this present session of Assembly, and the descendants of the females of them."[38] Sellers who ignored this legislation faced a fee of one thousand pounds per enslaved person, and buyers, five hundred pounds, making the entire interaction financially unviable as well as illegal.

At first glance, this code might appear to abolish slavery altogether. However, the law specifies that all future generations of children born to enslaved mothers in Virginia would be enslaved. The "free" part only applied to "negroes and mulattoes" who were brought into the commonwealth from outside its borders and remained inside Virginia for a year. Far from abolishing slavery, the intent of the law in June 1779 was to decrease the international slave trade's financial earnings within the state. Slave traders who wanted to disembark with their cargo at Virginian ports and sell them in other states were not affected because they would pass through the state before the allotted year passed.[39] Virginia wanted to control all the financial proceeds from the institution of slavery, including tithes and other taxable elements, instead of diluting their "take" with national and international traders.

A side effect was individual Virginian planters going in the business of "growing" their enslaved communities by natural means. For men like William, the two strategies were to force enslaved mothers to give birth to more and more "property," and to buy and sell Virginian slaves within the commonwealth from neighbors or professional slave traders. Of the people he inherited, according to the 1787 Census of Virginia, six of the ten enslaved African Americans living at Tusculum were over sixteen years old. This means some of these adults could have been born in Hanover County and traveled with David II to Amherst in 1753. This multigenerational black community with deep interconnections may have been relieved when William decided to call Tusculum home, providing them with a small modicum of stability, rather than to move on farther west, as many white landowners did.

As the new country grappled with its growing pains, Northern and Southern states fought over how enslaved men would be counted when determining legislative representation and taxation. While many Southerners treated their slaves as animals, not humans, they wanted their presence to go toward determining the number of seats their states would have in the population-based US House of Representatives. An insidious agreement was reached in 1787 when they arranged the "three-fifths compromise," which accounted for the lesser humanity of enslaved individuals. Thus, the first federal census showed a Virginian "population" of 420,000, which included three-fifths of 280,000 African Americans. If they hadn't counted African Americans at all, the population would have been only 252,000, whereas the actual number of white and black Virginians in 1790 was 532,000. If they had let their racist views of personhood guide them completely, Virginian lawmakers would have had less representation than Massachusetts and Pennsylvania (each with a population of 360,000), as well as New York (with its population of 238,000).[40]

Amherst County continued to grow, with an actual population of more than 13,700 people in 1790; almost a third were enslaved African Americans (3,852). By 1810, the county's 5,200 slaves accounted for half the population. A new arrival to the county seat of New Glasgow in 1811 described the homes as "not so large & elegant as in many places," and the businesses as limited to several stores and mechanic shops.[41] At Tusculum, much of the growth was under the auspices of a sadistic overseer. In 1792, William had hired a man, referred to in documents simply as Vaughn, to organize his enslaved laborers. This may have been twenty-nine-year-old James Vaughan, the son of Matthew Vaughan, a large slave owner who lived in Goochland County.[42] Vaughn is described in various correspondence as "disgraceful to civilized human society," exceptionally cruel, and such a menace that William's father-in-law, Gabriel Penn, told him to fire Vaughn at once.[43] When Gabriel Penn died at age fifty-seven, William was named one of the executors of his will but declined the offer. Whether this was a consequence of ill feelings from the earlier intervention in his plantation dealings is not clear.

We don't know precisely what horrors the enslaved community at Tusculum suffered under Vaughn's cruel oversight, but reports of injuries suffered by their contemporaries at other Amherst County plantations give us an idea. On 13 January 1796, an enslaved man named David ran away from his owner, Denny Christian. One of David's identifying features was "a scar on the face occasioned by the stroke of the switch, likewise one or more on the breast." This twenty-six-year-old man had already suffered horrible beatings and decided to risk it all and broke free from his chains and escaped. Similarly, an enslaved man named John ran away from his Amherst County owner, John F. Lewis, in the winter of 1796. He had "a large scar on his chin" from unspecified causes.[44] An enslaved twenty-five-year-old man named Jupiter ran away from one of William Crawford's nearest neighbors, William Spencer, in the summer of 1798. Jupiter lacked toes on his left foot "occasioned by burning in his youth."[45] Other eighteenth-century runaways had suffered branding, burns, scalds, beatings, or broken teeth at the hands of the owners or overseers.

With the help of Vaughn and the people he enslaved, William Crawford became a successful farmer and performed political services for his community, serving as local sheriff and county clerk for many years. After the birth of his nine children and an increase in his enslaved community from ten to seventeen people, he decided to expand his home. He experimented with an unusual architectural feature to double his space: he built a breezeway (covered with a roof but open at each end) to connect the existing five-room house with a square, two-story addition. To provide entrances into both parts of the addition, the breezeway wrapped around part of the new addition, creating a covered porch.

The showpiece of the new addition was a wood-paneled dining room, a specialized domestic space only found in elite homes, on the ground floor. Upstairs were more bedrooms. By doubling the size of his home, William also increased the daily cleaning tasks for his enslaved labor force. Based on other, well-documented examples, we can easily imagine that one or more black women were in charge of the "house servants," while the overseer probably organized the "field hands" on a daily basis to ensure they completed their onerous work.

By 1805, William had also built more cabins to house the growing enslaved labor force, a separate office for his business as clerk of the Amherst County court, a structure to store corn, an overseer's house, and probably an additional and/or deeper well (Figure 2.2). Mot of the backbreaking work for these construction projects—carrying hops of bricks, cutting down trees, erecting fences—would have been done by the enslaved community. To meet these labor requirements, William purchased and quite possibly encouraged the "natural increase" of his

Figure 2.2. One of the outbuildings at Tusculum, shown here in a 1905 photograph. Sweet Briar College Library Archives.

slaves, leading to a dramatic increase from seventeen to forty-three people over just five years (1805–1810). Part of this increase was from the settlement of his father's estate, which finally concluded in 1810, eight years after David IV's death. By then, William and Sophia had thirteen children, requiring decades of nursing, feeding, minding, and, eventually, domestic caring by a lady's maid or a manservant.

The numbers tell only part of the story of the growth of the enslaved community at Tusculum: ten, seventeen, forty-three. To track generations of African American families, however, I needed names. I started with the names listed in David II's 1762 will. An infant or young child named in 1762 would have only been in their fifties in 1815 when David's great-grandson died. I dutifully recorded the names of the men, women, and children recorded in subsequent wills: David II (died 1762), David III (died 1766), David IV (died 1802), and William (died 1815). While there was no direct connection between a name in 1762 and one in 1815, I found numerous connections between 1766 and 1802 and, in turn, 1802 and 1815. Later, I would trace six names from the mid-eighteenth century all the way to an 1852 will.

The financial document that settled David IV's estate in 1802 provided the most insightful genealogy for the Tusculum enslaved community. David IV "died in the enjoyment of the support of the Christian religion and with much tranquility and composure," but his enslaved community faced separations and heartbreak. In the estate settlement, the executor divided the enslaved into two groups: descendants of Mingo, and descendants of Ned (probably a shortened version of Edmund). As you would expect after multiple forcible separations, these were not two intact family units but rather groupings of spouses, sometimes accompanied by daughters and sons, but also individually listed girls and boys, as well as older men and women who may be the grandparents of other people on the list. For example, Ned is listed with his "youngest child," Moses. No wife is listed, leaving one to wonder if he was a widower or if his wife lived elsewhere. The "Descendants of Ned" list continued with two boys named Bartlet and Armistead and a pair of girls named Molley and Nicey. Nicey and Armistead are on the same line and might be siblings. But the relationship between Bartlet and Molley and among the each of the four children is less clear.[46]

Generations of Crawford wills suggest that the white men who owned humans in bondage did try to keep families together when death or debts in white families threatened to affect the black communities. The executors of William S. Crawford's 1816 settlement stated explicitly that "the Commissioners have been guided by two objects 1st that slaves should be kept in families." They failed to state their second objective, instead admitting in the next line, "It was impossible to avoid [separating families] from fractions or surpluss [*sic*] in the several lots." They clearly prioritized the financial balance sheets over the integrity of black families.

On Christmas Eve 1811, the enslaved African American cooks and house servants would have been busy preparing and serving the morning's "egg punch" (a local tradition) and, later in the day, the Christmas "dinner." That evening, in the fancy, wood-paneled dining room built five years earlier, they served the family along with a visitor, the newly arrived schoolmaster at the nearby New Glasgow Academy. The master of the house, William Crawford, was a trustee at the private school, along with a dozen neighbors including Samuel Meredith, William H. Cabell, and Edmund Penn.[47] William's daughters were taking classes in French and Latin with the newcomer, a recent transplant from Vermont who was spending the holidays far away from his family. In his journal, Elijah Fletcher reported on the day's festivities: the customary egg punch, a church sermon, and a lavish dinner party that continued into the wee hours of the next morning. It was then that he met his future wife, Maria Antoinette, sending him down a path entirely different from that of an educator from a slavery-abhorring Northern family.[48]

Notes

1. The advertisement was posted in the *Virginia Gazette*, 4 August 1774, published by Purdie & Dixon, Williamsburg, Virginia. Gabriel Penn was the father of Sophia Penn Crawford, who married Williams S. Crawford and moved to Tusculum, mostly likely with some of her enslaved maids who had lived with her at the Glebe. Sophia was the mother of Maria Antoinette Crawford, Elijah Fletcher's wife.
2. "An act concerning Servants and Slaves," in Hening, *The Statutes at Large*, 3:447.
3. "An Act concerning Servants, and Slaves," in Hening, *The Statutes at Large*, 5:547.
4. "An act to amend the act for the better government of Servants and Slaves," in Hening, *The Statutes at Large*, 8:135–137.
5. Calculated at "Duration of Daylight/Darkness Table for One Year," Astronomical Applications Department of the United States Naval Observatory, last modified 29 July 2015, http://aa.usno.navy.mil/data/docs/Dur_One Year.php.
6. Billings, *The Old Dominion in the Seventeenth Century*, 177, 105 (quote).
7. Esposito, "Clifford–New Glasgow Historic District," section no. 7, 1.

8. Crawfurdiana, *Memorials of That Branch of the Crawford Family*, 13, 55.

9. The British colonist John Rolfe wrote of the arrival of a Dutch ship with "20. and odd Negroes." Cited in Kingsbury, *The Records of the Virginia Company of London*, 243.

10. Vaughan, "The Origins Debate," 312, citing James C. Ballagh's legal research.

11. Palmer, "Servant into Slave," 361.

12. E. Morgan, *American Slavery, American Freedom*, 299.

13. P. Morgan et al., *Don't Grieve After Me*, 19.

14. E. Morgan, *American Slavery, American Freedom*, 308.

15. Kulikoff, *Tobacco and Slaves*, 340.

16. P. Morgan, "Slaves in Piedmont Virginia," 217.

17. "An act for preventing the farther importation of Slaves," in Hening, *The Statutes at Large*, 9:471–72.

18. *Virginia Gazette* [Williamsburg], 7 November 1771, 4.

19. National Archives of the United Kingdom (Kew, England), Office of Registry of Colonial Slaves and Slave Compensation Commission: Records, class T71, piece no. 149.

20. Genealogical connections courtesy of Derek Nicholas, Nelson County genealogist.

21. Shefveland, *Anglo-Native Virginia*, 62.

22. "Study Aid: Slavery and the Law in Seventeenth-Century Virginia," Gilder Lehrman Institute of American History, accessed 27 December 2018, https://www.gilderlehrman.org/history-by-era/origins-slavery/resources/slavery-and-law-seventeenth-century-virginia.

23. Percy, *The Amherst County Story*, 7.

24. Brown, *The Cabells and Their Kin*, xx; Houck, *Indian Island in Amherst County*, 38.

25. Percy, *The Amherst County Story*, 8.

26. Board of Supervisors, *Facts of Interest about Amherst County, Virginia*, preface.

27. Seaman, *Amherst County Environmental Studies*, 64.

28. Esposito, "Clifford–New Glasgow Historic District."

29. McDonald, *Tusculum, Amherst County*, 23–27.

30. Vlach, *Back of the Big House*, 43.

31. Will of David Crawford [III], 21 June 1765, proved 4 August 1766, Will Book 1: 76–79, Amherst County Courthouse.

32. Will of David Crawford [IV], August 1802, Will Book 4: 49–52, Amherst County Courthouse.

33. Crawford, *The Crawford Family*, 126–130.

34. Seaman, *Tuckahoe and Cohee*, 290.

35. 1787 Land Tax files, Amherst County Courthouse. 1787 Personal Property Tax indicates that he owned ten enslaved individuals as well as sixteen taxable animals.

36. Kraus, "The Glebe."

37. "An act for establishing a town on the lands of Smyth Tandy, in the county of Amherst," in Hening, *The Statutes at Large*, 12:229.

38. "An act for preventing the farther importation of Slaves."

39. "An act concerning slaves," in Hening, *The Statutes at Large*, 12:182–83.
40. Wright, *The History and Growth of the United States Census*, 11.
41. Von Briesen, *The Letters of Elijah Fletcher* (hereinafter *TLEF*), letter to his father, Jesse Fletcher, 29 November 1811, 44.
42. B. Davis, *The Deeds of Amherst County Virginia*, 277. Reference to Matt Vaughan who paid Hudson Martin for two slaves lent to Vaughan's son, Jas, on 16 May 1793.
43. Letter from Gabriel Penn to William S. Crawford, 27 July 1792. owned by Wes McCarty. Cited in Amherst County Heritage Book Committee, *Amherst County Heritage Book*, 213–14.
44. *Virginia Gazette and General Advertiser*, 13 January 1796.
45. *Virginia Argus (Pleasants)*, 29 June 1798.
46 Will and settlement of David Crawford IV, 1810, Will Book 4: 146, Amherst County Courthouse.
47. *TLEF*, 38n4.
48. *TLEF*, letter to his father, 23 December 1811, 49.

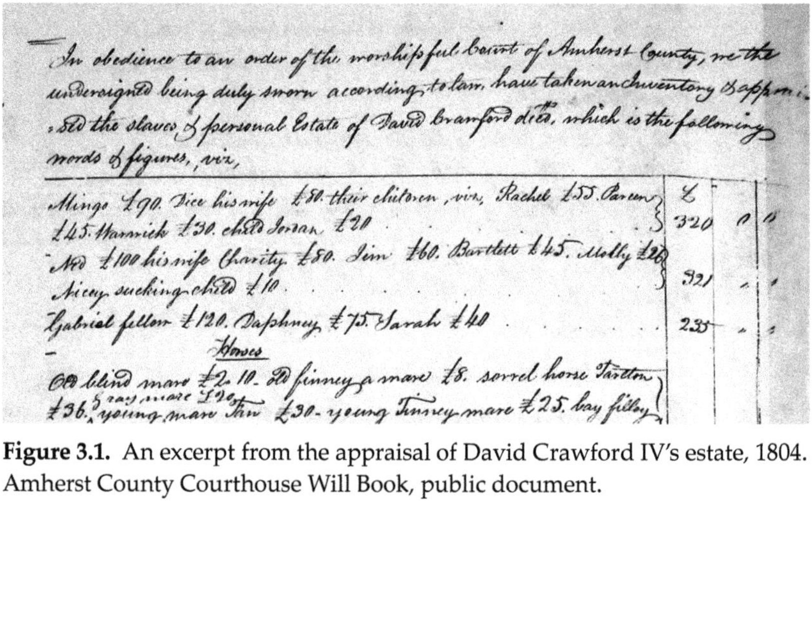

In obedience to an order of the worshipful Court of Amherst County, we the undersigned being duly sworn according to law, have taken an Inventory & apprai:sed the slaves & personal Estate of David Crawford dec'd, which is the following words & figures, viz,

	£		
Mingo £90. Dice his wife £80. their children, viz, Rachel £55. Parcen £45. Warrick £30. child Jordan £20	320	"	"
Ned £100 his wife Charity £80. Jim £60. Bartlett £45. Molly £26 Nicey sucking child £10	321	"	"
Gabriel fellow £120. Daphney £75. Sarah £40	235	"	"
Horses			
Old blind mare £2.10. old finney a mare £8. sorrel horse Tarlton £36. gray mare £30 young mare Jim £30. young Finney mare £25. bay filley			

Figure 3.1. An excerpt from the appraisal of David Crawford IV's estate, 1804. Amherst County Courthouse Will Book, public document.

3

Virginian Slavery, 1811–1830

In the years after David Crawford IV's death, his property and belongings were recorded in a series of legal documents. As mentioned previously, David IV divided his enslaved labor force into two family groups: those related to an enslaved man named Ned, and those related to an individual named Mingo. We have no means of determining whether these genealogical groupings mirrored the preferences of the enslaved families. Nonetheless, we can learn a great deal about Mingo's family tree from his owner's will and estate inventory (Figure 3.1). A woman named Dice (appearing also as "Dicey" in other documents) is identified as Mingo's wife, and four of their children are listed: Rachel, Pareen, Warwick, and Jordan. The range of their assigned monetary value corresponds roughly to the distribution of their ages. Ned and his wife Charity are also mentioned, along with a list of their children, including a "suckling child." The names on this document match individuals listed on other legal records associated with David IV and his close kin and inheritors. Following this paper trail reveals the fractured nature of kinship ties among these men, women, and children.[1] The ruthless separation of enslaved families was one of the many reasons why a newcomer from the North, Elijah Fletcher, initially approached the South's "peculiar institution" with suspicion and dismay.

Elijah Fletcher was born in 1789, one decade after his home state of Vermont became the first to end the practice of holding humans in bondage.[2] Elijah grew up with a strict father who was against slavery, and as a young man, Elijah wholeheartedly endorsed this antislavery view. He was educated at New England schools that considered themselves untouched by the "peculiar institution" that tainted the South. Elijah attended classes in New Hampshire at Dartmouth College and in Vermont at Middlebury College, finally receiving his BA from the University of Vermont. He was the only one of his fifteen siblings to receive a secondary education. Beyond bearing the expense of tuition and boarding, his mother and sisters husbanded resources and time to spin and weave him an appropriate wardrobe. One of Elijah's younger brothers,

Calvin, recalled jealously that "all was done that could be to give him a college education" and that the rest of the family lived "very poorly."[3]

On 10 June 1810, Elijah Fletcher finished his last class at the University of Vermont and began searching for a job to repay his father for financing his education. As the sixth of fifteen children, Elijah's childhood had been a hardscrabble existence, so when he received an offer from the Raleigh Academy, Elijah headed south toward North Carolina. Elijah traveled on horseback often dozens of miles in a day with only $19 or $20 to finance his seven-hundred-mile trip.[4] By the time he reached Washington, DC, he had less than $4 to his name. To save money, he claimed, he ate only "five regular meals from Albany to the City of Washington" (a trip of several weeks), boasting to his father that he "ke[pt] my mare well and starve[d] myself."[5] When he arrived in Washington, DC, he still had three miles to go and planned to sell his horse as soon as possible to finance those last miles. Instead, he had a fortuitous encounter with another tutor, and they decided to switch positions. Elijah took his colleague's job teaching fifteen "scholars" in Alexandria, Virginia, while the other man continued on to Raleigh, North Carolina.

In Alexandria, Elijah stayed at Hollin Hall, a large plantation built by George Mason's third son, Thomson Mason (1759–1820).[6] George Mason had been a "founding father" and an author of the 1776 Virginia Declaration of Rights. During his visit to Hollin Hall, Elijah observed Thomson living an opulent lifestyle on a large 676-acre estate, enabled by the work of dozens of enslaved individuals.[7] As was typical on a large antebellum farm, the plantation operated as a miniature village with dozens of slave cabins, an icehouse, barns, orchards, a blacksmith's shop, a dairy, a bathhouse, a smokehouse, and even a kiln to produce lime on-site.[8] In a letter to his father, Elijah appears troubled by his first impression of this lifestyle: "I saw herds of negroes in fields—men, women and children, some dressed in rages [sic], and others without any cloathes [sic] . . . Rich planters have from fifty to an [sic] hundred negroes" whom they buy and sell "as we do our cattle." He continued by describing slave "drives" that wrenched individuals away from their birthplaces and propelled them to South Carolina or as far as Georgia to maximize the owner's profit. Elijah observed whippings "for every little offence most cruelly" and concluded that each enslaved worker "knows his place and business and every thing is conducted with the greatest order."[9] After more than a year in Virginia, Elijah declared slavery was "a curse to any country."[10]

Elijah's Alexandria home was just eight miles from Mount Vernon, the former home of George Washington, who had died a decade earlier. Washington's nephew, Bushrod Washington, was managing the plantation when Elijah was in Alexandria. After several visits, Elijah calculated, "A negro man is worth five hundred dollars, a woman not so much." He concluded that slaves were "very valuable" and admired the "rich and neat apparel" of Virginian planters, although he believed they lived in "idleness and some in dissipation." At the same time, Elijah observed that the enslaved laborers had "very little to eat and are under the constant eye of an overseer, who makes them work from sunrise, till sunset."[11]

After several months in Alexandria, Elijah accepted a position farther south, in central Virginia, to teach Latin in New Glasgow. As he traveled, he passed by the homes of other US presidents. Three of the first four presidents were Virginians: Washington, owner of Mount Vernon; Thomas Jefferson, owner of Monticello; and the sitting president, James Madison, owner of Montpelier. At Montpelier, Elijah observed laborers rolling hogshead of tobacco to market and critiqued the farmlands as "nothing but barren, poor, uncultivated land." He had agricultural and sociological observations to make when he reached Albemarle County, as well. Jefferson had just completed his two terms as president and retired to his Charlottesville plantation. Although Elijah professed he lacked "an exalted opinion of [Jefferson]," he was delighted to be welcomed by Jefferson himself, who took Elijah on a tour of his "Library, Museum of curiosities, Philosophical apparatus, &c." Despite his warm welcome, Elijah left with an even poorer opinion of Jefferson. Elijah explained his reaction in a letter to his father: "The story of black Sal is no farce. That he cohabits with her and has a number of children by her is a sacred truth, and the worst of it is, he keeps the same children slaves, an unnatural crime which is very common in these parts."[12]

It was a great shock for a man from Vermont, which, in the 1810 US Federal Census, reported no slaves and only a small, nonwhite population of 750 people. This free population of African Americans and Indians represented less than a third of 1 percent of the state's total population.[13] As Elijah traveled in the South, he encountered plantations with enslaved communities that were almost as large as Vermont's entire nonwhite population. Virginia's 346,671 slaves made up 39 percent of the population, while an additional 20,493 free blacks made another 2 percent.[14]

Elijah's new job as the principal of a private academy in a small town at the base of the Blue Ridge Mountains began conventionally enough. He was delighted with the community, which he described as "a village of about 50 houses butifully [sic] situated, high and healthy," and he was "pleased" with the inhabitants.[15] He found accommodations with a local physician who lived only a short distance away from New Glasgow Academy. Although his own quarters were modest and plain, his students were the children of nearby wealthy plantation owners. At the end of his first term teaching French and Latin, he received an invitation to join William S. Crawford and his family for a Christmas dinner. Crawford was one of several trustees at the academy. Another was his neighbor and in-law, Edmund Penn, who lived at the Glebe.

When he reported on that evening to his parents, Elijah said he had "become acquainted with a young Lady in this place of amiable manners and disposition for whom I have more than common [regard?] & with whom I am on terms of intimacy." The budding relationship between a Southern belle and an antislavery Vermonter would have long lasting impacts on the enslaved families living at Tusculum and their kin on neighboring plantations. Weeks after his auspicious Christmas dinner at the Crawford home, Elijah wrote to his parents back in Vermont and assured them he was no "love-sick boy" but rather a practiced suitor.[16] That winter, he began to spend more and more time with Maria Antoinette Crawford, and by the spring term of 1812, several of her sisters joined her at Elijah's academy to take classes in French. In August, Elijah dropped a hint to his mother about making a "wedding coat."[17] And then in November, he made his case to his parents: "I have long been intimate with a most amiable, accomplished, sensible Lady, of one [of] the most rich, extensive, respectable families in the state." Elijah's argument contained adjectives like "respectable," "sensible," and "mature deliberation." He mentioned "happiness" in passing and followed up with a separate letter to his sister Lucy, in which he confessed they "expect to be married the middle of next April [1813]."[18] Apparently, when there were almost seven hundred miles between a suitor and his family, the formal process of requesting and receiving permission was circumvented.

It is not clear whether William and Sophia Crawford initially approved of this somewhat curt, cold New Englander as a suitor for their daughter's hand. After all, Maria Antoinette was a fifth-generation American Crawford, a family that originally emigrated to Virginia only a few decades after the establishment of Jamestown. In contrast, Elijah grew up in poverty on the Vermont frontier. But his family had equally deep roots in the New World. Family historians have traced the Fletcher family's line to "The Immigrant Robert Fletcher," born in England in 1592. His surname means "arrow maker" and may relate to his profession.[19] Robert emigrated to Massachusetts and died in Concord in 1677. Five generations later, his great-great-great-grandson twenty-year-old Jesse Fletcher served in the Revolutionary War. After his service, he left Massachusetts and settled on the Vermont frontier, where he helped carve out a newly founded American town and raised his fifteen children with his wife, Lucy Keyes. Raising children in this harsh environment left little time to coddle them or even, as it turned out, to show much affection at all. One of his younger sons, Calvin, described Jesse as "a real Puritan in many things," studious, and "uncommonly rigid in relation to the Sabbath."[20]

The Vermont Fletchers plainly had misgivings about the union between their son and a Southerner. Although we do not have his parents' letters to their son, Elijah's tone in his responses suggests they did not approve of his marrying into a slave-owning family. Still, the courtship continued. Two months after Elijah's marriage, he wrote home to assure his parents they were always first in his affection: "If I have chosen a companion recently, my highest esteem, dear to me as life itself, my filial regard for you is unaltered."[21] Elijah may have been worried his family would cut off communication with him when they learned more about his new bride. Indeed, after his marriage, Elijah's allegiance remained with his Vermont family, especially his father. On 5 September 1813, he cryptically wrote to his father, "I have complied with your request and never shown Maria your letters. There are a great many family secrets that I never shall communicate."[22] Given the great distance, physical and emotional, between father and son, it is hard to imagine how Maria's knowledge of a Vermont family secret could be so earth shattering.

Throughout his life, Elijah maintained an active correspondence with his father until the latter's death in 1825, when Elijah was just thirty-six years old. These letters reveal a very strained relationship between father and son.[23] But Elijah dutifully sent money back to his father and siblings. Jesse's letters do not survive, but Elijah's letters suggest Jesse was continually disappointed in his son. Elijah struggled to live up to Jesse's expectations right up until his father's death. His relationship with his mother, Lucy, was more oblique. He professed his love for her in letters, but she was never a central figure in his adult life.

For Maria, the first few years of married life were rather tumultuous. She married Elijah when she was nineteen years old, having grown up on a plantation with only limited and enjoyable chores such as feeding the chickens, collecting eggs, picking and stringing vegetables for drying, preserving food, knitting and sewing, and learning to read and write from private tutors. Elijah was her French and Latin tutor. Very few of her letters survive, so it's hard to determine if she was in love or simply being practical in marrying Elijah. His descriptions of her are measured rather than passionate; he described Maria as "devoid of all the affectation and common prudery of modern girls." Instead, he saw her as "sincere, candid, intelligent, and sensible."[24] They were married for almost four decades, but they remain separate in death. Elijah is buried at his beloved Sweetbrier, while Maria is at Tusculum.

Their union was devastating for at least one black family. We will never know what criteria William Crawford used in deciding whom to pick as the newlyweds' servants. It was unthinkable for him that his nineteen-year-old daughter could set up house without a lady's maid. Unfortunately, by selecting such young enslaved children, they were certainly prematurely separated from their parents. Although we cannot say precisely how old they were or whether they were in fact siblings, Elijah describes them in a letter to his five-year-old brother, Stoughton, and his nine-year-old sister, Louisa, in which he says his new "servants" are roughly their age, and happily tells Louisa that the "black girl . . . may be her waiting maid" if she comes for a visit. He was quickly acclimating to his new surroundings. That same summer of 1813, Elijah boasted to his family that he lived "something in the Virginia style," which he defined as well stocked with food (a barrel of mackerel and a round of cheese), beverages (plentiful whiskey, wine, Imperial tea, and coffee), and with "black servants enough."[25] Not surprisingly, Elijah modified his earlier opinion of slavery as "a curse" to seeing it as "a misfortune [not] a crime." In one apologetic letter to Vermont, he shares a philosophy he would espouse for the rest of his life: "The present holders of slaves are not censurable for their fathers [*sic*] crimes of introducing them. They are only censurable for not treating those they possess well." This simplistic reasoning left out the option of freeing slaves, emancipating them in one's will, pursuing a different type of occupation in Virginia, or leaving the South all together. In the same letter, he acknowledges, "I know what horrid ideas I formerly had of slavery and how I despised the man who would traffic in human flesh."[26]

Despite Elijah's protestations that he would "never be perfectly reconciled" to this human trafficking, he decided to quit his position as president of the academy and instead turn to farming. He was determined to become a successful businessman, no matter the human cost. In the spring of 1814, he began cultivating the grounds of a plantation on the land that would eventually become Sweet Briar. In a letter home, he proudly reported he had "a very good garden and take pleasure to work in it myself."[27] But over the next three decades, he would increasingly rely on the labor of others as his human holdings increased to 155 men, women, and children.

Owning two young children was, as it turned out, just the first step in his transformation from an ardent antislavery proponent to a large slave owner. Less than two years after Elijah's marriage into the Crawford family, his father-in-law died suddenly without a will at age fifty-five. An enslaved man named Cornelius cared for William during his last illness and was awarded $2 from Crawford's estate. Sophia Crawford arranged to have her son-in-law manage the complicated estate, which took decades to settle. The arrangement required Elijah to spend a large amount of his time working on the estate and settling William's debts. Four months after his father-in-law's death, Elijah complained to his Vermont family, "the management of all Mr. Crawford's affairs devolving upon me makes my task arduous."[28]

The estate included a very complicated set of financial transactions in progress, most notably a large number of debts William was holding and on which he was collecting interest. As Elijah began calling in these debts, his shrewd determination rubbed many people the wrong way. Elijah was stepping into the shoes of a successful Virginian planter without knowing the rules of engagement or the boundaries of acceptable fiduciary duties. Yes, William had loaned money to dozens of Amherst residents, but he was expected to continue holding the debt, earning interest on the loan, rather than calling in the entire payment. When Elijah attempted to settle William's estate so that it could be probated and divided among his heirs, he encountered resistance and bitterness. Over the next two decades, Elijah's mercurial and brusque personality became legendary in Amherst County. He was called repeatedly as a defendant in front of the county clerk for lawsuits brought against him by unhappy families who had lost their land to his strict financial accounting/accountability. Elijah referred to his debt-ridden neighbors as "rascals" and "depraved" humans as he struggled to manage seven plantations, three of which he leased out to other farmers.[29] In a letter to his father, he confessed, "My enemies cared little for me and my friends distrusted me."[30]

Around 1817, Elijah and Maria moved twenty miles south to Lynchburg. Although Maria may have pressured him to move to a city, he also may have felt more comfortable negotiating the tricky and acrimonious estate settlements from a distance. From her letters, Maria apparently enjoyed cosmopolitan living and did not plan to return to Amherst. Elijah adapted easily to city life. He bought a newspaper called *The Virginian*, helped found the first Episcopal Church in Lynchburg, was elected mayor, and served as president of the Lynchburg Auxiliary Society, which aimed to send some enslaved African Americans "back to Africa." During this time, the Fletchers owned three people in their city home, one of whom may have been the same girl they received as a "gift" in 1815. The 1820 and 1830 Censuses recorded enslaved individuals only by gender and a general age range. In 1830, one of the twelve people Elijah owned in Lynchburg was listed as a "female, age 19 to 23," consistent with a girl who would have been around nine years old in 1813. In the 1840 Census of the Fletcher family, we find a "female, age 24 to 35," also consistent with the same girl, and now perhaps the mother of a young girl listed as "under the age of 10." She is the only enslaved child under the age of ten in Elijah's household recorded in the 1820, 1830, and 1840 censuses. This suggests that while in the city, he was buying adult slaves for specific tasks rather than trying to increase his human holdings by natural increase. From these quantitative tallies, the young boy who entered his household in 1815 apparently did not survive, or perhaps Elijah sent him to work on one of his new rural landholdings or he ran away; no male of the appropriate age is listed in 1820, 1830, or 1840.

The men Elijah owned in 1820 were very valuable to white owners. It is unclear if Elijah purchased them—a large expense for an urban household—or brought them from Tusculum to help in the Lynchburg household. It is unlikely that Elijah purchased the older woman; she more likely worked at Tusculum. Years earlier, Elijah had pledged to "use every endeavor to make their [slaves] situation as agreeable and comfortable as possible," so perhaps she was the enslaved girl's mother and Elijah was reuniting them in his household.[31]

Elijah, ever the shrewd businessman, followed in his father-in-law's footsteps by lending money to his rural neighbors. His scattered financial notes over two years (1818–1819) demonstrate a complicated series of financial transactions in which he called in notes, lent out money, collected interest on earlier loans, and purchased fine china for his home. He also hired out his enslaved men: Alfred was sent to Fluvanna County for one day with John Patten, while Davy was sent on a three-month indenture to a relative, Nelson Crawford. And just as his father-in-law did, Elijah increased the number of enslaved servants to provide his children with maids and manservants. Between 1821 and 1830, Elijah and Maria had six children, of whom four survived: Sidney (born 1821), Lucian (born 1824), Indiana (born 1828), and Elizabeth (born 1830). To accommodate this growing family, Elijah and Maria moved, in 1826, into a $3,500 townhouse on Elm Avenue, on the corner of Commerce and 13th streets in Lynchburg.[32]

Elijah boasted to Calvin in 1828, "I have spent a heap of money in the course of the last year or two in improving my house and lot and making it one of the most convenient and handsome in this place."[33] Some of the furniture from this two-story, red brick home survives. The fed-eral-style pieces reflect the Fletcher's growing wealth and social status. Their guests would have been received in the formal parlor, sitting on French-style chairs (fitting for a woman named after Marie Antoinette), reclining on Empire sofas (adorned with "sinuous acanthus leaves" and the US national symbol of a bald eagle), and playing cards on the "hairy paw foot" table.[34] This level of daily luxury required the labor of enslaved individuals who lived in sparse outbuildings in the yard.[35] The enslaved laborers at Elijah's Lynchburg home would have worked to manage his domestic affairs, including cooking, gardening, cleaning, sewing, and carrying a regular supply of water to the house and hu-man waste away from it. Elijah and Maria almost certainly relied on a manservant and a maid, and they purchased at least one young African American boy, Archer, to serve their sons.

Although Elijah mentioned a handful of enslaved individuals by name, many more were mentioned only by referencing their impact on his financial ledger. Unfortunately, we do not have obituaries for the enslaved individuals on Sweetbrier Plantation. Instead, their deaths were recorded annually in county ledgers ("Slave Deaths") and, even more rarely, in letters Elijah wrote to his Vermont-based parents. In the summer of 1825, Elijah wrote to his father about the death of a "Negro Boy about ten or 12 years old" who had been sick for some time. In-stead of lamenting the death or discussing the boy, he focused on his bottom line: "Such a boy is worth in case from $350 to $400. This kind of property is now rising."[36] Later that fall, two more enslaved toddlers died, while Elijah boasted that he enjoyed "fine health."[37]

Given Elijah's increasingly successful financial dealings, it comes as no surprise that the 1830 Census listed a dozen slaves in his home, a fourfold increase from 1820. These individuals ranged from ten to more than fifty-five years old. Four were between the ages of ten and twenty-three. He also owned five men between the ages of twenty-four and fifty-four, and one woman in that age range; two of these adults might have been a couple. Finally, he owned a man and woman, over fifty-five years old, who also might have been a couple, assuming Elijah made an effort to keep spouses together.[38] The large number of enslaved adult men is a demographic more commonly associated with plantations or industry (such as ironworking). In this urban situation, the strange de-mographic of several enslaved men is probably a result of Elijah's debt settlements. To increase his cash flow, he hired the men out to other slave owners to work in the city's quarries, blacksmith forges, or canals.

From 1830 to 1840, Elijah further increased the number of slaves he managed on his father-in-law's plantations and in his own household, an increase again attributable to his management of William's debts. Elijah guiltily explained to his father: "I have likewise increased the number of my slaves very much. I have found it necessary to take them in payment of debts."[39] Dozens of enslaved families were separated from relatives, as their owners used them in lieu of cash to pay the debts for which Elijah demanded payment. Elijah pledged to "treat them with humanity" by feeding and clothing them well but made no provision for, or even reference to, their separation from family members.

He also began selling surplus slaves. On 14 February 1831, Elijah advertised a "first rate Cook and House Servant" for sale.[40] If she were the young girl he and Maria received as a wedding gift, then she would have been twenty-seven years old. Later that year, Elijah posted another advertisement in his Lynchburg newspaper, *The Virginian*: "For Sale, a Family of Negroes, consisting of a Woman and three Children."[41] This profile fits four of the residents on the census, the "female slave" age ten to twenty-three, and the four young men under the age of twenty-three. If these were the "Negro Family" in 1830 and if Elijah were successful in selling them, then he would have been left with five single men between the ages of twenty-four and fifty-four and one woman, again an unusal demographic for an urban slave owner.

With his increased cash flow, Elijah reinvested in land, steadily buying up thousands of rural acres scattered over several contiguous counties. On 22 December 1830, he was the highest bidder on about eight hundred acres of land then called Locust Ridge.[42] Located just eight miles south of the Tusculum plantation, the former owner, Thomas Crews, had defaulted on his mortgage payments, and the courts ordered the property to be put up for sale.[43] In the decade before his financial insolvency, Thomas lived at Locust Ridge with his wife, Sarah, and their eight children.[44] He owned twenty-five African Americans, many of whom worked almost daily in the fields. Buying up yet another bankrupt farmer's plantation did not endear Elijah to his future neighbors. Meanwhile, he bragged to his brother that he was debt free, except in some "small matters."[45]

Although genealogically convoluted, Maria was related to Thomas's wife, Sarah Penn. Sarah and Sophia (Maria's mother) were two of Gabriel and Sarah Penn's children; they grew up at the Glebe. When Gabriel's estate was finally settled in 1829, Thomas inherited a girl named Betsy, who may have passed to Elijah as part of his purchase of Locust Ridge. Two decades later, when Elijah itemized the enslaved families living at this location on Sweetbrier Plantation, he included a woman named Betsy who, as later documents show, is Betsy Rose, born around 1830. While Betsy was a common name in Virginia during this period such that it may not be the same woman referenced in 1829 and 1852, I use this example to demonstrate how understanding the complicated kinship connections among white families is important in unraveling the sparse historic records for black families during this period.

After two decades of city living and frustrating attempts to settle his father-in-law's estate from afar, Elijah decided to try his own hand at being a "gentleman farmer"—a wealthy businessman who could delegate much of the backbreaking work to others. Accordingly, at age fifty, Elijah Fletcher retired from politics, the newspaper business, and his urban social commitments. This allowed him to spend most of his time at Locust Ridge, which he eventually renamed Sweetbrier to honor his wife's favorite species of rose. Other than influencing the name of her husband's new project, Maria preferred life in Lynchburg and, on occasion, visiting her mother in distant Kentucky. As a result, the large plantation Elijah had intended as a family retreat became home for Elijah and his two daughters, Indiana and Elizabeth. Meanwhile, he sent his sons, Sidney and Lucian, away to secondary school: Sidney to Yale and Lucian to a private boarding school.

This new plantation included "a large brick house on it, containing about 1000 acres of pretty good land."[46] The plantation house was a modest Virginian farmhouse, dating to the 1790s. At first, Elijah might have been able to manage the farm with some of his urban slaves and perhaps forcing some of the Tusculum slaves to join him at Sweetbrier. But his agricultural vision for the property, which included crops, livestock, orchards, and even beekeeping, was going to require a sharp increase in enslaved labor. Over the next two decades, Elijah began purchasing additional slaves from domestic traders, receiving enslaved individuals in lieu of payments on debts owed to him and benefiting from the "natural increase" of the women he owned. By the time of his death, in 1858, Elijah was well known as a slave owner. One of his neighbors, Samuel M. Garland, observed that Elijah was "the owner of many negro women & . . . therefore often in need" of a midwife.[47] One particular woman he purchased ended up outliving all of Elijah's direct descendants and was one of the few enslaved individuals at Sweetbrier who also worked for Sweet Briar College.

Notes

1. Settlement of David Crawford IV's estate, 1804, Will Book 4: 146, Amherst County Courthouse; David Crawford IV's will, 1802, Will Book 4: 49–52, Amherst County Courthouse.

2. While not always enforced, the 1777 Constitution of Vermont freed enslaved women when they reached age eighteen, and men at age twenty-one. "1777 Constitution," Vermont Secretary of State archives, last updated 29 October 2018, https://www.sec.state.vt.us/archives-records/state-archives/governm ent-history/vermont-constitutions/1777-constitution.aspx.
3. Thornbrough, *The Diary of Calvin Fletcher*, 1:xxi.
4. *TLEF*, letter to his father, 6 July 1810, 4–5.
5. *TLEF*, letter from "Washington City" (Washington, DC) to his father, 17 July 1810, 6.
6. "Children of George Mason of Gunston Hall," Gunston Hall, accessed 7 January 2019, http://www.gunstonhall.org/georgemason/mason_family/thomson_mason.html.
7. "Hollin Hall," Gunston Hall, accessed 7 January 2019, http://www.gun stonhall.org/georgemason/landholdings/hollin_hall.html.
8. Taken from the advertisement to sell Clermont after the death of General John Mason, *Alexandria Gazette*, 19 April 1849, 3. Von Briesen concludes the plantation was Hollin Hall. *TLEF*, 15.
9. *TLEF*, letter to his father, 29 August 1810, 12, 14.
10. *TLEF*, letter to his father, 29 November 1811, 45.
11. *TLEF*, letter to his father, 29 August 1810, 13–14.
12. *TLEF*, letter to his father, 24 May 1811, 34, 36.
13. "Slave, Free Black, and White Population, 1780–1830," Terry Bouton's University System of Maryland user page, accessed 28 December 2018, http://userpages.umbc.edu/~bouton/History407/SlaveStats.htm.
14. "Population of Virginia: 1810," Inter-University Consortium for Political and Social Research, accessed 28 December 2018, http://www.virginia places.org/population/pop1810numbers.html.
15. *TLEF*, letter to his father, 24 May 1811, 36.
16. *TLEF*, letter most likely intended for his father, 23 December 1811, 49.
17. *TLEF*, letter to his sister Laura Fletcher, 16 August 1812, 61.
18. *TLEF*, letter to his sister Lucy Fletcher, 6 November 1812, 67.
19. 1881 Fletcher Family History, photocopy version given to the author by a descendant.
20. Thornbrough, *The Diary of Calvin Fletcher*, 1:xx.
21. *TLEF*, letter to his father, 20 June 1813, 73.
22. *TLEF*, letter to his father, 5 September 1813, 77.
23. Thornbrough, *The Diary of Calvin Fletcher*, 1:xx.
24. *TLEF*, letter with no recipient specified but delivered to his father, 7 February 1813, 72.
25. *TLEF*, letter to his father, 20 June 1813, 74–75.
26. *TLEF*, letter to his father, 5 September 1813, 77–79.
27. *TLEF*, letter to his father, 2 May 1814, 80.
28. *TLEF*, letter home, 4 July 1815, 83.
29. *TLEF*, letter to his father, 31 August 1815, 85.
30. *TLEF*, letter to his father, 5 August 1810, 7.
31. *TLEF*, letter to his father, 5 September 1813, 78.
32. Livingston, "Elijah Fletcher of Nelson County, Virginia," 16.

33. *TLEF,* letter to his brother Calvin, 10 August 1828, 102.
34. Furniture styles as described in Denva Jackson's 2005 exhibit brochure, "The Fletcher Parlor," 2003.
35. Based on the memories of a woman born in 1850 whose father purchased the house from Indiana Fletcher in 1860. *TLEF,* 103n9.
36. *TLEF,* letter to his father, 23 July 1825, 97.
37. *TLEF,* letter to his father, 7 November 1825, 98.
38. *TLEF,* letter to his father, 5 September 1813, 78.
39. *TLEF,* letter to his father, 14 November 1824, 92.
40. *The Virginian,* 14 February 1831.
41. *The Virginian,* 20 October 1831 to 17 November 1831.
42. Amherst County Deed Book, vol. T, 455. Elijah rounds up the acreage of his purchase to one thousand in *TLEF,* letter to his brother (most likely Calvin), 29 March 1831, 123.
43. Amherst County Deed Book, vol. T, 323; *TLEF,* 123n2.
44. 1820 US Federal Census, Amherst, Virginia: p. 21, NARA Roll M33_131, Image 33.
45. *TLEF,* letter to his brother (most likely Calvin), 29 March 1831, 122–23.
46. *TLEF,* letter to his brother (most likely Calvin), 29 March 1831, 123.
47. Deposition of Samuel M. Garland, 3 December 1864, Simpson v. Fletcher case, Amherst County Courthouse.

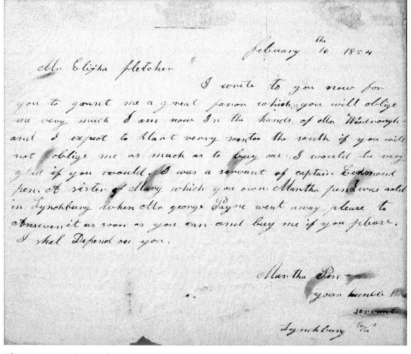

Figure 4.1. A letter from Martha Penn ("Pen") Taylor to Elijah Fletcher,
16 February 1854. Sweet Briar College Library Archives.

Transcription:

february the 16, 1854

Mr. Elijha fletcher,
I write to you now for

you to grant me a great favor which you will oblige
me very much. I am now In the hands of Mr. Woodrough
and I expect to start very soon too the south if you will
not oblige me as much as to buy me. I would be very
glad if you would. I was a servant of captain Edmond
pen. A sister of Mary which you own. Martha pen. I was sold
in Lynchburg when Mr. george Payne went away please to
Answer it as soon as you can and buy me if you please.
I shal Depend on you.

Martha Pen
your humble
servant
Lynchburg Va.

4

Survival Strategies, 1831–1857

Martha Penn was born around 1833, just a few years after the birth of Elijah Fletcher's eldest daughter, Indiana. Throughout the remainder of the nineteenth century, Martha and Indiana lived two very different but intersecting lives. If not for a bold act by Martha, she would have been sold into the Deep South and separated from her family, including her sister Mary. In the letter reproduced as Figure 4.1, Martha begs Elijah to purchase her so that she will not be removed from her sister. From Martha's letter, we learn Elijah had purchased Mary at some point after leaving urban life behind and beginning to engage in "pursuits more congenial to his feelings than the heartless politics of the day."[1] By the time he received this remarkable plea from Martha "Pen," he owned more than one hundred African and Native American men, women, and children. Very few of them had any choice about their circumstances, which made Martha's letter even more remarkable. Her efforts to control her destiny illuminate the subtle connections among enslaved families and white families in antebellum Virginian communities.

The first time I read this letter, it presented more questions than answers. Did Martha have any previous personal connection to Elijah Fletcher or to Sweetbrier? Did she expect a slaveholder to agree to buy her just because he owned her sister? To whom did she hand the letter for delivery, especially as she apparently wrote it after being confined to a Lynchburg building—possibly the jail—while awaiting her forced departure into the hands of "Mr Woodrough" (Seth Woodruff, an infamous Lynchburg slave trader)? At a time when enslaved families were regularly separated by the sale of family members, and when countless coffles of slaves were forced to make the treacherous journey to the Deep South, what made Martha think this particular white man would respond positively to her request? Did she simply have nothing to lose?

As I began to research this unusual woman's life, I wanted to untangle the vicissitudes of her early years, when she was in thrall to white families and their financial decisions. Scholars reconstructing accounts of enslaved individuals often take one of two approaches: (1) they use "etic" (external) sources, such as the personal letters and secondhand bureaucratic accounts of white slave owners and governmental records, or study the occasionally preserved photograph; or (2) with a lot of work and usually a bit of luck, they locate and analyze "emic" (internal) records, such as genealogical information recorded in family Bibles or oral histories compiled by descendants that reveal the everyday life of enslaved families. Some researchers try to combine both types of sources, leaving the impression of two entirely separate universes on a Southern plantation: that of the white decision-making residents of the "big house," and the constrained daily lives of the black residents of the slave cabins.

However, if we could interview Martha in 1853, on her twentieth birthday, we would find these universes intimately connected. The system of slavery required enslaved black residents to heighten their powers of observation. They had every reason to watch, listen, and care deeply about the ups and downs of slave owners' lives. Conversations overheard while serving meals, cleaning chamber pots in the master bedroom, or announcing visitors to the head of the household were also opportunities to gauge the relative happiness, economic prosperity, and health of slaveholders. When their moods or circumstances changed, enslaved individuals could find themselves facing a beating, the sale of a family member, or—as in the Fletchers' case—a white family wedding that required African Americans as dowry.

Martha was born around 1830, most likely at the Glebe. Martha's first owner was Edmund Penn, who had inherited the plantation from his father, Gabriel. When I first read through page after page of account records, chancery suits, and genealogical charts that outlined, in great detail, the successes and failures of the Penn family in Amherst and Lynchburg, I filed it all away as Martha's "background" material. The hundreds of white Penn documents contained only one or two references to Martha or her sister Mary, so I skipped over most of the details associated with the white family's births and deaths, social successes, and financial failures. Then I realized I was looking at this information the wrong way. The minutiae of Penn family bankruptcies, guardianship appointments, out-of-state moves, and white marriages and deaths would have been daily fodder for Martha. She ultimately used this knowledge at just the right moment, contacting just the right person to exert control over her future.

Those decisions all lay ahead. As a child in the 1830s, as she stood in the doorway of the Penns' large house, Martha would have surveyed a full complement of outbuildings, an orchard, gardens and fields, and, in the far distance, the foothills of the Blue Ridge Mountains. When

Gabriel purchased the Glebe, he owned thirty-nine slaves. We can piece together only some of their names: Mary, Sam, Lucy, George, Jack, Siller, Frank, Charlott, William Brody, and Bartlett. Martha may have known some of these people only briefly, while others were removed from the plantation before she was born; Lucy, for example, was already listed as an "old woman" by 1826, while Bartlett, listed only as "Jenny's son," was sold in 1828 for $262 to settle the debts from Gabriel's estate.[2] Martha would have grown up in a multigenerational community, with elders like a woman referred to as "Old Jude," who was so old in 1827 that instead of being valued for sale, her owners set aside $50 annually to care for her. Reading between the lines of the inheritance documents, Mary and Sam were likely a couple, as were Lucy and George. William (or Billy) Broady, born around 1790, shows up in multiple sources as a talented blacksmith. He grew up at the Glebe, and passed on his skills to several of his sons.

After inheriting the Glebe in 1798, Edmund married Jane Johnston in 1806 and started a family. Each of the couple's four daughters—Sarah, Ann Fox, Jane J., and Catherine Gabriella—would have required a lady's maid. As a young man, Edmund had been given six slaves by his father, only one of whom, Charlott, was female.[3] So between 1794 and the birth of his last daughter in 1819, Edmund likely purchased several enslaved women, one of whom may have been Martha's mother. Although her name is not recorded, she would have been born at least as early as 1810. Perhaps mother and daughter shared stories about Edmund and his impecunity. They would have known and lived in fear of his growing debts, which he paid off by selling land and people. Perhaps in response to his growing family, or maybe just as a symptom of his poor money management, Edmund enhanced the Glebe around 1825, adding wainscoting, wooden trim and moldings, a new floor, and fireplace mantels.[4] Mary was an infant at the time, and her father may have been one of the carpenters brought in to chop down trees, remove their bark, and carve them into decorative wainscoting, trim, and moldings. Or he may have been one of several blacksmiths who handwrought nails for construction projects or made and repaired plows, axes, and other agricultural tools.

Edmund's mother, Sarah Calloway, came from a powerful Bedford family that had earned its wealth as leading iron merchants. Sarah died in 1826 at the Glebe, and Martha's mother may have been one of the slaves called on to wash and prepare her body for burial. Sarah's obituary opined, "This amiable lady . . . has left numerous offspring and many feeling friends to lament a blank in their society."[5] Her death also would have created uncertainty and anxiety within her household, causing the enslaved women who served her to wonder whether they would be sold or hired out by their next master.

During her first fifteen years, Martha would have witnessed first-hand the large, white Penn family expand and then contract at the Glebe. As a small child, she may have helped clean the sheets when two of Edmund's daughters gave birth in 1838; as a teenager, she may have cooked for his growing family. As Edmund and Jane's brood grew up, Martha and her enslaved family members at the Glebe may have grown nervous as several of the Penn children moved farther south, to Kentucky, Florida, and Tennessee. Edmund joined one of his sisters in Tennessee after Jane's death in 1847.[6] These migrations caused disruptions and separations within Martha's social network and, most likely, her extended family. Martha's sister Mary escaped the threat of these out-of-state departures because she was given to Elijah Fletcher in 1844. One of Edmund's sons-in-law, Hugh Brown, had borrowed money from Elijah and, in 1844, paid the debt in flesh, transferring ownership of Mary as payment. The document reveals a prior injury or perhaps a hereditary malady: Mary had only one eye.[7]

Because of the many kinship and fiscal ties between the white families, Martha would have grown up hearing tales from enslaved cooks, manservants, messengers, farmhands, and housekeepers about not only the Penn family but also the Fletchers and the Crawfords. The enslaved workers would have heard which owners were rumored to be kinder or crueler, and would have been aware that many white landowners scorned Elijah as a money-grubbing Northerner.

For the remainder of the 1840s, the six-mile distance between the Glebe and Sweetbrier separated the two sisters. But this proximity was in jeopardy. In 1850, Edmund died, leaving his finances in disarray. One of his heirs, George B. Payne, the husband of Edmund's daughter Catherine, was appointed to settle the estate. The Paynes had moved to Florida a year or two earlier and were not seeking more Virginia slaves. It was then that Payne decided to sell Martha to the local slave driver, "Woodrough," "Woodroof," or "Woodruff." He was a central Virginia "soul driver" who profited from the exportation of black and native peoples to the Deep South, destroying many family ties in the process.[8] This was very likely Seth Woodroof, one of the most active slave traders in Lynchburg, who worked as a commission merchant in the 1850s, specializing in a "market for NEGROES, of both sexes, between the ages of 10 and 30 years."[9]

Martha's letter to Elijah Fletcher stands out not only for its desperation but also for its bravery. Had Woodroof learned of her efforts, she could have been punished or beaten to death for interfering with his business. Moreover, Elijah could have read the letter and worried that this enslaved woman was too determined to achieve her goal. Given these circumstances, it was a considerable gamble to hope Elijah would respond affirmatively. And yet, he did.

Martha was likely to have been put to work as a domestic upon her arrival at Sweetbrier (Figure 4.2). She was just a few years older than Indiana, so Elijah may have expected her to serve as his daughter's personal maid. The "mansion house" Martha had arrived in was a reno-

Figure 4.2. Martha Penn Taylor, circa 1880s. Sweet Briar College Library Archives.

vated farmhouse, transformed by the addition of two Italianate towers. Elijah's children were inspired to add these architectural adornments after returning from a European tour through several countries. The "imposing structure" was "very capacious, and so arranged as to combine elegance with every convenience." The enslaved domestics may have preferred a smaller residence, without the multitude of associated outbuildings that required tending: "Kitchen, Laundry, Extensive granaries, Tobacco Houses, Stables, Carriage House, and Cabins, with gardens attached."[10] Their daily labors supported the white family: cooking, digging wells, serving water to the paid workforce, and making the bricks, digging the foundations, or hammering out nails.

Despite the large number of enslaved laborers at Sweetbrier in 1850 (about ninety-eight, according to the US Federal Census that year), men and women relied on a larger community to locate potential marriage partners. The challenge lay in getting permission to assemble in large numbers. Between the mid-eighteenth century and the 1830s, most states strengthened laws that prohibited the gathering of more than a handful of slaves, and required funerals to be conducted during the daytime or when a white man was present to officiate. These laws were passed primarily because of the fear that enslaved people would meet to plot rebellions.[11] Mounted patrols enforced the restrictions on gatherings and sometimes used these laws to disperse mourners at the site of a funeral. The American historian Eugene Genovese pointed out a significant outcome of successful funerals: "the extent to which they allowed the participants to feel themselves a human community unto themselves."[12] Perhaps partly for this reason, and certainly because of the rarity of large gatherings of enslaved individuals, the occasion of a funeral was also one of the few times enslaved people could meet potential marriage partners.

If we turn to contemporary accounts from other Virginia and Carolina plantations, we can sketch an outline of the rituals that accompanied the death of an enslaved individual. For example, a North Carolina farmer recalled a funeral held for a young boy who had died in a wagon accident. The family held a wake on the first evening after his death, which the farmer—then a young boy himself—described: "Late into the night the voices of those who were keeping watch over the dead could be heard singing their mournful songs, and it was very late before sleep came to any of us, so deeply moved were we by this sad occurrence." The next morning, two enslaved carpenters constructed a coffin and buried the child in a separate cemetery that the farmer referred to as "God's Acre."[13] While we do not know what sermon was preached, a contemporary example from another Southern plantation is a sermon delivered for "sister Dicey": "I commit your body to the ground, earth to earth, ashes to ashes, dust to dust, but on that Great getting up Morning, when the trumpet of God shall sound, we will meet you in the skies and join the hosts of saints who will go marching in."[14] These sermons were often preached in the middle of the night, when the enslaved labor force was most likely to be free from work requirements. One observer described these "midnight funerals" as a celebration "in the deep night-darkness of some dense old wood, made doubly dismal by the ghostly light of the pine torches and the phantom-like figures of the scarcely visible mourners."[15] Female domestics may have prepared the body, while an enslaved blacksmith or carpenter with access to tools would have made the coffin and carved the gray fieldstone. Finally, friends and neighbors of the deceased would have served as pallbearers, walking uphill through the crops to a rocky and irregular summit.

Although Elijah occasionally described the everyday lives of enslaved individuals in his copious letters, he did not allude to any of their funerals. He did mention, very casually and in passing, the death of enslaved children and adults but never indicated where their bodies were buried or whether he gave mourners time off to prepare the deceased for burial or to carve a marker for their gravesite. Martha herself may have suffered a loss; by 1860, no "Mary" appears on the list of Elijah's property. In August 1852, just six months after Martha's fateful letter, Elijah wrote to a brother that two of his "servants" had died recently, "one a very old man, the other a young woman, who had been sick a long time."[16] Thus, Martha may have lost her sister before they could be reunited. Mary's death, whenever it came, would have received little documentary attention. Some slave owners recorded the deaths of African Americans in their farm books, and once-a-decade "mortality" reports recorded the names of individuals, both black and white, who had died in the year leading up to the census. Since Martha never mentions a surname for Mary, it is almost impossible to track her sister, a black "Mary" in Amherst after the Civil War, and to prove she is the correct Mary.

The records that could shed light on crucial parts of Martha's life, such as whether she and her sister were successfully reunited, may not have been preserved. This could limit our ability to answer other questions: What was the nature of their relationship in 1854, having been separated as children a decade earlier? Did the sisters have siblings living on other plantations? Were their parents enslaved together at the Glebe? And, more broadly, where had the family come from? Were some of their grandparents forced to accompany the white Penn family as they settled in western Virginia? If so, were they originally purchased at slave ports on the Eastern Seaboard, or in New Orleans? What about the ships that brought them? Did their journeys originate in the Caribbean or Africa? Were any of the stories from these tumultuous voyages passed down to Martha? For now, historic and oral histories are silent. But we can guess at a different aspect of Martha's midlife experience. Working backward chronologically, the archival trail suggests Martha met her future husband, Henry, in the first few years after she arrived at Sweetbrier, perhaps at the funerary vigil for her sister.

Although we may never know the exact trajectory of the courtship between Martha and Henry, they were married in the mid-1850s. A central Virginia slave owner named Abraham Fost possibly mentioned their marriage in postscript to a letter written to Elijah Fletcher around 1854 "The married servants will be . . . [illegible] to go home, in about two days. They are all well and doing well."[17] The union of two enslaved individuals in marriage was not legal because, in the eyes of white lawmakers, they were property, not people. Yet, there are countless examples of enslaved communities and even their masters who recognized lifelong commitments between enslaved men and women. Perhaps influenced by his Vermont roots or his sense of guilt, Elijah allowed servants to "perform the marriage ceremony." Perhaps one of the elders at Sweetbrier presided over a ceremony to acknowledge the union between Martha and Henry Taylor.

Elijah also permitted his slaves "to hold religious service among themselves . . . There are some among them who take a lead in these meetings, who perform . . . the funeral service over their deceased fellow servants, with much propriety and solemnity."[18] Elijah may have been influenced by Maria Antoinette's brother-in-law, Rev. Charles H. Page (who married Sophia Crawford's sister, Gabriella Penn), who arranged a church service for his own slaves in 1831. Page explained: "For the benefit of the coloured population, regular services are held in the churches upon the Lord's day, and occasional services in private houses." He considered the services a success, since "the coloured people attend numerously and it is hoped, with benefit to their souls."[19] Enslaved worshippers were constrained by Virginia law, which required a white preacher to be present, and social mores directed that the white preacher lead black services. In cities, black parishioners were often taken to church with their owners and made to sit in the balconies or other segregated places within the church. On rural plantations, enslaved individuals had slightly more privacy, and many were able to host nighttime religious services in "brush arbors," hastily constructed outdoor chapels, which often went undetected by slaveholders.

Throughout most of his years at Sweetbrier, Elijah arranged elaborate Christmas festivities for the enslaved community, when African and Native Americans hosted quilting bees, played instruments, sold products from their gardens, visited relatives at nearby plantations, met prospective spouses, or hosted marriage ceremonies (socially binding but not recognized by law). The year after Martha arrived at Sweetbrier, Elijah described his preparations "for a happy Christmas for our servants. They have all to sell their crops, which consist principally of corn, and it takes many wagon loads and each wants to go with it and lay in their finery and small comforts."[20] Maria noted that both her own children and the enslaved families "claimed and received their Xmas presents."[21] The record preserved by the white owners does not reflect any recognition of the bitter irony that an enslaved individual would have put "freedom" on their "Christmas list" if asked their preference.

The holidays were a rare occasion for enslaved families who were separated on different plantations to join for a visit. Accordingly, at Christmastime, Elijah observed, "Our Servants are now enjoying themselves in perfection and I do every thing to make it a merry time with them. They all started from here this morning to Tusculum Plantation to a Quilting, and as it was muddy the girls went in a four horse Wagon. They will stay all night and dance to the Banjo and be back tomorrow."[22] His note confirms that the enslaved individuals at Sweetbrier had social and kinship ties to the nearby Tusculum plantation, and could occasionally pursue them, dependent on the financial and managerial whims of their owners.

Between Martha's arrival at Sweetbrier, in 1854, and the birth of her and Henry's first child, Lorena, in 1858, Henry would have been frequently sent to work away from the plantation, as much as a day's walk from Sweetbrier. Elijah hired out Henry and several other enslaved young men on the plantation to work on canals, stone quarries, and railroads. Although Elijah expanded the scope of Sweetbrier Plantation throughout his life, he, like many of his Piedmont neighbors, did not have enough year-round work to make the ownership of dozens of slaves economically viable. Instead, he made money from their work on other plantations, railroads, and iron forges. This system separated men like Henry from their families for months or even a year at a time, while they worked on the other side of the Blue Ridge Mountains.[23] Virginia slaveowners like Elijah regularly hired out skilled laborers to earn extra money during slow seasons. From the paper trail—receipts, letters, and the relatively large number of adult men in his Lynchburg household in the 1830s and 1840s—Elijah apparently used hiring out as part of his business model. This practice continued after he settled permanently at rural Sweetbrier Plantation. Several of his enslaved men appeared to spend more time away from the plantation than on it.

In central Virginia, slave hiring increased throughout the 1850s because of labor shortages in specific sectors of the economy, including public works projects (e.g., railroads and canals), mining, factory work, and seasonal agricultural labor. And while individual contracts between slave owners and renters varied, most included the same basic obligations: the hirers had to provide "food, lodging, and two new suits of clothes, one for summer, the other for winter." These contracts usually began on New Year's Day and lasted as long as one year.[24] By 1860, one of the most common placements for hired laborers was in one of the 252 tobacco manufacturing facilities distributed throughout Virginia. Fletcher never mentions sending his enslaved workers to a specific site, but Lynchburg was one of the five largest tobacco-manufacturing centers in the world. The demand from employers for that type of work would have been high, affording slaveholders $100 to $150 a year, in addition to paying for clothing, food, and medical care for the leased worker.[25]

There is no evidence that Elijah shared any of these profits with his enslaved workers. But some of the men who were rented out in this way exercised a remarkable degree of agency and took considerable risks to manage their lives. For example, in 1857, Elijah hired out Jimbo, Murrow, and William (who was perhaps Billy Broady) to work in a canal. Sending men to the canals was, Elijah admitted, "a sort of punishment . . . to those who do not please me at home."[26] We do not have a first-person account of their work in the canals, but other slave owners reported that the work was difficult and that diseases such as smallpox were prevalent.[27]

The three Sweetbrier men may have been sent to work along the Lynchburg to Buchanan canal, which began just a few dozen miles from Elijah's plantation. Decades earlier, in 1836, the James River and Kanawha Canal project had reached Amherst County.[28] Originally surveyed and planned by George Washington in 1785, the canal was intended to improve the ease and economy of moving passengers and freight by water from western Virginia to the coast. After multiple financial delays and flood damage along the routes, the original towpath became a roadbed for the new railroads. By 1850, plans had been initiated for the Orange and Alexandria Railroad (later the Southern Railway) that was to pass by Sweetbrier on the Lynchburg-to-Charlottesville track; these projects would be finished by 1860 and required the labor of hundreds of enslaved men, including some of those owned by Elijah.[29]

The same year that Elijah sent the three men to work on the canal, an "N. Gill" asked about hiring "a large force of Black hands" to work in a stone quarry the next year. Gill assured Elijah that "good wages will be given and satisfactory security given for the payment of the hires."[30] The "wages" and "payment" accrued, of course, to Elijah and not to the laborers. The work was arduous and required long periods away from home. In the late 1840s, Elijah earned $110 a year for each man hired out; skilled workers brought in more—$200 for a blacksmith and $150 for a carpenter. He had "so many youngsters [enslaved children] growing up to take the place of the older ones that I can spare them without interrupting the usual course of plantation work."[31] The "older ones" would have included many of the fathers and grandfathers of the "youngsters," who were then separated from their families for a year at a time.

Although Gill did not indicate how distant the stone quarry was from Sweetbrier, a work site located even a dozen miles away would make it difficult for an enslaved man to return to visit family and friends. Slave patrols—first formed as public guards after the 1800 Gabriel Prosser rebellion and then reorganized and reinforced by a series of laws passed in 1832—regularly watched the main byways. Slaves required passes to travel and were subject to harassment and occasional false imprisonment even when carrying them.[32] Hiring out was thus one more aspect of slavery that created emotional and social hardship for enslaved families. For example, an enslaved man named Sampson was hired out to Bezaleel Brown, an Albemarle County farmer who lived more than seventy miles from Sweetbrier.[33] Even if Sampson were given two days off and a pass, he could not have walked home and returned in time. In other cases, Elijah hired men out to the ironworks on the other side of the Blue Ridge Mountains.[34] Their return trip would have been even more risky and arduous.

Sometimes, Elijah separated mothers from their children using this system of "hirings." In 1854, the Lynchburg resident Willis Mays wrote to Fletcher on behalf of an enslaved woman named Betsey: "Sir through the request of Betsey I here wish to inform you that Mr. [Wingfield] who hired her and her daughter will move from Lynchburg about the first of next month and consequently intends hiring out Betsey for the remainder of the year and intends taking with them Betsey's daughter. Betsey seems to be unwilling for Mr. [Wingfield] to carry her daughter over the mountains and therefore would be glad if you would prevent her being removed." Based on dozens of other instances when Elijah hired out an enslaved laborer, Wingfield very likely had paid Elijah for one year of Betsey and her daughter's labor. Wingfield's subsequent decision to separate mother and daughter is one example of the traumatic consequences of hiring out enslaved individuals. Elijah received this request around the same time he purchased Martha Penn in response to her petition. If he agreed to this second request, this "Betsey" and her daughter might be the same woman "and child" inherited by Elijah's daughter Elizabeth in 1860.[35]

In other instances, enslaved men used this system of hiring out to enhance specific skills. When asked to contribute information for a book about prominent Virginians, Elijah boasted about the abilities of his enslaved workers, explaining that every building on the plantation, except the "big house," was constructed by these men, "having among them almost every description of mechanic."[36] Some of the enslaved laborers on Sweetbrier Plantation realized that because their specialized labor brought in cash for Elijah, this position could allow them to assert some control over their circumstances. We can piece together the names of several of these skilled workers, including Henry and his colleagues, Phil, Joshua, Granville, and Preston.

In 1854, Preston used his exceptional smithing skills to bargain about the nature of his return to work after running away. That January, Abraham Fost had sent Elijah a bond for the hire of several "Negro men," including Preston. In February, Jacob M. Ruff (possibly Fost's overseer) wrote to Elijah enquiring about "Preston & the man I hired from you in place of Granville, neither of them have made their appearance." Elijah had trusted the pair to travel the fifty miles from Sweetbrier to Pattonsburg unaccompanied. Ruff complained that their services in the smithy were "much needed" and that, because of their absence, "the company has been to the expense off [sic] the hire to a shop no way connected with the work." In other words, the agency of two enslaved men caused a white blacksmith to shut down operations. Moreover, Ruff complained, "the company could better have spared the services of any four other hands than the two smiths." The specificity of the request illustrates that some enslaved men at Sweetbrier were known from as far away as the other side of the Blue Ridge Mountains for particular skills. Preston and his fellow smith never arrived at Fost's enterprise, so Elijah sent several other "hands," including a carpenter.[37]

Preston managed to stay at large for months. Due to a miscommunication between Elijah and Fost, no slave patrol had been sent after him. When Preston did not show up at Fost's work site in Pattonsburg later in the summer of 1854, Fost sent one of his men to Sweetbrier to inquire further. Elijah's African American overseer reported that Preston was not there and that it was "very doubtful if he could be caught." Fost stopped searching for Preston thereafter. From the letters (we have only the sender's inquiries, not Elijah's responses), Elijah apparently assumed Preston was working for Fost, while Fost assumed Preston's absence implied he had remained behind at Sweetbrier. By August, Fost was demanding that Elijah locate Preston and send him back to Pattonsburg "in charge of a constable or some good man" because "he deserves punishment."[38] Fost complained that Preston "left me without cause" and that his departure caused more trouble than "any other that has occurred" in his transactions with Elijah.[39] The letter implies that Fost and Fletcher regularly dealt in hired slaves and that, while Fletcher's enslaved labor force was in high demand because of their skills, they were willing to leave a job if the conditions were not bearable. Other Shenandoah Valley businesses, like William Weaver's Buffalo Forge located in Rockbridge County, also faced labor shortages and relied heavily on their own enslaved workforce. These skilled men were one of the most valuable assets in Virginia's ironmaking industry.[40]

Despite his efforts to run away, Preston must have been worth the inconvenience to Elijah, since Elijah, in 1857, instead of selling him off, hired him out to Weaver's forge and the James Rice Company in nearby Lexington. For Preston, too, there must have been reason to return to Sweetbrier, perhaps because Elijah owned his wife, Phoebe, and possibly other relatives. Still, it seems he won a sort of victory; he was no longer hired "over the mountains," far from loved ones and under more brutal working conditions.

At Sweetbrier, most of the enslaved men labored in the fields, where Elijah planted wheat and barley, experimented with viticulture, raised livestock, tended orchards, and ordered the construction of a water-powered mill—and he bought dozens of slaves to provide the labor for his enterprises. Elijah preferred black workers to white ones. He explained, "Our white men are so lazy and heedless and good for nothing there is no reliance upon them." Instead, Elijah had "more dependence in my Servants than in most any White man I procure. They become intelligent in their work and never tire at their work."[41] Although he employed white overseers initially, by the 1850s he required some of his black workers to assume this role. An unnamed visitor and magazine writer observed in the mid-1850s: "He has abandoned the custom of employing white men to oversee and manage his lands. Under his kind treatment, and with his instructions, his servants have learned all the operations of good farming."[42]

As Lynn Nelson points out in his research on Virginia agriculture, many "practical farmers" experimented with techniques to improve soil quality, even though "book farming" reformers—elite, knowledgeable planters who published articles on farming practices in regional and national newspaper and magazines—tended to receive most of the credit.[43] Elijah fell in between these two types of agroecologists, as he tried to adapt newly touted soil conservation techniques to centuries-old European-American agricultural methods. Throughout the 1840s, Elijah experimented with various crops, animals, and production techniques. He tried to increase his revenues by rotating crops, establishing manure schedules using guano from Peru, and implementing anti-erosion efforts on Monument Hill.[44]

By the time Elijah had turned to farming in earnest, most Virginian planters understood they had to leave fields fallow for a period of time, planting clover to restore vital nutrients and rotating English crops with cereal grains.[45] Elijah was a local expert on the matter, having published dozens of articles in his newspaper, *The Virginian*, that promoted agricultural innovations. He was part of a larger group of Virginian farmers who belonged either to the Agricultural Society of Albemarle (founded in the eponymous county in 1817) or the Agricultural Society of Virginia (founded in 1818). Both groups were concerned about the fertility of their fields and the nutritional exhaustion of soils. They worked at developing techniques to ameliorate these conditions and end their reliance on monoculture so that they could reverse the agro-economic decline of their state.[46]

Former Sweet Briar College curator and museum director Karol Lawson reviewed almost two decades of Elijah's writings and published treatises and concluded that he advocated "the importance of pruning; how best to manage timber; bee keeping; planning kitchen gardens; improving fencing; controlling weevils and lice; cultivating hemp; raising poultry, sheep and dairy cows; feeding livestock on carrots; growing pumpkins; experimenting with new types of grass; and using leaves as manure (e.g. compost.)" In recognition of his efforts in these areas, the Agricultural Society of Amherst County awarded him prizes in 1836 for raising the "best Devon bull, ram, and ewe."[47] But even with these agricultural advances, Sweetbrier's fields were subject to the central Virginia affliction of wheat rust, briars, and cockle, all of which required more backbreaking labor to prevent.[48]

Enslaved laborers implemented the projects Elijah devised in his role as a gentleman planter, building a "great barn" in 1844 (one hundred feet long by forty feet wide, with a rock basement story) as storage and work space for this growing operation. By 1850, through purchases and natural means, the enslaved labor force at Sweetbrier grew to 105 people, including nine adult men and an additional three men sixty-five years or older. These "servants," as Elijah continued to call them in his letters, performed a wide array of services for him and his family. In 1842, African Americans were managing a henhouse for the enjoyment of his twelve-year-old daughter, Elizabeth. Six years later, they grafted and inoculated a large nursery of fruit trees at Sweetbrier.[49] Under Elijah's direction, African Americans were building and running a fast-growing plantation. By 1854, Elijah himself was keeping a leisurely schedule: "I spend my time in planning and giving directions to my hands, ride out into the field in the morning, spend an hour or two, then return and read and amuse myself till middle of the afternoon, then go again and spend a short time, and time passes very agreeably."[50]

After long days of toil in the Fletcher fields and home, enslaved families returned to their cabins to cultivate food on a smaller scale. I have chosen not to use the verb "garden," which suggests cultivation was a leisure activity or primarily for decorative purposes. Gardens were a lifeline for enslaved laborers who often expended thousands of calories during work but received an insufficient quantity of food rations.[51] For enslaved families, these small patches of earth may have been the only resource that lay between starvation and satiety. At Sweetbrier, while Elijah had sufficient wealth to send large quantities of money home to Vermont for decades, as well as to make loans to neighbors, the enslaved community apparently did not receive sufficient food allotments. All the workers planted gardens to supplement their rations, and some were so hungry that they resorted to other means. In 1854, one of Elijah's neighbors complained that Elijah's "negro gerles" Nancy and Juley had come to his house and stolen three watermelons.[52]

While no documentary evidence suggests Elijah ever freed any of his slaves, he apparently allowed some to try to earn money on the side. For example, Elijah claimed he helped laborers who "had bad luck with their crops"[53] and rewarded some "who have been so faithful and useful" by allowing them to "outfit and set them up for themselves." However, he concluded that "every instance proved a failure" and that the men felt "worthless and unhappy."[54] There is no documentation of the obstacles the enslaved men faced in their entrepreneurial efforts.

We do know what Elijah's white neighbors thought about his business practices. As he called in debts with what he called "diligence prudence and integrity," he bankrupted several of his father-in-law's former partners.[55] The testimony of Elijah's white neighbors in various court cases is vitriolic: in one case, the lawyer for a defendant stipulated that "a certain Elijah Fletcher, who will hereafter be called a defendant, whose character is that of a shaver, and usurer, and whose cunning & duplicity, is proverbial, in the part of the country, in which he resides."

The lawyer said Elijah took advantage of his clients, Peter and Milly, when he "seize[d] upon the ignorant, and unsuspecting, and never . . . release[d] his hold, until they [we]re stripped, of all their property . . . and all their estates."[56] The case revolved around the ownership of several slaves whom Elijah claimed to have received in payment for a debt but whom the defendants claimed were unfairly seized from their possession. These cases help explain how Elijah was able to amass so many enslaved workers over a relatively short period of time, growing from the eight enslaved individuals who lived with him in Lynchburg in 1840 to a fifteenfold increase in captive labor by 1850. The litigation also provides first-person accounts of Elijah and his behavior. He admitted, "I was frequently called a hard-hearted, ungrateful, unfeeling child."[57] Once he became an adult and a prominent landowner, white neighbors and business partners made similar characterizations of his personality.

No surviving records indicate how members of Sweetbrier's enslaved community regarded their owner and his family. I am frequently asked, "Was Elijah a good or benevolent slave owner?" This is an extremely problematic question. There is no such thing as a "good" slave owner. Setting aside the evident immorality of owning another human being and the common practice of employing violence to exert control over enslaved individuals and populations, I will attempt to answer a slightly different, historically grounded question: Compared to their enslaved Amherst neighbors, was life moderately easier or harder for the enslaved men, women, and children at Sweetbrier?

Sweet Briar College historians have universally concluded Elijah was a "good master."[58] After my cursory survey of his letters, wherein he wrote he gave gifts to his enslaved workers at Christmas, sponsored holiday feasts, and provided garden plots for each enslaved family, I concluded that Elijah treated the enslaved community with a modicum of respect. However, after looking more closely at subtle clues in the letters, I came to a different conclusion. Soon after Elijah's arrival in Virginia, we can trace a change in his attitude toward slavery. In 1813, just months after marrying into a large slave-owning family, Elijah retreated from his earlier strong sentiments that "slavery is a curse on any country," advising his father: "The present holders of slaves are not censurable for their fathers [*sic*] crimes of introducing them. They are only censurable for not treating those they possess well."[59] Elijah clearly aspired to meet those benevolent expectations by attending to the perceived wants and needs of his slaves.

While he tried to reinforce this positive approach in letters to family members in the North, his sense of guilt is evident in a letter to his abolitionist brother: "Your Friends would many of them be surprised to see their [enslaved women] return cargoes, many of the women with fine Black silk dresses, costing $10 to $15, and some nice things for every child."[60] Here, Elijah appears to be describing a rare day pass given to enslaved women, allowing them to visit a nearby urban market. His defensive tone suggests an effort to describe ameliorating elements within the system of slavery. In his letters home and in the preserved observations of familial and unrelated visitors to Sweetbrier, the plantation apparently ran smoothly, with few complaints from the enslaved labor force. One visitor noted: "He has convinced them it is better to do their duty voluntarily than by compulsion; tried to instill into them principles of morality; made them fond of their homes; encouraged matrimony and attention to their families."[61]

But court and census documents provide a different perspective. Between 1813 and 1850, Elijah Fletcher became one of the largest slaveholders in the region. His purposeful purchase and sales of enslaved people began soon after his marriage, and he searched for bargains whenever possible. In January 1833, he bought a boy named Roland at a sheriff's sale, the equivalent of an auction for debtors. Roland was described as a "good sized plow boy" with a perceived value of $20 or $25 a year. The next year, he ran away from Elijah and sought refuge at the neighboring Cashwell household, perhaps in an attempt to rejoin members of his family. When Elijah's overseer John Bolling went to retrieve Roland, a "lady of the house" refused his demand, claiming she had raised the boy, and offered to hire him from Elijah so that he could remain at the Cashwells. Apparently, Elijah acquiesced, because Roland did not return to Sweetbrier Plantation.[62] This appears to have been an act of kindness on Elijah's part. If not for a lawsuit, *Bourne v. Fletcher*, filed in 1845 by an elderly woman named Charity Bourne, the archival evidence for Roland's fate would be limited to a tally for "slave males under 10" in the Cashwell household, listed in the 1840 Census. The rest of his story—his sale, purchase, successful escape, and possible reunion with his family—would have been lost. This one exchange also provides a window into the complicated human exchanges that were at the heart of the slave trade and the South's "peculiar institution."

Elijah's purchase of Martha Penn appeared to be another act of kindness. When I first read Martha's letter and saw the comments on the verso, I perceived Elijah's terse summary, "Martha, asking me to buy her," as an affirmative response indicating his intent to reunite the two sisters. But a closer examination of the 1850 Census shows that Elijah was trying to purchase a disproportionately large number of young women to increase the enslaved community by "natural means." This may have been why Elijah agreed to buy twenty-year-old Martha, who would go on to bear at least one child while enslaved at Sweetbrier.

Another purchase made by Elijah reveals the rising value of enslaved African Americans, when he bought a twenty-year-old man from a different neighbor in 1838. Described as a "simple field hand" without any of the more valuable "mechanic" skills and only "tolerably liked," the enslaved man was still worth about $1,000.[63] Over the next two decades, Elijah continued his practice of accepting enslaved individuals, usually men, in lieu of debts owed to him by his neighbors. When these payments "in kind" were not forthcoming, he sued. Court cases demonstrate that many of his Amherst neighbors were also regularly lending money and calling in debts, but Elijah appears to have turned to legal recourse more frequently than others.[64]

As the years passed and his slavery-based profits grew, Elijah's efforts to justify his actions became more insistent. Taking stock of his human chattel just days before Christmas in 1855, Elijah opined to one of his brothers: "None [of the servants] fear that they will suffer or have any little want which will not be gratified."[65] Could Elijah possibly have believed by this time that "any little want" of a human being did not include freedom? How had he managed to dissociate himself so completely from the antislavery stance of his own earlier years? The answer may lie in the reshaping of his familial role. Elijah appears to have cast himself as a patriarch, perhaps in partial compensation for his disastrous relationship with his son Lucian and his increasing alienation from his Vermont relatives. His paternalistic relationship to the people he owned lasted until the day he died, when, Indiana recalled, Elijah went into his cellar at Sweetbrier to "ascertain what groceries were necessary for the Servant portion of our family, for he had not been able to think of their wants, during his illness."[66]

The extent and nature of physical punishment at Sweetbrier can also offer clues to Elijah's character. Elijah claimed he never mistreated a slave. In letters to his Vermont and Indiana relatives, however, he admits he punished them on occasion, although he delegated the task to others. When enslaved children needed correction, he turned to their parents to mete the punishment.[67] At other times, his overseer delivered severe beatings. In his letters, Elijah often appears to express concern for enslaved families, claiming he tried to keep families together. But, as noted previously, the facts are more complicated. In a letter to abolitionist relatives, Elijah says he rarely sold anyone, "except the incorrigible."[68] His claim is supported by his will, which grouped individuals into families, such as "Archy and Rhoda," or "Tom and Hannah" and their six children. In 1860, when the estate was settled and these individuals and dozens of other families were divided among Indiana, Elizabeth, and Sidney, some of these families were indeed sent on to their new owners mostly intact. At the same time, these lists of nuclear families do not consider the connections between siblings, grandparents and grandchildren, and cousins, which may have been disrupted by the dispersal of these families.

These connections are obscured by the practice of many white owners who failed to record surnames for the enslaved community. Thus, the question of names becomes vital in attempting to reconstruct the stories of enslaved individuals. The selection of a child's name reveals individual, family, and cultural values. In the case of enslaved children, their names may contain links to other generations and even to the geographic origins of their distant ancestors. The novelist Toni Morrison explains, "There's a whole history, I think, in naming. In the beginning of black people being in this country, they lost their names. They were given names by their masters and so they didn't have names and they began to call one another, decades later, by nicknames."[69] Indeed, one of the first differences between researching white and black servants in seventeenth-century Virginia was the absence of names for black individuals in historic records. As the historian Alden Vaughan observes, the 1624 census of Virginian colonists included the first and last names of white residents, but of the twenty-two Africans listed, "none is accorded a last name, and almost half are recorded with no name at all."[70] This dehumanizing practice continued well into the nineteenth century, and the absence of recorded surnames makes it difficult to track enslaved individuals through decades of archival records.

The use of short and common first names, like the appellation "Uncle Tom," was part of the larger effort to dehumanize enslaved individuals. When Elijah listed sixty-six African and Native Americans in his 1852 will, he provided what appear to be surnames for only two individuals, Nancy Wyatt and Nancy Collins. Given inconsistent punctuation, there is a small chance he meant Nancy and a man named Wyatt, or Nancy and a man named Collins, for a total of four people, not two. Slaveholders occasionally selected first names for enslaved babies, sometimes using this opportunity to challenge the African identities of enslaved individuals by choosing European names. At Tusculum, this forced assimilation at times resulted in nondescript first names like Tom, John, and Mary. In other cases, enslaved parents may have wanted to solidify the connection between a newborn and the slave owner to discourage a future sale. Thus, in the case of the Crawford family's slaves, girls were named after Jane, the wife of David I, and after Sarah, the daughter of David III.

A curious incident reveals how parents enslaved by the Fletchers were subject to their owners' whims in selecting names for their children. In 1850, Elijah's brother Calvin suggested to a Swiss acquaintance, a "Mr. Guysor," that he travel to Virginia to seek employment as a teacher.[71] Guysor arrived "without Friends and without money," having been robbed during his journey. Elijah assisted and befriended him but several months later complained that Guysor visited Tusculum only once. But he noted: "His romantic turn pleases Maria very much. She thinks him a wonderful man."[72] This is one of the most effusive comments Elijah ever makes about Maria in print, more commonly describing her "sensible" nature.[73] Might he have been jealous? Later, informing one of his brothers about local gossip, Elijah opines: "I think it no misfortune to Professor Guysor that he does not succeed in his matrimonial plans. I think he is about the last man that would increase his own happiness or the happiness of his Partner by forming a marriage connection."[74]

By the fall of 1851, Guysor—by then referred to as Prof. Guysor—had returned to Indianapolis. In his absence, Maria honored him by giving one of the women servants a new coat for her child, as an inducement to name the infant "Guysor." The story is strange and may be apocryphal, for several reasons: the introduction of the name of a random Swiss passerby into a central Virginia enslaved community; the idea that an enslaved woman would have been able to refuse her white owner's command without a substantial bribe; and the absence of any information about the outcome. The name and fate of the child is uncertain, as no Guysor appears on a list of enslaved individuals Elijah drew up just seven months later, or in later Amherst census records.

In another instance, Elijah writes to his brother Calvin, "Among the new born of this year there is a Calvin, the first time I ever heard that name given to a colored person." After hours of searching postbellum census documents and marriage/birth records, I was able to trace the parentage of the younger Calvin to a child born to John Rose and his wife, Bettie, in 1851. It is difficult to recover the reason for their choice of name, since the white Calvin had visited Sweetbrier only once or twice in his life. Perhaps John or Bettie overheard Elijah talking about his beloved brother and selected the name as a sign of status or homage to their owner, or in the hope that Elijah would thus look more kindly upon young Calvin. Elijah comments derisively on naming practices among enslaved community members at Sweetbrier: "The negro women all claim the privilege of naming their children and are many times very choice and fanciful in bestowen names." In questioning parents' right to name their children ("claim the privilege"), Elijah suggests he, as their owner, might more appropriately claim that right, and his reference to their "choice and fanciful" method of name selection implies that white parents used more rigorous criteria in making this decision. More specifically, Elijah continues, "They are very apt to name them after departed and absent relations, particularly the male children."

Now we can review the 1852 census list in a new light: the African-inspired names may reveal earlier generations of ancestors, and thus generations who were more closely tied to their Caribbean and African roots. Unfortunately, it remains very difficult to locate eighteenth-century records of the ancestors of black families at Sweetbrier. If further sources are located, such as family Bibles, stories, or slave lists, it would be interesting to see if names like "Bristol" or "Isham" appear. Elijah's observations about female names is not reflected in his own 1852 list: "For the female children they select long double names and must have an Ann attached—'Phillis Ann,' 'Elizabeth Ann,' etc."[75] If true, this suggests the list in his will should be modified so that Phyllis is inscribed as Phyllis Ann and Betsy as Elizabeth Ann. Each of these interpretive decisions influences the likelihood of successfully following the paper trail for emancipated individuals after 1865.

After hundreds of hours spent studying documents revealing the everyday life of enslaved families at Sweetbrier, my aim was to trace their descendants into the present day. As described above, I have already identified questions regarding the veracity of Elijah's own insistence that he "kept families together." Although Elijah's 1852 will described several families, including a single father with his eight children and several apparently childless couples, I wondered where the elders were—the parents of these adults. And where were the adult siblings, the extended networks of nieces and nephews and cousins?

Investigating this question was difficult, since Elijah included only a handful of surnames. But it stood to reason that several black families had been separated in 1813 when Elijah and Maria were given two young children from William S. Crawford's Tusculum estate, again in 1815 after William's death and the intervening years it took to settle his estate, and yet again in the 1820s and 1830s when Elijah began to purchase new workers and distribute others around his multiple plantations. To test the theory that most, if not all, enslaved families owned by Elijah were separated from some of their close kin, I tried to identify the individuals enslaved at Tusculum in the 1850s.

Like many plantations, Tusculum had stayed in one family for generations. The Crawfords lived in the house for two hundred years when—due to the sudden death of William Crawford in 1815—Elijah

Fletcher became co-executor of the estate, assisting his mother-in-law, Sophia Penn Crawford, in settling his father-in-law's complicated estate, including debts, lands, and individuals. Elijah spent decades trying to locate debtors and creditors. In the meantime, Sophia moved to Kentucky, joining members of the Penn family who had migrated west a generation earlier. This left Elijah as de facto owner of the Tusculum plantation, although he did not formally purchase the property until the 1840s. By 1820, just after William's death, twenty-one enslaved men, women, and children lived at Tusculum.[76] Some of these individuals remained on the plantation as its ownership passed from William to his widow, Sophia, to Elijah as executor of William's estate, and finally, to Sidney Fletcher.

By the time Elijah became the owner of the Tusculum plantation, he was busy working on his own large farm, Sweetbrier. His eldest son, Sidney, had graduated from Yale University in 1841. The newly minted "Dr." Fletcher returned to Amherst and half-heartedly began practice as a physician; Elijah proudly announced to his brother that Sidney "has obtained [knowledge] in the healing art, and has already begun his practice among the Servants."[77] It is rumored that Sidney practiced medicine in the "cottage" located next to Sweet Briar House, but his only patients were members of the enslaved community. Medicine was not Sidney's passion. In 1836, when he was fifteen and attending school in Lynchburg, he had traveled to his father's Sweetbrier plantation each week, staying from Friday evening through Sunday to satisfy his love of farming. Within months of graduating from Yale, Sidney began spending time at Tusculum.[78] Meanwhile, Elijah clung to the hope that his son would become a practicing physician, encouraging him to attend medical lectures in Richmond between November 1841 and March 1842.[79] Instead, Sidney took over the management of Sweetbrier in 1842 and worked there for three years until he and his sisters decided to take a world tour.

The three children left Virginia in October 1844, leaving their fourth sibling, Lucian, to manage Tusculum during their absence and, presumably, help their father at Sweetbrier. After a whirlwind trip from Egypt to Russia and from Britain to Italy, the Fletchers returned to Amherst in November 1846. Sidney probably spent the next few months assessing conditions at both plantations and deciding what to do next. He still had time to return to the practice of medicine or to turn to commerce or politics, as had his father. In March of 1847, Sidney traveled to Florida to visit a sugar plantation, possibly to assess the viability of diversifying his agricultural holdings. Two years later, he took one last trip, this time to California. He and his brother, along with more than

sixty-seven thousand other Americans, hoped to strike it rich in the recently discovered gold mines. Sidney returned to Virginia after only a
brief stay in the West. He was back for good.

In 1850, Elijah observed, "Sidney is devoting himself to Farming
with great zeal," acknowledging that "farming is the only vocation in
life that pleases him or which nature seemed to adapt to his taste."[80]
Accordingly, on 20 February of that year, Elijah formally conveyed the
Tusculum plantation to Sidney.[81] Sidney turned twenty-nine in 1850,
with an MD, 1,500 acres of land, and twelve thousand dollars to his
name.[82] Twenty-eight enslaved men, women, and children worked the
fertile fields, ranging in age from newborn to seventy-five years, with
an average age of thirty; thirteen individuals were female, and fifteen
were male.[83] Given this age distribution, there may well have been four
or more multigenerational families living at Tusculum.

The 1850 Census Slave Schedule provides limited information for
Tusculum. The entire enslaved community is listed under "Sidney
Fletcher," with no names given for any of the African American individuals, who are identified only by age, gender, and race. If we take this
limited information and try to "sort" it into families, inventing relationships among the individuals, we could produce a hypothetical community, accounting for each man, woman, and child listed on the census.

The first family might have included a pair of grandparents, a
seventy-five-year-old man and a seventy-year-old woman, who could
have been the parents of a man aged forty-five and the in-laws of his
younger, twenty-five-year-old wife. Sidney owned a disproportionate
number of men in their twenties and thirties who worked on the farm,
and there apparently weren't sufficient female contemporaries to make
appropriate matches. This family could have had two children: a boy
(seven) and a girl (five). These six people might have lived in one of
the cabins that stood within a dozen yards of the Tusculum plantation
house. A second family might have included an elderly couple, aged
seventy-five and sixty, whose adult children had been sold to another
farmer. A third family could have been younger, with a man (twenty-
seven) and woman (twenty-five) and three young children between the
ages of two and seven. A fourth family might have been a childless couple in their twenties, aged twenty-seven and twenty-four.

The fifth family could have included a woman of fifty-five, living
with her forty-year-old son and his daughter (twenty-one), whose
mother had died in childbirth. The sixth family might have been an
older couple (a sixty-year-old man and a fifty-year-old woman) living
with a twenty-two-year-old daughter and her infant girl. The seventh
pair could have been a male/female pair of twins, aged nineteen, who

might have been separated from their parents years earlier. The eighth group could be two young men, ages sixteen and fifteen, who might have been purchased to dig a well for Sidney's agricultural projects and to build some new barns at Tusculum. The last group accounts for three unattached men, ages twenty-nine, thirty, and forty, whose wives and/ or parents might have died and who had yet to find a new partner, or whose new partners were living on adjacent plantations.

The above "families" are of course entirely hypothetical, and the individuals could be reorganized into many possible family groupings, but the exercise is intended as a way to envision Sidney Fletcher's twenty-eight enslaved people as human beings with families, rather than as itemized property. This possible distribution of the twenty-eight enslaved individuals follows kinship patterns commonly found on other plantations from this time. Even in this attempt to construct intact family units, there are clearly gaps in the relationships described, absences that can only be accounted for by assuming family members were often separated from one another. Whatever their exact relationships, these black families labored on about one thousand acres of improved land, using seven horses, eight asses and mules, and six working oxen to plow and pull wagons for collecting the harvests, according to the 1850 Census Agricultural Schedule. Another sixteen milk cows, seventy-five assorted cattle, and thirty-three swine were used for their dairy and meat products. The combined human and animal labor enabled Sidney to produce 120,000 pounds of wheat, 1,250 bushels of corn, 22,400 pounds of oats, 4,000 pounds of tobacco, 60 pounds of peas and beans, about 5 bushels of Irish potatoes, and 300 pounds of butter in 1860.

Over the next decade, as Sidney lost both his parents, he increased both his acreage and his slave holdings dramatically. The cash value of his land nearly tripled in just ten years, from $12,000 in 1850 to $41,000 in 1860, and in the 1860 Census Slave Schedule, he is listed as owning seventy-four slaves. Based on age and gender distributions, many of the individuals Sidney owned in 1850 were apparently still living at Tusculum a decade later.

At Elijah's thriving Sweetbrier, around 1850, one of his white overseers threatened to cut off the fingers of an enslaved woman named Mary if she didn't finish her work. Such punishment was not a singular occurrence. But in this case, Mary (not the same Mary who was Martha's sister) began to weep and told Lucian, Elijah's younger son, age twenty-six, of the threat. Lucian immediately came to her rescue, allegedly declaring, "No such thing will happen because I will run off with you."[84] Thus, the family learned that the two apparently had a preexisting relationship. Lucian kept his promise, running away with Mary and taking along his own manservant, Archer. The couple fled to West Virginia, where Archer apparently died of an illness; Lucian and Mary then continued on to Canada, where slavery was illegal and they could establish a household together. Eventually, they would start a family. We can only imagine how angry Elijah and how embarrassed Lucian's socially astute sisters would have been. Elijah promptly disinherited Lucian, never again mentioning him in letters to relatives. Indiana nourished a hatred of her brother that stayed with her until the day she died, refusing to help him and his children on numerous occasions and literally barring the windows of her home to prevent their entry.

While Archer's surname is never mentioned, later documents reveal that Mary's full name was Mary Elizabeth Woodfork. This surname is not very common, but "Woodfolk" or "Woodruff" is, and there were a handful of white Woodfolks or Woodruffs in nineteenth-century Amherst County. Perhaps the most tantalizing connection is a white man named David Woodruff Jr. (also spelled Woodroof) who died in 1814 at age fifty-two. His much younger second wife, Judith McDaniel, died three decades later, at fifty-eight, in 1844. This couple owned the domestic predecessor to Sweetbrier, a farmhouse called Locust Ridge, and are buried on Monument Hill, the burial ground associated with these plantations, later the burial location for Elijah Fletcher himself. It is tempting to suggest that Mary and her parents were enslaved by Judith Woodroof and possibly given to Elijah as part of a property transfer during the 1830s. While I cannot conclusively identify at what date Elijah bought Mary, she was born in 1828, just four years after Lucian, so they possibly grew up together, albeit on unequal social footing.

When Lucian, Mary, and Archer fled Sweetbrier, they left behind family members and a community of almost one hundred souls. For those left behind, everything was about to change with the coming of the American Civil War.

Notes

1. "Another Veteran of the Press Gone," Elijah Fletcher's obituary, *Daily Dispatch*, 7 February 1858, 1.
2. Gabriel Penn's will, 1798, Amherst County Will Book 3, 506.
3. Ackerly, *Our Kin*, chapter 9.
4. Kraus, "The Glebe," 2.
5. *The Virginian*, 2 February 1826.
6. "Capt Penns Family have all sold out and moved away." *TLEF*, letter to his brother, 4 November 1848, 216.

7. Loose Papers, Brown v. Penn lawsuit, "Report to the court as follows," April 1847, Amherst Courthouse.
8. Johnson, *Soul by Soul*, 215.
9. *Lynchburg Daily Virginian*, 27 September 1854, cited by L. Morgan, *Emancipation in Virginia's Tobacco Belt*, 59.
10. Details obtained from one of the estate sale advertisements, *Richmond Enquirer*, 24 January 1860, 1.
11. Genovese, *Roll, Jordan, Roll*, 194. The first law that prohibited enslaved blacks from gathering for funerals, "The Act of 1680 on Negro Insurrection," was passed in Virginia. Subsequent legislation fine-tuned this law, such as the 1804 statute that prohibited "nighttime religious meetings of slaves" in Virginia. May, "Holy Rebellion," 237, 247.
12. Genovese, *Roll, Jordan, Roll*, 195.
13. Avirett, *The Old Plantation*, 129.
14. Roediger, "And Die in Dixie," 171.
15. Richards, "The Rice Lands of the South," 735.
16. *TLEF*, letter to his brother, 4 August 1852, 237.
17. Undated letter (ca. 1854) from Abrm I. Fost to Elijah Fletcher, Archives.
18. Livingston, "Elijah Fletcher of Nelson County, Virginia," 18. Note: this title is inaccurate; he lived in Amherst County, as correctly listed in the volume's table of contents.
19. *Journal of Proceedings of the Convention of the Protestant Episcopal Church*, 32, 24.
20. *TLEF*, letter to his brother, 20 December 1855, 257.
21. *TLEF*, letter from Maria Fletcher to Calvin Fletcher, 25 December 1841, 177.
22. *TLEF*, letter to his brother, 26 December 1843, 188.
23. Piedmont Virginian examples of hiring out practices and their impact on enslaved families include Dew, *Bond of Iron*; Dusinberre, *Strategies for Survival*; Blassingame, *Slave Testimony*.
24. L. Morgan, *Emancipation in Virginia's Tobacco Belt*, 60–62.
25. Swanson, *A Golden Weed*, 68–69.
26. *TLEF*, letter to his brother, 18 August 1849, 219.
27. L. Morgan, *Emancipation in Virginia's Tobacco Belt*, 63.
28. "They are now excavating a Basin for this town at the foot of my bed." *TLEF*, letter to brother, 6 March 1836, 139.
29. *TLEF*, letter to his brother, 28 December 1850, 227.
30. Letter from N. Gill to E. Fletcher, Esq, 13 October 1857, Archives.
31. *TLEF*, letter to his brother, 18 August 1849, 219.
32. Schwarz, *Twice Condemned*, 12–13, 27.
33. Letter from Bez[aleel] Brown to Elijah Fletcher, 27 December 1848, Duke University Libraries, Indiana Fletcher Williams Papers, 1804–1900, Small Manuscript Collections, Section A, Box 136, Items 1–38, c. 1.
34. Lewis Harrison's deposition in *Bourne v. Fletcher*, loose papers, n.d., Amherst County Courthouse; Dew, *Bonds of Iron*, 69.
35. Letter from Willis N. Mays to Elijah Fletcher, 28 July 1854, Archives.
36. Livingston, "Elijah Fletcher of Nelson County, Virginia," 17.
37. Jacob M. Ruff to Elijah Fletcher, 3 February 1854, Archives.

38. Abrm. I. Fost to E. Fletcher, 9 August 1854, Archives.
39. Abrm. I. Fost to E. Fletcher, 18 August 1854, Archives.
40. Dew, *Bond of Iron*, 42–44.
41. *TLEF*, letter to his brother, 18 August 1849, 219.
42. Livingston, "Elijah Fletcher of Nelson County, Virginia," 17.
43. L. Nelson, *Pharsalia*, 12–13.
44. *TLEF*, letter to his brother, 24 October 1847, 210; on manuring practices in central Virginia, L. Nelson, *Pharsalia*, 95–96; on soil erosion, Stoll, *Larding the Lean Earth*, 31.
45. L. Nelson, *Pharsalia*, 76–77.
46. Cohen, *Notes from the Ground*, 132–37.
47. Lawson, "'I have lately bought me a Plantation.'"
48. L. Nelson, *Pharsalia*, 137.
49. *TLEF*, letter to his brother, 10 April 1848, 212.
50. *TLEF*, letter to his brother, 28 July 1854, 248–49.
51. Coelho and McGuire, "Diet Versus Diseases," 234.
52. Obadiah Gregory to Elijah Fletcher, n.d., Archives.
53. *TLEF*, letter to his brother, 20 December 1855, 257.
54. *Elijah Fletcher of Nelson County*, 18.
55. Amherst County Will Book A-1, 55. For an account of the Crawford estate, see the Administrator's Account, in *TLEF*, appendix V.
56. *Bourne v. Fletcher* lawsuit, loose papers, Amherst County Courthouse. A dozen pages that begin with "To the Honorable Lucas P. Thompson." Image of the circuit Supt. A. of law & chancery for Amherst County, hand-numbered, 1–11. Compiled in August 1852, but the events described date between 1825 and 1852.
57. *TLEF*, letter to his father, 23 December 1811, 48.
58. Whitley, *Indiana Fletcher Williams*, 7; Stohlman, *The Story of Sweet Briar College*; Long, "Our Colored Folks."
59. *TLEF*, letter to his father, 5 September 1813, 77.
60. *TLEF*, letter to his brother, 20 December 1855, 257.
61. Livingston, "Elijah Fletcher of Nelson County, Virginia," 17–18.
62. Based on John D. Bolling's testimony, *Bourne v. Fletcher*, 21 April 1845.
63. Charles D. Stratham's testimony, *Bourne v. Fletcher*, 10 May 1845.
64. For example, in *Fletcher v. Pendleton*, Elijah sued James S. Pendleton for money owed on a $1,000 debt from 1842. In the suit, eighty-nine other individuals are listed as creditors of Pendleton, but only Elijah puts forth a legal petition to claim his money. In the end, he accepts an enslaved man named Isaac in lieu of a cash payment.
65. *TLEF*, letter to his brother, 20 December 1855, 257.
66. *TLEF*, letter from Indiana Fletcher to Calvin Fletcher, 15 March 1858, 270.
67. Livingston, "Elijah Fletcher of Nelson County," Virginia, 18.
68. Livingston, "Elijah Fletcher of Nelson County," Virginia, 18.
69. "'I Regret Everything': Toni Morrison Looks Back on Her Personal Life," *Fresh Air*, 20 April 2015, http://www.npr.org/2015/04/20/400394947/i-regret-everything-toni-morrison-looks-back-on-her-personal-life.
70. Vaughan, "Blacks in Virginia," 472.

71. *TLEF*, letter to his brother, 20 August 1850, 225.
72. *TLEF*, letter to his brother, 28 December 1850, 226.
73. *TLEF*, letter to his father, 6 November 1812, 65.
74. *TLEF*, letter to his brother, 5 January 1852, 233.
75. *TLEF*, letter to his brother, 10 November 1851, 232.
76. 1820 US Federal Census, Sophia Penn Crawford: six whites, twenty-one slaves.
77. *TLEF*, letter to his brother Calvin, 13 March 1842, 181. Although Sidney studied medicine at Yale University and later attended medical lectures in Paris in the 1840s, he never received a formal medical degree. Regardless, he was often called "Dr. Fletcher" in census records and other historic documents. For his academic background, see "Sidney Fletcher," 1341.
78. In 1837, Elijah Fletcher put Tusculum up for sale.
79. *TLEF*, letter to his brother, 26 November 1841, 174; letter to his brother, 10 December 1841, 176; letter to his brother Calvin, 13 March 1842, 181.
80. *TLEF*, letter to his brother, 21 January 1850, 224.
81. Amherst County Deed Book, vol. BB, 70.
82. 1850 Agricultural Census, Sidney Fletcher, Eastern District, Amherst, Virginia, p. 194, line 21.
83. 1850 Slave Schedule, Sidney Fletcher, Eastern District, Amherst, Virginia, p. 719.
84. Testimony of Mamie Warner (a friend of Sarah Fletcher Thornton), Chicago Court Case (file 185), 72–73.

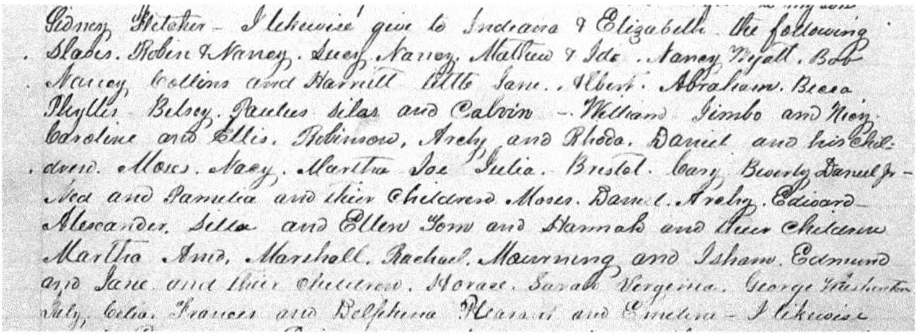
Sidney Fletcher – I likewise give to Indiana & Elizabeth the following
Slaves. Robin & Nancy. Lucy. Nancy. Matthew & Ida. Nancy Wyatt. Bob
Nancy Collins and Harriett. little Jane. Albert. Abraham. Becca
Phyllis. Betsey. Paulus. Silas and Calvin – William Jimbo and Nicy
Caroline and Ellis. Robinson, Archy and Rhoda. Daniel and his chil-
dren. Moses. Nacy. Martha. Joe. Julia. Bristol. Cary. Beverly Daniel Jr –
Ned and Pamelia and their children. Moses. Daniel. Archy. Edward –
Alexander. Silla and Ellen Tom and Hannah and their children
Martha. Anid. Marshall. Rachel. Mourning and Isham. Edmund
and Jane and their children. Horace. Sarah. Virginia. George Washington
July. Celia. Frances and Delphena. Pleasant and Emeline – I likewise

Figure 5.1. Excerpt from Elijah Fletcher's 1852 will. Amherst County Courthouse Will Book.

Transcription:

I likewise give to Indiana & Elizabeth the following
Slaves. Robin & Nancy. Lucy. Nancy. Matthew & Ida. Nancy Wyatt. Bob
Nancy Collins and Harriett. little Jane. Albert. Abraham. Becca
Phyllis. Betsey. Paulus. Silas and Calvin. – William – Jimbo and Nicy
Caroline and Ellis. Robinson, Archy and Rhoda. Daniel and his chil
dren. Moses. Nacy. Martha. Joe. Julia. Bristol, Cary. Beverly, Daniel Jr. –
Ned and Pamelia and their children. Moses. Daniel. Archy. Edward –
Alexander. Silla and Ellen. Tom and Hannah and their children
Martha. Anid. Marshall. Rachel. Mourning and Isham. Edmund
and Jane and their children. Horace. Sarah. Virginia. George Washington
July. Celia. Frances and Delphena. Pleasant and Emeline.

5

Families Divided, 1858–1865

Six years before his death, Elijah Fletcher wrote his last will and testament, dividing his belongings among three of his children and thereby disinheriting his second son, Lucian. After specifying the distribution of his animals, land, and furniture, he turned to his human property, the enslaved families. In the excerpt shown in Figure 5.1, he gives his daughters Indiana and Elizabeth "the following Slaves," listing sixty-six men, women, and children. Few are identified by surnames, making it difficult to untangle individual family relationships. One large family is comprised of a couple and their nine children, specified by Elijah as "Edmund and Jane and their children." An interesting list of names follow, ranging from the geographical (Virginia) to the historic (George Washington), and from calendar months (July) to names shared with members of Elijah's family (Horace, named for Horace A. Fletcher, a distant cousin) and Frances (named for Frances Penn, a relative of Elijah's wife, Sophia). After emancipation, siblings sometimes selected more than one surname, making it difficult to locate these families in the historic record after 1865. In the case of this large family, Indiana and Elizabeth divided the siblings when they selected their portions of Elijah's estate in 1860. By then, some of the children were missing from the tally of bondage, having perhaps died or run away. But we do know Indiana selected Edmund and Jane, as well as July, while Elizabeth acquired Celia and Frances.

As Indiana and Elizabeth were separating Edmund and Jane's family, tension was increasing between the North and South. For the white and black residents of Sweetbrier, another kind of tumult loomed. On the morning of 13 February 1858, Elijah Fletcher arose, feeling well rested after a "refreshing" night's sleep. He had just returned to Sweetbrier from a trip to Lynchburg on business, but on his way back, the weather had turned "stormy and cold." After riding a mile or two on horseback, he had been "taken with a congestion of the Stomach." He had stopped in at a farmhouse for care, while his daughter and son rushed to his side. It had taken him two days to improve enough to continue his ride back. Now home, he dressed himself, "ate his morning meal, gave directions about the affairs of the Farm, put on his hat, visited his cellar, and on his return prepared to shave." Indiana heard him fall and rushed to his side, quickly enough that she "received his head in her arms."[1] He was sixty-nine, and his sudden death shocked the family; his sister Lucy said she had "always thought that Brother Elijah would live to a great old age."[2]

Elijah's unexpected death would have sent a different kind of shock wave through the black families living at Sweetbrier. As word spread rapidly through the slave quarters, the questions on the minds of the enslaved mothers, fathers, brothers, sisters, cousins, grandparents, and children would have been: Who will inherit me, and where will I be sent to live? Will my family be able to stay together?

In death as in life, Elijah relied heavily on his enslaved workers. They were the ones who carried out the funeral rituals. Enslaved women would have prepared his body and laid it out on a cooling board. After a family viewing, he would have been placed in a coffin. Later, four of "his favorite Servants" carried this bier to his chosen resting place, atop Woodruff Mound, which overlooked his beloved Sweetbrier mansion house. At the funeral, Indiana observed, "all from the neighboring plantations & those at a greater distance, hastened as soon as tidings reached them & were here to join that humble procession, wending its way, to the chosen spot where their beloved Master & friend was to be laid."[3] A month later, she wrote to Elijah's brother Calvin, lamenting the loss of her "beloved departed Father" whose spirit, she believed, had gone "to the happy land of good and just men."[4] Her description of Elijah's death fits the model of the "good death," prized by survivors who felt that one's moral fiber was reflected in one's death. As in life, Indiana idolized her father in death.

But Elijah had known, as he wrote in an 1812 letter to his sister Lucy, other people saw him as a "cold phlegmatic being" and "the most grave ministerial ouster fellow in the world."[5] And after the funeral, the African Americans belonging to Sweetbrier likely returned to the estate not grieving their departed master but with somber and sad recognition of their future: as settlement to pay his creditors and as inheritance for his children.

Elijah's will was probated on 19 April 1858; it disinherited the wayward Lucian and specified that his estate should be divided among his remaining three children. It took several years to pay off creditors and settle affairs, so not until June 1864, a year after the Emancipation Proclamation and in the throes of continuing civil war, did Samuel Garland and Robert Tinsley preside over the distribution of land and enslaved families. For the white inheritors, this was a financial interaction. For the enslaved families, it meant a division of their 137-person community among three plantations: Sweetbrier, Tusculum, and Elizabeth's future home. Four years later, Elijah's beneficiaries reported back to the county clerk about their agreed distribution of enslaved people. The list of human property to be divided contains the names and certain details of every enslaved man, woman, and child at Sweetbrier, and each was accorded a perceived value, from $100 to $1,500.[6] It differs somewhat from the list in Elijah's will, written in 1852, well before his death, and it differs from the census record of Sweetbrier residents in 1860. Still, by comparing these three lists and other pre- and postwar documents, it is possible to piece together some of the stories of African Americans in this period.

Sidney selected his portion of the human chattel first, initially picking only four of the most valuable men: Peter (valued at $1,450), Henry King ($1,400), Henry Miller ($1,200), and Squire ($600). Using later records, it is possible to piece together more of their identities. I later deduced that Peter was one of Permelia and William "Billy" Broady's children. Born around 1814, the skills of this fifty-year-old, second-generation blacksmith accounted for his high valuation. His father, along with Martha Penn, was owned by Edmund Penn, one of Sophia's brothers. Yet again, the complicated genealogical connections among white families had a lifelong impact on the trajectories of African American ones.

Henry King was thirty-five years old when he was freed after the war. He formalized his union to Nancy, an enslaved woman about ten years younger than he. One of their first children was born in 1863, followed by three more after the war ended: Nazareth, Laudress, and "Babe." Squire, born around 1810, was one of a handful of adults who took the Fletcher surname after emancipation. He and his wife, Catherine, had at least two children, including a son named Lemartine. In other cases, enslaved men with first and last names are still difficult to locate after 1865 in the historic record. For example, Sidney also selected a man named Henry Page, but no such individual is listed in the 1870 Amherst Census, leading me to surmise that he died between 1860 and 1870 or he selected a different postbellum surname. This was one of the frustrating realizations about deciphering antebellum naming practices: pre- and postwar surnames (and occasionally even first names) of enslaved individuals did not always match.[7]

The men and women chosen by Sidney would have walked for about two hours to travel the eight miles north from Sweetbrier to Tusculum to settle into their new home.

Indiana selected sixty-eight enslaved African Americans to remain on the plantation where many had been born and most had multigenerational ties. At first, this list seemed an insurmountable genealogical and ethnographic task: How could I trace the family histories of the individuals who were given to Indiana, seeing as few had last names, and even the first names were not correlated with the age and sex of the 132 enslaved individuals listed on the 1860 US Federal Census Slave Schedule? How could I ever learn the fate of a "Louisa" or a "John"? But, gradually, patterns emerged and other pieces of documentary evidence helped fill in some of the family trees.

Indiana's selection of human chattel began with two men, Daniel and Daniel Jr. Both were assigned a middling value of around $700. My initial expectation that this was a father and son was reinforced by a similar pair listed on Elijah's will. On the 1852 will, Daniel is listed along with the names of nine children, concluding with Daniel Jr. The next three names on Indiana's list also correspond to three of the nine children listed alongside Daniel Sr. in 1852, suggesting a single-father household. Using the 1870 Census, I found that this was Daniel Bibby, an African American man born around 1805 and, after emancipation, a neighbor of Elizabeth's. His son, Daniel Bibby Jr., was born in 1849, a young age that correlates well with his moderate value of $700 in 1860 when he would have been around eleven years old. The senior Daniel was given $10 when the estate was settled, for "fidelity to his master"; he may well have been one of the four men who carried Elijah to his final resting place.

Having already raised at least nine children, Daniel remarried a woman named Jane after the war and helped raise her children (Amanda, Esmeraldo, Peter, Broder, Elsie, Jane, and Sarah). Amanda and Esmeraldo are also on Indiana's 1860 inheritance list; they were born in 1852 and 1858. Daniel's 1870 household reveals another strain on postbellum African American families: caring for extended kin with limited employment opportunities in rural Virginia. Later, in 1887, Daniel's son Broder ("Bradden") married Mary Taylor, one of Martha Taylor's children. The kinship networks in this rural community were tightly woven.

Elijah also enslaved several of Daniel's siblings and cousins. One such family was headed by Tom and Hannah Bibby. In 1852, they were listed with several children: Martha, Anid, Marshall, Rachel, Mourning, and Isham. In 1860, Tom is valued at $400; Hannah and their youngest child, Thomas, are valued together at $750; and Marshall, Rachel, Mourning, and Isham ("Sam") are listed individually, with Martha and Anid no longer appearing. The organization of Daniel and his children into a family unit on the list was a helpful clue in deciphering the rest of the list. As I scanned Indiana's inheritance, many of the names appeared to be spousal pairs, larger family units (usually two parents followed by their children), and occasionally sibling pairs. In some situations, the appraiser added a comment to signify a relationship. For example, "Lucy and child" were valued jointly at $750, and "Margaret, Rodrick, child" were valued much higher, at $1,400.

In a handful of cases, I have been able to track an enslaved family from the 1860 estate list all the way back to the Crawford family's slave holdings at eighteenth-century Tusculum. Such was the case with a boy named Edmund, born in the early 1800s. In 1815, when William S. Crawford's estate was settled, the appraiser filled many pages describing his household belongings, furniture, animals, and, unavoidably, slaves. From the pithy entries "1 Negro Man named Gilbert" and "1 Negro Boy named Edmund, son to Aggey," we learn there were at least two enslaved families at Tusculum. Gilbert and Nicey's household included their four children: Lily, Patrick, Kitty, and Jack. A single mother, Aggey, had with her two children, Jenny and Edmund. This Edmund is likely the man who appears four decades later in Elijah's 1852 will, along with his wife, Jane, and six children. Even with the smallest bits of information about Edmund, we can flesh out aspects of his life. Although Elijah's 1852 list does not include ages, the fact that Edmund and Jane had six children would suggest that Jane had reached puberty a decade or more earlier, making her birth date sometime in the 1820s. Husbands were usually older than their enslaved wives, so Edmund's birth year may have been in the 1810s.

The enslaved community at Tusculum was small, so Aggey and her children probably lived in a cabin near the big house. She was probably in her twenties when she gave birth to Edmund. The value assigned to her by white owners in 1815 was $350, indicative of her childbearing capacity; it was just $50 less than the highest valued slave, Gilbert. Young Edmund grew up with at least one sibling, Jenny. In 1815, Edmund is listed at $200 and Jenny at $150; Edmund is listed first on the list, which, together with his slightly higher price, suggests he was the older sibling. As young as two or three years old, he would have been helping with household chores and probably assisting in harvests and feeding animals. His childhood would have been beset by the perennial concern that he might be sold away from his mother and/or sister, as Tusculum was undergoing changes after William Crawford's death, when Elijah took over the management of the estate. Eventually, Elijah consolidated most of his enslaved labor at Sweetbrier, where Edmund came to live sometime after 1840. By then, Edmund was almost certainly a father; his first child was probably born in the 1830s. When Indiana selected Edmund as part of her inheritance, his perceived value of $750 included Jane and their youngest child, Lafayette. Their daughter July was still listed alongside them in 1860, but the other children were missing from the list.

These tendrils of family branches are the clues that African American genealogists rely on to make connections between generations of enslaved families in the absence of more formal records. While a difficult process, genealogy has become an essential tool in identifying enslaved families and their descendants.

Elijah's death left not only his human property but also his vast land holdings to be divided among his creditors and heirs. Elijah owned dozens of rural pieces of farmland, providing him income from crops as well as rent. Two years after his death, Indiana altered the name of the plantation and placed the crown jewel up for sale. The "Auction Sales" section of central Virginian newspapers listed "Sweet Briar Estate for Sale," accompanied by the opening sentence: "The valuable Plantation of Sweet Briar, the late residence of Elijah Fletcher, Esq., is offered for sale."[8]

The story line of Indiana's adult life is so solidly enshrined in Sweet Briar culture that a fundamental question is often ignored: Why did she continue in her father's footsteps as a slave owner? One of her brothers, Lucian, had already eschewed the slave-owning gentry and escaped to Canada with an enslaved woman. Indiana was in regular contact with her Northern relatives who were firmly antislavery. Moreover, one of her uncles, William Crawford (one of her maternal grandfather's sons), felt that women were particularly ill suited to manage the responsibilities of slave owning. William wrote to her in 1859, encouraging her to sell: "The management of a Farm with a large lot of Negroes is wholly incompatible with female comfort & convenience when that labor devolves on her & I know from experience generates a perpetual state of vigilant care & anxiety."[9]

A year after she received this advice, Indiana advertised the "sale" in the local newspaper. Was Indiana trying to shed the yoke of slave ownership? Granted, she would have lost money if she manumitted the sixty-eight people she inherited, and they would have been forced to leave the state per an earlier legal statute for freed slaves. Neither was an ethically uncomplicated decision, but she would have avoided a lifetime of owning other people. She could not have known that the end of this "peculiar institution" was a handful of years away.

Apparently, however, the real reason behind the proposed sale was conflict within the family. With one son in disgrace and the other comfortably ensconced at Tusculum, Elijah had intended his two daughters to share in the management and profits of Sweetbrier Plantation for twenty years after his death. This may have suited the sisters in 1852 when he wrote the will. But a year and a half after Elijah's death, on 30 September 1859, Elizabeth married William H. Mosby, a Virginian slave owner.[10] It was by contemporary accounts a loveless, opportunistic marriage. Indiana objected strenuously to her sister's choice and quickly decided Mosby was not to be trusted. She feared he was a gold digger who would somehow squander his own assets and then turn to Elizabeth's share of Sweet Briar.

In December 1859, just months after Elizabeth's marriage, Elizabeth and Indiana settled the matter, with Indiana deciding to buy out Elizabeth's share in Sweet Briar, trading other land in exchange for 1,300 acres.[11] Following the counsel of her uncle, she put the estate up for sale—in order to buy it back herself, in its entirety. This "severed as far as practicable" her financial entanglements with her sister. Thus, on the eve of political, economic, and military crisis, Indiana reaffirmed the values she was raised with: that it was part of the natural order for plantation owners to own slaves and to use their labor to ensure a productive agricultural harvest and a life of comfort for a few.

The advertisement provides an invaluable window into the state of the plantation on the eve of the Civil War, and supplies insight into the fact that blacks and whites experienced the Sweet Briar landscape in very different ways. The white Fletchers consistently described their environs with a remarkable lack of recognition for the dozens of enslaved people who worked and lived on the plantation. Conversely, as the African studies professor Rebecca Ginsburg points out, "enslaved workers knew the land through a different set of cognitive processes than whites."[12] At Sweet Briar, these differentially experienced landscapes and segregated geographies were quite stark. Although we do not have any first-person accounts by enslaved workers, we have a unique window into Indiana's perception of her home from the ad.

Obviously written to appeal to elite, white buyers, the advertisement urges high-status readers to seize this "rare and excellent opportunity ... to secure a country seat. Distinguished in a high degree for comfort and elegance as well as to make a profitable investment." The ad describes the many buildings within the extensive village that housed more than one hundred enslaved African Americans without once using "slave," "black," "negro," or even "servant." The descriptions could fit in a modern-day issue of *Home and Garden* without revealing the true inhabitants of the plantation: "The outhouses of every description, Kitchen, Laundry, Extensive granaries, Tobacco Houses, Stables, Carriage House, and Cabins, with gardens attached." The description doesn't even bother to mention the enslaved laborers who ran the farm's day-to-day operations: it would have been an accepted assumption unworthy of attention.

"Cabins, with gardens attached" is a veiled reference to the quarters where enslaved African Americans lived and where they had laboriously created gardens to supplement the rations provided to them by their white owner. The "outhouses of every description," as well as every other building, were all managed by African American labor. Indiana's advertisement also describes the 1,300 "heavily timbered acres" as "newly enclosed." In other words, she or her father had ordered enslaved men to erect fences. And these fenced acres were "well watered and in a high state of cultivation." Because of Elijah's successful experiments with various crops and fertilizers, the ad promises soil "of very superior quality" for future efforts. Indiana even boasted that "improvements most excellent" were made by the late owner "almost regardless of cost." The advertisement does not indicate whether the cost was measured in dollars or human lives.

Enslaved people also tended the natural environment Indiana described in glowing terms. Countless hours of labor were behind the "pleasure garden," which was "tastefully arranged, handsomely improved." Only daily, hard work under the hot Virginia sun would have produced a "well stocked and highly productive" vegetable garden. Even the reference to a nearby "market" masks the long trips on horseback or by foot that enslaved African Americans would have taken, with a pass that prevented them from being picked up by the local slave patrol, a dozen miles to Lynchburg or a hundred miles to Richmond to sell Elijah's produce on the open market.

The ornamental shrubs, surrounding geometric pathways, and stately house would have been irrelevant to the daily life of enslaved workers. Their families lived in the cramped cabins lined behind the "big house" and stretching down along the rolling hills toward the agricultural fields, positioned to give the field hands better access to their place of work. The complex of cabins, outbuildings, and workshops was located close to the mansion so that the house slaves could answer the beck and call of whites in their bedrooms and parlors, and be supervised by whites. Though the kitchens were separate buildings because of fire hazards, they nevertheless were located close enough to the dining room table to ensure hot food for the white family.

In negotiating her complete control of Sweet Briar, Indiana might have worried, but she could not have known she was taking ownership of a slavery-dependent plantation on the eve of a war that would end slavery. We have little documentary evidence for what must have been a tumultuous time at Sweet Briar, when a thirty-two-year-old single woman inherited sixty-eight enslaved men, women, and children on the eve of the Civil War. Virginia was at the center of many of the pivotal military engagements, although Amherst County was on the periphery of this action. The closest battles were at least a dozen miles away, but local sites were militarized due to the constant fear of Union attacks. Fort Riverview was built in Madison Heights, about five miles south of Sweet Briar, to protect a strategic bridge.[13] Breastworks were built about five miles north of Lynchburg at Duckbill Farm. There was one tense moment along the Tye River (the northeastern boundary of Amherst County) on 11 June 1864 when the Botetourt Artillery protected a railroad bridge from destruction by the Federal cavalry.[14]

Otherwise, the daily physical and emotional trauma of the war years in Amherst would have come from the uncertainty of the conflict for black and white citizens. Large numbers of African Americans in Amherst took advantage of the chaos and ran away to the North, often to join the Union Army. Virginians who stayed put faced food shortages and economic struggles as Confederate currency became almost worthless. Elizabeth's husband, William Mosby, fought for the Confederate States Army (CSA). Even Lucian returned to his roots and enlisted in Captain Hardwicke's Company (Virginia Light Artillery, nicknamed the Lee Battery) on 28 May 1861. He was promoted to first sergeant later that year and fought until he was captured by the Union Army, serving out the last few years of the war as a prisoner in a Northern jail.

Sidney remained on his farm during the war and successfully applied for a pardon on 4 August 1865, just months after the war ended and earlier than many other Southerners. Sidney met several of the criteria outlined by President Andrew Johnson for a pardon: he owned property valued at over $10,000, he had never held any position (civil or military) in the Confederate government, and he took the "amnesty oath," pledging his allegiance to the United States. Indiana, meanwhile, most likely faced challenges to her authority as she tried to manage enslaved African Americans while gossip about contrabands and the possibility of a Union victory began to reach her rural homestead. Half a dozen African Americans formerly enslaved by the Fletchers accompanied their Civil War era masters into battle as manservants or were forced to work on Confederate fortifications.[15]

Givens Rose left his parents and brother behind at Sweet Briar when he was forced to work on a nearby defensive breastwork. Givens is part of a small, poorly understood group of African American men who fought for the CSA. Some participated as manservants alongside their owners. Others, likes Givens, were part of a corps of laborers who were impressed into service to construct Confederate defenses. On 11 March 1864, the Confederate States Congress issued "an Act to Increase the Efficiency of the Army by the Employment of Free Negroes and Slaves in Certain Capacities." This enabled the Bureau of Conscription to draft up to twenty thousand enslaved men to work on fortifications.[16] And while they hoped to accomplish this work with free black labor, enslaved men filled in the gaps.[17] Elizabeth may have been one of the Southern slave owners who initially volunteered the services of their enslaved laborers. Once these owners realized the high likelihood of injury and death, most demanded compensation, and states eventually passed slave impressment legislation. Accordingly, for each enslaved man Elizabeth provided to the CSA from 1862 to 1864, she would have received $16 a month; the amount increased to $25 in 1864, and, still lacking sufficient labor, a final impressment act in 1865 provided owners with $60 a month in compensation.[18] The enslaved soldier would have received food rations and medical treatments. The enslaved African Americans from Amherst who fought in the CSA were, most likely, coerced into service, either by physical threats or by the worry that their families, left behind on the plantations, would be harmed.

Another Sweet Briar laborer, one of Billy Broady's sons, William H. Broady, also fought in the Civil War. In the years after his 1847 birth in Amherst, William H. had been sold to Charles Claiborne. During the war, William H. was forced to serve as a hostler, caring for horses, in Lynchburg and carried dispatches between Greensboro and Columbia, South Carolina, for Major William Parton and Major William H. Kriker. Both William and Givens survived the war and raised families in Amherst County afterward.[19]

Some of the enslaved men impressed into service were using their forced servitude to plot their escape. For example, on 1 June 1861, thirty-six-year-old Abraham escaped his work detail in the service of the Virginia and Tennessee Railroad Company. He was owned by Captain John Buford of nearby Bedford County, and local gossips concluded that he escaped to Richmond, where he could join one of the Union encampments.[20] One unexpected outcome of this service with the Union Army was the decision of some formerly enslaved Virginians to sue the federal forces after the war ended. For example, a formerly enslaved man from Warrenton, Virginia, asked to be compensated for the use of his horses and stock by the Union Army. His request was brought before the Senate, but the record of the case decision has been lost.[21]

A rare story about wartime Sweet Briar is preserved in a twentieth-century newspaper article. In 1931, at the age of about eighty, Lawrence Freeland talked with an Indianapolis reporter about his memories of being enslaved at Sweet Briar during the war. Lawrence's parents selected an interesting surname, "Freeland," perhaps as a tribute to their migration to the Northern and thus "free" state of Indiana. In the years leading up to the war, Lawrence's mother, Jane Powell, had worked as a cook for Indiana Fletcher. Lawrence recalled that he "was born in a little cabin just back of the big house." If his memory is accurate, he is one of a handful of individuals we can tie to the slave cabin that still stands behind Sweet Briar House. He fondly remembered Indiana being "mighty kind to me" and that she "used to take me riding on her horse with her and I was always at her heels when she was out in the grounds." He recalled less pleasant memories from the war years, which he described as "pretty dark for my folk." He concluded his interview with a memory of a frightening occurrence: "One night the Yankees came ridin' down on us and set fire to the barn and the smokehouse. I was just about scared to death, too. I was awful 'fraid of the Yankees."

This is a fascinating story on many levels: no other source located to date mentions any altercation at Sweet Briar during the war, this is the first mention of a "smokehouse" on the property, and Lawrence is admitting his fear of the Yankees to a Northern reporter during the Jim Crow era of the 1930s. And the last amazing part to this story is the accompanying photograph (Figure 5.2). In it, Lawrence is holding one baby shoe. Apparently, the catalyst for the article was a "home show" he attended in Frankfort, Ohio, where he won a blue ribbon for his display of the oldest footwear. The shoe in question (only one survived) was his baby slipper, dating to the 1860s, when he was enslaved at Sweet Briar, which he carried with him for luck.[22]

It was surprising to read that an enslaved infant owned a pair of shoes (many enslaved children did not wear them), let alone that his parents preserved them and their son carried one with him to Ohio, where, eighty years later, he still had it. Lawrence's story is so remarkable that it almost seems impossible. But the reporter added an important familial link, reminding the local Ohio reader that Indiana was related to Stoughton Fletcher, "one of the pioneer citizens of Indianapolis." Stoughton was one of Elijah's brothers. So, when Lawrence proudly pointed to a small picture of Sweet Briar College on his wall, it is entirely believable that he somehow preserved the shoe from his en-

FORMER SLAVE 'TOTES' HIS BABY
SHOE AS CHARM TO BRING LUCK

LAWRENCE FREELAND.

Figure 5.2. Lawrence Freeland, formerly enslaved at Sweet Briar Plantation. *Indianapolis News*, 18 April 1931.

slaved childhood and then kept himself informed about the subsequent founding of a college on the plantation where he was born.

After four bloody years, the CSA formally surrendered at the Appomattox Court House. Even though the historic event occurred only twenty-five miles away from Sweet Briar, some Amherst County slave owners may have tried to withhold this news from the families enslaved on their plantations. Again, we have no firsthand accounts of the spring of 1865 at Sweet Briar, but we can shed some light on this moment using the remembrances of other enslaved Virginians. This material comes from oral histories conducted by employees of the Works Progress Administration, a New Deal agency that employed Americans during the Great Depression to carry out public works projects. A subgroup called the Federal Writers' Project was formed; locally, this was organized as the Virginia Writers' Project. In 1936, this state-level agency formed an all-African-American unit, led by the thirty-two-year-old Hampton Institute professor Roscoe E. Lewis. He and his sixteen colleagues interviewed more than three hundred formerly enslaved individuals and conducted research in archival repositories throughout the state. This material was synthesized in *The Negro in Virginia*, published in 1940, and later reprinted in various forms.

Thus, although we have no account of how the news of the surrender was received at Sweet Briar, in nearby Franklin County, a soon-to-be-famous enslaved boy was hearing the news from his mother. Booker T. Washington grew up on a plantation near Hale's Ford, where his mother was enslaved as a cook. One morning, after the war had just ended, members of the enslaved community were told to go to the big house. Washington, his siblings, and his mother, listened while someone read "some papers and [gave] a little speech." Washington said, "This was the first public address I had ever heard, and I need not add that it was the most effective one to which it had ever been my privilege to listen." Afterward, his mother whispered the most welcoming news to him: "Now, my children, we are free."[23] Fighting in Virginia with the US Colored Troops in May 1864, Sergeant George H. Hatton witnessed an astounding reversal of history near Jamestown: "The slave can now apply the lash to the tender flesh of his master." Hatton may have based his observation on a single plantation where freed women and one man were invited by a Union commander to whip their former slaveholder, captured the day before.[24]

Almost two years before the surrender, President Abraham Lincoln had freed three million slaves in ten Southern states by issuing the 1863 Emancipation Proclamation. While a welcome first step, this statute was somewhat restrictive and only freed "all persons held as slaves within any States, or designated part of the State, the people whereof shall be in rebellion against the United States, shall be then, thenceforward, and forever free." In other words, the passage of the Emancipation Proclamation freed slaves only in the ten states rebelling against the United States; Lincoln passed it under the auspices of his war powers, not with the legal support of Congress. And while Virginia was one of those ten states, these legally freed people were in some of the most precarious and dangerous wartime communities: Southern plantations whose owners had taken up arms against the US government. The Thirteenth

Amendment, which formally abolished slavery, was not passed in the Senate until the next year (8 April 1864) and did not become law until it passed the House a year later (31 January 1865).[25]

With the surrender at Appomattox and the gradual return to the unified states, formerly enslaved families were informed of their newfound freedom. At Sweet Briar, we are unable to answer even basic questions: When did the enslaved community at Sweet Briar hear about their legally ratified freedom? When did they learn the Union had won the Civil War? What "promise and peril" did freedom represent? But based on the experiences of other enslaved Virginians, we can imagine they probably heard from their own network of kin and enslaved neighbors who, in turn, would have had access to overheard conversations and, in some cases, newspaper stories. After the initial euphoria wore off, the Sweet Briar families had sobering tasks ahead of them: trying to locate and reunite with long-since sold or runaway kin, securing jobs in the financially depressed South, and formalizing prewar relationships through the institution of marriage. If the enslaved individuals at Sweet Briar followed other broad patterns among freed people, we would expect a certain percentage of the families left Virginia to travel to Northern cities. For example, dozens of individuals who left nearby Monticello established a community in Chillicothe, Ohio. Over time, the law caught up with their new freedoms: on 9 July 1868, the Fourteenth Amendment granted African Americans citizenship, and on 30 March 1870, the Fifteenth Amendment gave black men the vote.

For Indiana, the end of the war brought economic challenges and a change in her personal circumstances. No records are preserved to tell us how she felt about the South's loss or her ownership of a large plantation during Reconstruction. But we do know she did not face these challenges alone. Although she had been engaged twice, she did not marry until the fall of 1865, when she was thirty-seven years old. In the end, an Irishman of the cloth caught her eye, Rev. James Henry Williams. Born to an Irish mother who immigrated to the United States as a widow with her three children, he grew up in New York City and attended Union Theological Seminary to train as an Episcopalian reverend. They courted via letters during the war but waited to marry, perhaps because of the difficulties in traveling between the South and North, until several months after it ended. In a nod to Indiana's background, they married at her childhood church in Lynchburg but later that day took a train to New York City, an urban locale that became their preferred residence. There, James Henry and his mother owned a series of rental apartments, and Indiana quickly became proficient at managing the properties. For the next two decades, they spent most of their time in New York, returning to Sweet Briar only to confer with the African American servants who were left to run the farm along with the occasional overseer and periodic visits by Sidney.

Indiana's wedding was just one of many that year, as enslaved individuals took advantage of the new rights to choose their own unions and have their marriages legalized. Before the war, countless couples met, fell in love, started families, and stayed together until they died — but the Southern states did not sanction marriages among slaves, leaving no formal records of these unions. After the passage of the Thirteenth Amendment, African Americans' marriages were added to local court registries. Many of these first marriages were probably men and women formalizing long-term relationships that most likely included children. In Amherst, the first African American marriages were transcribed on their own page in the register labeled (actually, handwritten over the preprinted label) "Col^d" (colored). By 1870, the union of African Americans had become commonplace, and these unions were interspersed with white marriages, row after row with the applicant's race indicated as "C" (colored) or "W" (white).[26] If we scan these earlier marriages, we find the very first black union formalized by Amherst County on 19 May 1866, almost a year after the end of the Civil War: R. Anderson "col.d" married Hester (?) Dawus (?) "col.d." He is twenty-four and lists his occupation as a woodcutter and farmer. She is twenty-three, listed as widowed—showing that even without legal status, she considered herself married pre-emancipation.

Indiana's husband, James Henry, was one of the first white pastors to unite newly freed slaves in marriage. He is listed as the officiant on several postbellum marriage certificates in Amherst's Coolwell community, suggesting that he used his very brief visits to Sweet Briar to perform the ceremonies. Most if not all of these individuals were men and women previously enslaved by the Fletchers. Combining these scant pieces of evidence suggests that James Henry was opposed to or at least uncomfortable with slavery and its legacy. One of the first weddings he presided over was on Christmas Eve 1866 between the former Confederate veteran Givens Rose and Nannie Davies. Givens was about six years older than his fifteen-year-old bride. Neither had been married before, and both were from Amherst. In the end, this was one of three matrimonial unions for Givens. Fourteen years later, at age forty in 1880, he married Mary; they had one daughter, Nancy, born in 1882. It's small details like this—naming his daughter after his first wife, Nannie, who also went by Nicey or Nancy—that help connect antebellum and postbellum black family members.

Throughout that first summer of freedom, many more African Americans met and married or formalized previously existing unions. Peter Higginbotham (age twenty) married Mourning Bibby (age eighteen); Mourning was the daughter of Tom and Hannah Bibby, a couple enslaved by Elijah Fletcher. Many of the older couples listed their marital status as "widowed," providing additional support for my earlier contention that many enslaved couples formalized their unions during slavery despite the lack of legal recognition for those partnerships. The postbellum marriage records also provide a fascinating sociological insight into the movement of recently freed individuals. The entries in the marriage register record where spouses were born (nearby counties like Appomattox, as well as ones farther afield like Rappahannock and even communities in North Carolina) and typically provided the names of parents, many of whom had been enslaved on nearby plantations for decades. Other entries demonstrate that surnames were more flexible than a modern-day historian might wish. For example, Caesar Jordan's 31 July 1866 marriage license records his parents as Sam and Jane Jordan, but his new wife, Mary J. Ruffman, listed her parents as Dar(ius?) and Bunch Bibby, without listing herself as a widow. In other words, her last name differed from her parents, with no obvious explanation. This would make it very difficult to assess the connections Mary has with Dar and Bunch in other records.

For Elizabeth and William Mosby, the postwar period was a time of growth. Back in 1860, at the dividing of her father's estate, Elizabeth had selected families and single workers. Interestingly, her first choice (of sixty-four people) was Sampson. He was almost certainly the same Sampson who was hired out to work for Bezaleel Brown in 1848, indicating he had been a valued worker, but by 1860, he was valued at just $100. Perhaps he was old, infirm, or both. Seeing him at the top of the list suggests Elizabeth had grown up with him or had some other attachment. Her next two selections were a woman and child valued at $750 and then a woman, Lucy, who was assigned the highest value given to a woman on the entire list, $1,000. And so it continued for dozens and dozens of men, women, and children. Elizabeth selected couples, women and their children, single men, and brothers. By the time she made her selections, Elizabeth would have spent her entire twenty-nine years being surrounded by enslaved African Americans at her disposal.

When Elizabeth and William had first married, they had land and slaves but no plantation. Before the war, they had finished building a home in northern Virginia. But, perhaps to avoid the ongoing battles, they ended up settling in Amherst County. The farm estate neighbored Sweet Briar and included several outbuildings, which are visible in the handful of photographs that survive. This would have been the workplace of sixty-four enslaved African Americans. And although there were just eight years between the death of Elizabeth's father (1858) and the passage of the Thirteenth Amendment (1865), these individuals suffered from the impact of slavery. During that short time span, Sidney, as the executor of Elijah's estate, was still selling and hiring out slaves, resulting in permanent separations.[27] As with other marriages between two white slave owners, Elizabeth's wedding disrupted the African American community. Elizabeth inherited sixty-four enslaved people in 1860. That year, the slave census shows Wm. H Mosby owning fifty-eight slaves. Most would have been Elizabeth's, but perhaps William brought an enslaved manservant or other laborers with him when he moved from Henrico County to Amherst to court and marry Elizabeth.

There is a strange pattern to the otherwise limited data—age, sex, race—contained in the slave census. Only five of the fifty-eight people are over the age of forty. The rest are young, ranging from twenty-nine to two one-year-olds. The oldest individuals are probably two couples, a woman aged seventy-eight, a man aged seventy-six, a man aged seventy-five, and a woman aged seventy-three. Born in the eighteenth century, just after the American Revolution, these elders may have helped raise Elizabeth or William and had probably been owned by one of their families for decades. The rest of the demographics are easier to interpret: twenty-four men and women over the age of fifteen, accompanied by twenty-seven children between the ages of one and fifteen. Apparently, Elizabeth avoided selecting too many of her father's older, and thus potentially less useful, laborers. She was investing in the future of slavery. The slaves Elizabeth chose were individuals with copious family ties: Givens and Nannie Rose; Ned and Pamelia Bibby and their children (Edward, Elick, Alexander, Silla, and Ellen); the siblings Abram, Becky, and Phillis; and Celia and Frances, who showed up as a pair on both Elijah's 1852 will and Elizabeth's portion of the estate in 1860.

By 1870, Elizabeth's land and material possessions were in disarray. On 21 May 1869, she and her husband filed the first of several forms to dissolve their marriage. The law restricted what property she, as a woman, could own in her name,[28] so Elizabeth arranged a trusteeship whereby H. Macon Steptoe would hold the deed on her behalf. Her efforts to untangle her financial connection to William did not go smoothly. On 18 January 1870, Elizabeth claimed a balance due to her of $149.43, plus $20,000 in Virginia registered bonds, "which with the real estate conveyed by me to him as my trustee excluding all previously sold by us jointly is the only [means] for which he is to account to me in the future."[29] Perhaps because of the social stigma attached to Victorian era divorces, Elizabeth and William continued to work together on their Amherst property but not as a happily married couple. Later that summer, William moved to his Henrico County estate in Varina, while Elizabeth began planning to build a home on the Amherst County land.[30]

Dozens of African Americans worked on the Mosby land for many years after the war. Most of these individuals rented land from their former owners; no evidence suggests that the Fletchers or Mosbys gave land to people they had once held in bondage. Receipts show that black tenants, such as Givens and his brother Moses Rose, rented houses from William Mosby. The pair purchased agricultural materials from him, including cows, mules, and cooking utensils. The Rose brothers were part of a large tenant farmer community that was renting out lands from the Mosbys. In return, the Mosbys claimed a share of the crops.[31]

Another family that worked on the Mosby land for a time was the McDaniels: Preston and his wife, Phoebe. Preston was the formerly enslaved blacksmith who had run away in 1854 from a far-distant plantation where Elijah Fletcher had tried to hire him out for several months. In the years after the war's end, Preston and Phoebe moved to Lynchburg. There, they rented a home from William Alvis, a baggage agent for the Norfolk and Western Railway.[32] In the 1870s, other African American families farming the Mosby land included Austin Quarles (born 1843) and his wife, Jennie (born 1850); they lived with their daughter, Eliza. While their birth dates suggest they may have been born enslaved, there is no record of an "Austin" or a conclusive "Jennie" at Sweet Briar before 1865. They rented a "house & Board" from William Mosby for $52.35 a month. Like the Rose family, the Quarles bought goods from William, as if he were in charge of a "company store." For example, in 1870, "Mrs. Quarles" bought $3.97 worth of feathers from William.[33]

Because the Mosbys were occasionally absentee landlords, William hired a Scotsman, "Mr. Murray," to manage his Amherst lands and tenants. Murray was responsible for managing the financial accounts, grazing the cattle, and overseeing the farm. But he was apparently not up to the task, as William complained he was "incapable of doing work one half the time."[34] Instead, dozens of tenants, primarily African Americans, were planting crops, raising and selling animals, and working on construction projects. While work on the farm was going smoothly, Elizabeth's marriage was not. Despite their divorce, eventually, in 1872, the Mosbys built a house on the land so that they could live at and supervise their estate directly. Built in 1872, they initially called it Hamlet Hall.[35] During the six months of construction, African Americans provided crucial services. William reported that the tenants produced "ample provisions," including corn, bacon, milk, butter, vegetables, and fruit. In many ways, William's postbellum account book sounds no different than an antebellum plantation record, with the labor of others providing subsistence to a white family. Moreover, in 1873, Givens Rose and Julius Scharr were "hired by the year" and during that time "made a fine crop of corn and oats."[36]

That same year, Elizabeth began living full time at Hamlet Hall. Accordingly, she employed a cook, an African American woman named Patsy Cabell.[37] Throughout the next two decades, Elizabeth managed black labor on the land to ensure successful harvests, healthy herds of sheep and cattle, and efficient management of her household. Most of these individuals had been enslaved at Sweetbrier, including Paulus, Givens, and Moses Rose; J. Royal; F. Richeson; and Horace Lucas. Over the years, the Mosbys were pleased with their labor, writing in 1876 that the "hands hired . . . did well."[38] In 1879, William Mosby died at age fifty while living apart from her at Brookland in Henrico County.[39] Elizabeth claimed ownership of the newly built plantation, which she renamed Mt. San Angelo.

Widowed, Elizabeth hired two white servants to live with her in 1880: Edward Carr (age twenty-one) and Serena Carr (age nineteen). Most of her rural neighbors were African Americans, several of whom her family had enslaved decades earlier. Daniel Bibby and his wife, Nannie, lived two doors away.[40] Daniel had been widowed while enslaved by Elijah Fletcher and raised many of his dozen or more children by himself before remarrying after the Civil War and purchasing about one hundred acres of land.[41] Another near neighbor, Squire Fletcher, had a tiny plot of twelve acres of land valued at just $100. In comparison, Elizabeth owned just over one thousand acres valued at $15,00.[42] Squire was one of the handful of individuals who selected the surname Fletcher after he was freed. Before William died, Elizabeth and her husband had regularly rented homes to African Americans such Preston McDaniel and Givens Rose. On occasion, they gave these men and their families a hog or a sheep or hired them to do farm jobs at Mt. San Angelo.[43] Many of these individuals were living in impoverished circumstances. The end of the Civil War had not ended agricultural networks and interdependent relationships between wealthy farm owners and African American laborers.

Meanwhile, Elizabeth's relationship with her sister across the road at Sweet Briar remained strained. Indiana's daughter, Daisy, however, wrote in her diary of visiting her aunt, whom she nicknamed Lilybell.[44] Daisy made her gifts (like a painted ceramic plate)[45] and sometimes wrote letters to her in French. Meanwhile, she wrote in her diary of her parents' critical comments about Elizabeth's lifestyle and mind-set. Elizabeth occasionally visited Daisy, but when Indiana and James Henry were out of town, Sidney was the primary caretaker of both Daisy and Sweet Briar. Elizabeth preferred Mt. San Angelo to either of her siblings' farms, rarely leaving her home base. Instead, she used her servants as go-betweens to carry messages and occasionally food. For example, in the spring of 1883, Daisy mentioned that Elizabeth had "sent Albert over with a great big pat of butter and some bread which she said she had baked fresh for us."[46]

Besides her siblings, most of Elizabeth's 1880 neighbors were African American. More than a dozen were her age or older, so it is likely that some of the women had helped raise her and that the men had worked the Sweetbrier fields for her father. Many of these African American neighbors were still dealing with the heart-wrenching separations imposed on their families during slavery. Even after enslaved individuals were freed, some parents struggled to reunite with their children. The efforts of Laura and Nelson Tinsley, born at Sweetbrier illustrate this distressing challenge long after the "peculiar institution" of slavery was abolished. On 7 May 1866, almost a year after the end of the Civil War, Nelson was still hard at work trying to reunite his family. During or before the war, three of his children had been taken out of the state by one of Edmund Penn's daughters, Sarah, and her husband, Hugh Brown. They were sent to Rome, Georgia, 490 miles away—a two-week journey on foot if you walked twelve hours a day. His young children were very likely led in a slave coffle, possibly chained together.

After the Civil War ended, Nelson put in a formal request to a local branch of the newly created Bureau of Freedmen, Refugees, and Abandoned Lands to recover his children. Commonly called the Freedmen's Bureau, it had been formed by Congress on 3 March 1865 to help formerly enslaved African Americans and poor whites in the South cope with the impact of the war. It played a crucial role in providing food, housing, and medical and legal assistance such as helping former slaves legalize their antebellum marriages. The bureau also opened freedmen's schools throughout the South; the nearest one to Sweet Briar was the Amherst/Lynchburg unit. The Freedmen's Bureau was instrumental in helping formerly enslaved families, until white Southerners successfully argued for its closure in 1872. But even the bureau's long reach did not automatically reunite families. Even after his initial, straightforward request (paraphrased: my children are in Georgia, here

are their names, please arrange for them to return to Virginia), Nelson
spent months begging the Freedmen's Bureau officers to carry through
with their promise to return his children. Even after a Freedmen's Bureau lieutenant, Lewis W. Stevenson, took up Nelson's case, almost a
year passed between Nelson's initial request and the final approval of
the "transportation order #498" for his children to be returned to him
and his wife.[47]

In the first few letters I transcribed from the Freedman Bureau Records, the children were not named in the application for assistance.
If this story had a happy ending, the children listed would have been
Charles Robert (born 1852), Emma (born 1854), and perhaps Nellie
(born 1860). These three children were listed in Nelson and Laura's
household in the 1870 Amherst County Census.[48] If the story had a
tragic ending, the three other Tinsley children, born between 1855 and
1859, and the children listed above were never reunited with their parents. At the same time, it isn't very likely that one woman had three
children in the space of four years, although twinning among Virginia's
African American population is common (central African populations
have one of the highest rates of twins in the world). Still, the more likely
scenario is that some or all of the three children living with their father
in 1870 were the three children who are referred to in the 1866 letters.

Unfortunately, a search of census records suggests a different ending, which ties into one of the themes of this book: slavery results in an
emotional and social trauma that can be passed down through many
generations and continue into the present. When I finished my search
of the 1870 Census for Nelson and his family and saw he was living
with six of his children, five of whom were born before 1865 and thus
could have been the "three children" referred to in the 1866 document,
it appeared as if this story had a happy ending—that is, Nelson had
located his children who were sent to Georgia and brought them back
to Amherst. But when I looked deeper, I found a 1910 listing for Emma,
the girl I originally thought was Nelson and Laura's eldest daughter.
In 1875, at age twenty-six, she married Daniel Jordan, a man just a few
years older than she and, most likely, born enslaved. Laura A. Tinsley,
listed as Daniel's mother-in-law, was living with them. She was widowed, so Nelson must have died sometime between 1900 (when he was
listed on the census) and 1910. But the 1910 Census contains another
column of data: "Number of Children" and its more telling counterpart, "Number of Living Children." Laura said she had eight children,
two of whom were still living in 1910. Those two children were Charles
Robert (died 1919) and Emma (died 1915). Using the 1870 and 1880
censuses, I had only accounted for six children. The other two possibly

were born after 1866 (their eldest son) and died in infancy (although, after 1866, the records for black births are as comprehensive as white births, and there is no record of her giving birth in Amherst), but they were more likely two of the three children Nelson tried so desperately to get back after the war.[49]

And then, just as I was writing the final draft of this book, a new series of records were released online—letters from officers in the Freedmen's Bureau. The revelations in those documents, thousands of which were uploaded to FamilySearch.org in the early fall of 2015, provided crucial links between antebellum and postbellum black families. I renewed my search for "Nelson Tinsley." Buried in almost a dozen letters to and from Rome, Georgia, and Amherst, Virginia, one of the procedural letters finally named the missing children. On 14 May 1866, with the children not yet reunited with their parents, an agent for the Freedmen's Bureau, L. D. Burwell, explained that he was very "particular" about listing their names because they "once had their transportation refused by the Rail Road here on account of some informality."[50] Nelson and Laura's children were finally treated as human beings, not lost luggage. Their *lost* children were Charley (about seventeen years old), Margaret (about fourteen), and Emma (about twelve). If we return to the 1870 Census, taken just four years later in Amherst, we see that Charley was then going by the name Charles; Margaret is not listed, and she most likely died as a teenager in the intervening years after all that effort to see her parents again; and Emma was married five years after her return to Amherst.[51]

By 1910, all of Charles and Emma's siblings were dead, as was their father. In the end, Charles lived fifty-three years in Virginia after his return from Georgia. In the early twentieth century, he was running a livery stable in Amherst.[52] Horses from his downtown barn were probably some of the steeds being rented by the first students at the newly founded Sweet Briar College, which did not yet have an on-site stable. Emma outlived her brother, dying at age sixty-one in 1915.[53]

Notes

1. *TLEF*, letter from Sidney Fletcher to Calvin Fletcher, 15 February 1858, 269.
2. *TLEF*, letter from Lucy Fletcher Williams to Calvin Fletcher, 28 February 1858, 269.
3. *TLEF*, letter from Indiana Fletcher to Calvin Fletcher, 15 March 1858, 271–73.
4. *TLEF*, letter from Sidney Fletcher to Calvin Fletcher, 15 February 1858, 269.

5. Letter from Elijah Fletcher to Lucy Fletcher, 15 May 1812, Archives.

6. Amherst County Will Book 16, 524–27.

7. For example, the Amherst resident Taft Hughes (1909–1999) reported that his grandfather took the surname Douglas after he was born in Rockbridge County; when he married and moved to Amherst, he changed his name to Hughes. Amherst County Heritage Book Committee, *Amherst County Virginia Heritage Book,* 174.

8. "Sweet Briar Estate for Sale," *Lynchburg Virginian,* 6 January 1860, 1; "Sweet Briar Estate for Sale," *Richmond Enquirer,* 17 January 1860, 1.

9. Letter from W. S. Crawford, Washington DC, to "Inda," 1 November 1859, 4–5, Archives.

10. 30 September 1859 marriage to William Hamilton Mosby (W. H. Kenkle), Amherst County Courthouse Marriage Records.

11. Amherst County Deed Book "E. E.," December 1859 deeds, 339. Karol Lawson is the first contemporary historian to have realized the sale was a facade for settling a more complicated family affair. Lawson, "I have lately bought me a Plantation," Archives.

12. Ginsburg, "Escaping through a Black Landscape," 52.

13. Works Progress Administration Historical Inventory, Library of Virginia (Richmond, VA), 28 April 1936.

14. Percy, *The Amherst County Story,* 116.

15. US Confederate Pension Applications (e.g., Alice Wright, John Berry, Archie Hollins, Anderson Carter Sr., Charles Ellis, William H. Broady), accessed via "Alabama, Texas, and Virginia Conference Pensions, 1884–1958," ancestry.com. Each applicant submitted a request at various times in the early 20th century.

16. Jordan, *Black Confederates and Afro-Yankees in Civil War Virginia,* 232–35.

17. Glymph, "Noncombatant Military Laborers in the Civil War," 28.

18. B. Nelson, "Confederate Slave Impressment Legislation," 395, 398, 402.

19. Library of Virginia; Confederate Pension Rolls, Veterans and Widows; Collection CP-3_192; Roll 192; Roll Description: Servants from Various Counties (surnames A–L): "William H. Broady."

20. *Richmond Daily Dispatch,* 1 June 1861 .

21. "Domestic News" section, *Daily Phoenix,* 21 June 1870, 3.

22. "Former Slave 'Totes' His Baby Shoe as Charm to Bring Luck," *Indianapolis News,* 18 April 1931, 15.

23. Booker T. Washington, *The Story of My Life and Work* (Toronto: J. L. Nichols & Co., 1901), 29–38, reprinted in Duke, *Don't Carry Me Back!,* 170.

24. Letter to the editor from "G. W. H.," *The Christian Recorder,* 10 May 1864, transcribed as "Retaliation in Camp," Africans in America, http://www.pbs.org/wgbh/aia/part4/4h3082t.html.

25. "The Senate passes the Thirteenth Amendment," United States Senate website, https://www.senate.gov/artandhistory/history/minute/Senate_Passes_the_Thirteenth_Amendment.htm.

26. While the 1870 US Federal Census used three "racial categories" (white, black, or mulatto), the marriage records used just "white" or "colored."

27. Amherst County Will Book 16, "The Estate of Elijah Fletcher," 57 (sale of

Ferdinand, 9 October 1858), 64 (hiring out Edmund and Joshua, 26 May and 1 June 1858), 67 (hiring out Betsy and Lydia, 3 and 27 January 1860).

28. Amherst County Deed Book "H. H.," 16, recorded 21 January 1870.

29. Amherst County Deed Book "H. H.," 22, recorded 18 January 1870. Apparently, when the census taker came through Amherst that summer, William was not at home, because the census incorrectly listed Elizabeth and William as "B" for "black."

30. 1870 US Federal Census, Varina, Henrico, Virginia; Roll M593_1655; Page 456A; Family History Library Film 553154.

31. *Mosby v. Mosby*, Exhibit "E" filed with The Bill of Elizabeth F. Mosby, 1870s, loose papers, Amherst County Courthouse.

32. The 1870 US Federal Census, Amherst Township, p. 42, line 11, documents Phoebe McDaniel as forty-five years old, living in the Edward Bibby household; the 1880 US Federal Census, Lynchburg, p. 7, Dwelling 51, Family 70, documents Preston and Phoebe McDaniel living in their own home in Lynchburg; the 1881 *Lynchburg City Directory*, 114, lists Preston as a laborer, living in a residence behind Wm. Alvis.

33. *Mosby v. Mosby*, Exhibit "E" filed with Bill, third (unnumbered) page, "1870: These Credits are not given in the Trustee's Report," loose papers, Amherst County Courthouse.

34. *Mosby v. Mosby*, Exhibit "E" filed with Bill, second (unnumbered) page, "1870," loose papers, Amherst County Courthouse.

35. According to the 21 May 1869 settlement between Elizabeth and Wm. H Mosby, Deed Book HH, 16, Amherst County Courthouse.

36. *Mosby v. Mosby*, Exhibit "E" filed with Bill, fifth (unnumbered) page, "1873," loose papers, Amherst County Courthouse

37. Deposition by Wm. H. Mosby about Patsy's employment in divorce suit between Edmund Cabell and Patsy Cabell, 1878, Amherst County Courthouse.

38. *Mosby v. Mosby*, Exhibit "E" filed with Bill, loose papers, Amherst County Courthouse.

39. Amherst County Deed Book 19, 439.

40. The 1880 US Federal Census, Amherst Township, p. 35, lines 1–14, 31–32, 36–46, 49 ("Mrs Elizabeth Mosby"), 50; also p. 36, line 1.

41. The 1880 US Federal Census, Amherst Township, p. 22, line 25; by 1880 he had increased his acreage to 320. The 1880 Agricultural Census, Amherst County, 15th District, p. 20, line 7.

42. The 1880 Agricultural Census, Amherst County, 15th District, p. 20, lines 2, 9.

43. *Mosby v Mosby*, Exhibit "E" filed with Bill, loose papers, Amherst County Courthouse.

44. Foreword," in Williams, *Daisy Williams*, 5.

45. Figure "Aunt Lilybell from Daisy," in Williams, *Daisy Williams*, 75.

46. "Daisy's Letters," 2 May 1883, in Williams, *Daisy Williams*, 80.

47. Records of the Field Offices for the State of Virginia, Bureau of Refugees, Freedman, and Abandoned Lands, 1865–1872, NARA Microfilm publication M1913.

48. The 1870 US Federal Census, Amherst Courthouse District, p. 78, lines 4–11.
49. The 1870 Federal Census, Amherst Courthouse District, p. 78, lines 4–11; The 1880 Federal Census, Amherst District No. 16, p. 16, lines 46–50; The 1910 US Federal Census, Amherst Courthouse District, p. 9, lines 12–15.
50. Records of the Field Office for the State of Virginia, Bureau of Refugees, Freedman, and Abandoned Lands, orders and circulars received June 1865–December 1868, NARA M1913, roll 109.
51. The 1870 US Federal Census, Amherst Courthouse District, p. 78, lines 4–11.
52. Advertisement in *Amherst Progress*, 22 December 1904, 1.
53. Death Certificate, 16 August 1915, filed by W.S. Watts, File No. 18081, Amherst County Courthouse.

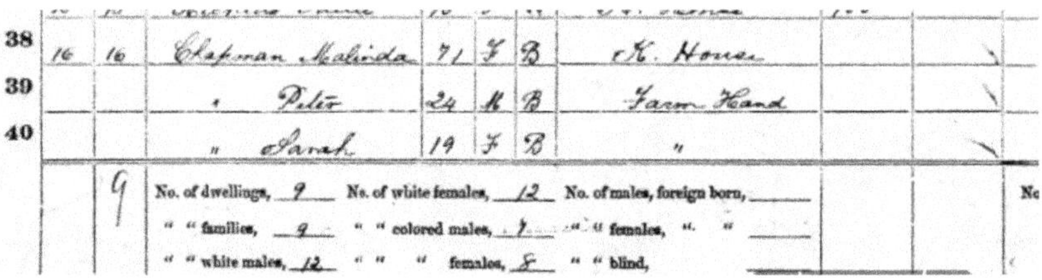

38	16	16	Chapman Malinda	71	F	B	K. House
39			" Peter	24	M	B	Farm Hand
40			" Sarah	19	F	B	"

9 No. of dwellings, 9 No. of white females, 12 No. of males, foreign born,
" " families, 9 " " colored males, 7 " " females, " "
" " white males, 12 " " " females, 8 " " blind,

Figure 6.1. Excerpt from the 1870 US Federal Census for Amherst County, Virginia. Roll M593 1633, Page 399B, Family History Library Film 553132.

6

Freedom Communities, 1866–1883

At the end of a long, hot day on 30 July 1870, J. C. Hearn, the assistant marshal of the US Census, recorded the names of the elderly Malinda Chapman along with three young adults, likely her grandchildren: Peter, twenty-four; Pamelia, twenty; and Sarah, nineteen (Figure 6.1). At seventy-one, Malinda was one of the older black residents of Coolwell, born around 1799. Although the connection is speculative, a Malinda is listed as "Daphney's child" on David Crawford IV's 1802 will. The neighborhood where Hearn recorded Malinda's household was just around the corner from Mt. San Angelo, where Elizabeth Fletcher Mosby lived with her husband, William. Malinda's geographical proximity to Elizabeth after emancipation might point to a longstanding relationship between the two women, dating to the Tusculum childhood of Elizabeth's mother.

Hearn had begun his day in the village of Coolwell at the home of two white brothers in their twenties who lived with a woman of color and her three young children, as well as an older boy, age fifteen, who may have been her brother.[1] Hearn's census forms did not include a means of recording family relationships, so a contemporary researcher is left wondering about the familial ties in some of these households. Hearn collected information about seventy people on 30 July, ranging from a seven-month-old baby to an eighty-one-year-old African American man named Jefferson Bibby. Over the next twelve days, he recorded the particulars of more than a thousand residents of the rural Coolwell community, about half of whom were of African or Native American descent. These federally mandated questions came just five years after the Fletcher family slaves were freed. As I approached the wealth of data collected in this first census of free African Americans in Amherst County, I wondered what type of occupational, educational, religious, or familial opportunities were available to them. Did freedom enable them to reunite their families? Where did they work? Did they have the luxury of sending their children to school?

Hundreds of pages later, I realized I needed to think more critically about the invisible yet significant role of the census taker himself. My questions were not his questions; the demographic and racial identity of these white men affected the type and accuracy of data they collected. The nineteenth-century census taker, or "enumerator," had an immense amount of power as he (always a he) traveled from house to house. He had the final word on which racial descriptor to apply to each individual, how to spell family names, how to describe socially awkward family relationships (such as unwed mothers and their children), and whether to take the head of household at their word if they identified household members who were not physically present on the day he stopped by to ask his questions. The end result of these efforts was a document containing thousands of names, family relationships, monetary assessments of wealth, occupations, and, before 1865, a tally of enslaved individuals per household and farm. To better understand the biases inherent in the process of collecting household data, it helps to shine a brighter light on the interaction between interviewer and interviewee.

The enumerator unknowingly created one of the only detailed records of the relationships that were being forged among newly freed individuals. He also documented the growing communities of African Americans as families purchased and rented land in newly formed neighborhoods. The subtle connections among households and the unrelated "boarders" or "servants" in postbellum homes in Amherst suggest lifelong connections that, while not related by blood, do reveal social and economic bonds among former slaves. And the order in which Hearn went about his research, in the age before the automobile, tells us which families were neighbors within a day's horseback ride, and illuminates the nearby associations among businesses, schools, and churches.

Driving through Coolwell today, it's easy to get turned around. The original, eighteenth-century residents relied on horses and carriages. And the postbellum African American community mostly relied on foot traffic. Driving around, even at the relatively sedate rate of 40 mph, is too fast to appreciate the character of the old neighborhoods, often centered around churches and double-wide trailers with old cars parked out front. The main roads today have route numbers and modern-day names like Bobwhite Road; in some cases, the routes of the old roads have moved or disappeared. But the real neighborhood character is found on the dead-end tendrils that fan out from the main roads. These lanes have more atmospheric names like Crabtree, Grandfather, Partridge Creek, and Glory Lane; most have a combination of modern homes and abandoned structures. The cultural centers of the community revolve around the churches, such as First Baptist and Bolling Hill Baptist.

The entire location derives its name from a well that still stands in front of a historic tavern. The few businesses in this area today include the Humane Society and an auto body shop. By asking questions of local residents, I began to peel back the layers of the historic landscape. For example, someone pointed out the falling down, clapboard-covered "store" in the woods, which used to sell everything from candy to moonshine. Of the approximately one thousand Coolwell residents, slightly more were African American (51 percent) than white (49 percent). Most of the black adults surveyed in Coolwell that summer of 1870 had been enslaved just five years earlier, and dozens of those families had ties to one of the Fletcher family plantations. For example, Thomas and Hannah Bibby—enslaved by Elijah and inherited by Indiana—were working on their Coolwell farm, assisted by three of their adult children: Sam, Frederic, and Thomas, none of whom could read or write. Their six-year-old daughter, Winnie, probably helped with some of the chores like feeding the animals, getting water from a nearby well, and preparing meals.

There is limited evidence that their former owners gave any land to the families enslaved at Sweetbrier. Although the Union had promised African Americans that freedom would come with "forty acres and a mule," the adage did not hold true in most places, and certainly not in Amherst County. Instead, postbellum property records reveal the parcels that freed people purchased when funds were available; until then, they traded their labor for wages to rent homes. While there are a few recorded instances of Fletchers giving money and land to African Americans, it was usually only after their death, many decades after emancipation, and only to "favored" or long-term servants.

African American residents of Coolwell applied the various skills they had acquired during the antebellum period to build their community. In 1870, most Coolwell residents worked on farms, as "hands" or laborers. Dozens of local men and women had developed specialized skills. Several men were blacksmiths or carpenters; two worked as coopers, and many others worked for the railroad. Many of the largest furnaces in the area were in the Shenandoah Valley and cities such as Lynchburg and Richmond, so these men probably spent months working at foundries, living far from their families. Almost eighty black Coolwell residents, a fifth of whom were men, worked as domestic servants, usually in white households. Sometimes these working relationships mirrored enforced ones from antebellum times. African Americans who had been preaching to their community in secretive "hush harbors" during the antebellum period founded brick-and-mortar churches after the war. Coolwell was home to one of Amherst

County's earliest postbellum African American churches, First Baptist, organized by Rev. P. Ferguson in 1866.

Soon after the church's founding, Indiana Fletcher's husband, Rev. James Henry Williams, donated money to the church. One Coolwell resident, Rev. R. D. Merchant, recollected in his 1935 memoir "very distinctly when [Williams] stood at an old oak tree in our church yard one day, oh! I guess sixty-five years ago [ca. 1870], he handed my father a five-dollar note for the benefit of our church, with these words, 'Here John, give this to your church with my compliments.'" Merchant referred to this as "that memorial act" —a weighty credit for a $5 donation. Later, the residents of Coolwell remembered Williams as "one of the gentlemen of the entire county." Many of the African American employees at Sweet Briar College over the years attended First Baptist, and today, there is a memorial offering table and window contributed by the college in honor of some of these longtime workers.[2] Several families in this congregation had been enslaved at Sweetbrier, and many of their descendants worked on the postbellum plantation and, later, for the college.[3] In 2016, when the church celebrated its sesquicentennial, members of the Sweet Briar community were invited to a Sunday service in recognition of the longstanding connection between the two institutions.

Between 1870 and 1907, about two dozen additional black churches were founded in Amherst County. Several local men served as deacons or reverends for neighborhood churches, but these were low or voluntary positions, so most took on other jobs. Several of the church graveyards contain rows of stones memorializing men and women who worked on Sweet Briar Plantation and/or the college. I often visit these postbellum black graveyards to record names and kinship connections, such as a stone that lists "James, son of Nannie and Peter." Names become crucial in comparing pre- and postbellum records. Like most slave owners, Elijah Fletcher and his children rarely recorded the full names of people they enslaved. Instead, he and his family sometimes added paternalistic pronouns such as "Auntie" rather than identifiers that acknowledged kinship among black families.

The 1870 Census represents an important milestone for genealogists of black families, because it was the first federal census to list formerly enslaved people by their full names, first and last. I have spent hundreds of hours combing the 1870 Census to locate the individuals who were formerly enslaved at Sweetbrier and her two sister plantations, Tusculum and Mt. San Angelo, and match them with earlier lists that typically include, at most, first name, age, and/or gender. A key step in trying to reconstruct more accurate kinship affiliations is to determine the surnames freed people selected when they registered in the 1870 Census.

About six adults enslaved by the Fletchers selected that surname as their own. One was man referred to during antebellum times as Squire, born around 1810. He was one of the four valuable men requested by Sidney in the 1860 estate settlement. His white captors valued him at $600, a relatively high figure for a fifty-five-year-old man, suggesting that his value to Sidney may have been measured by his time spent with the Fletchers over many decades. Two dozen other men and women selected a surname that harkened back to an earlier owner, such as Crawford or Penn. Far more popular were last names like Rose, Jordan, Bibby, Taylor, Reid, and Pendleton. To be clear, these surnames were also those of eighteenth-century white families that migrated to Virginia generations earlier. But these surnames were selected by families that were enslaved by the Fletchers for most of their lives, so the reason for their choices may represent an effort to map out their own claims to Virginian ancestry.

The names are just the first key to tracing the social and economic trajectories of formerly enslaved families after the Civil War. African Americans who had been enslaved at Sweetbrier selected a variety of paths to reestablish their kinship connections and build their own communities. Some moved into the town of Amherst and found work, others tried to search for family members who had been sent to plantations in the Deep South, and still others remained at Sweet Briar in the paid employee of Indiana or her siblings. The 1870 Census provides a window into each of these scenarios. Perhaps half or more of the thirteen dozen African and Native Americans at Sweet Briar in 1860 found postbellum employment beyond the gates of Sweet Briar. Several moved out of the Commonwealth of Virginia, finding work in the coal fields of West Virginia, the railroad in Pennsylvania, or as domestics, washerwomen, and nursemaids for New England families in Massachusetts. By 1900, almost seventeen thousand black residents in West Virginia were Virginians by birth; and over a twenty-year period (1890–1910), more than twenty-five thousand Afro-Virginians had arrived in West Virginia to work in the coal mines.[4] This exodus was part of a new system of free labor whereby former slaves were willing to emigrate elsewhere in search of higher wages or better working conditions.[5]

Others stayed in the general region but not at Sweet Briar itself. One of these families, headed by James and Lavinia, took the surname Fletcher and settled on Turkey Mountain, several miles northwest. Lavinia had been enslaved by Elijah and given to Indiana as part of the 1860 estate settlement. Her first child, Nelson, then age four, accompanied her, but it is unclear where James was enslaved. Both James and Lavinia were born around 1835, and neither appeared on Elijah's 1852 will, so they may have been enslaved elsewhere. Part of the challenge in locating eighteenth-century ancestors of African Americans who selected the surname Fletcher is that none of their grandparents would have used that name. Elijah was a first-generation "Fletcher" transplant to Amherst County, so I would not expect any enslaved individuals at eighteenth-century Tusculum or the Glebe to have used that name. Instead, James's or Lavinia's parents may have used more common Amherst names like Rose, London, or Davis. People using those surnames and born in the early 1800s lived next to James and Lavinia in both 1870 and 1880. In other cases, nearby neighbors in those Reconstruction era communities are relatives. So Frank (born 1800) and Bettie (born 1805) Davis, who lived next door in 1870, might have been one of either James's or Lavinia's parents. A decade later, most of the members of this family had died, including most of Lavinia and James's children. Two of James and Lavinia's surviving sons, Patrick Henry and Hammond "Amon," were working as laborers for a white farmer named Benjamin Rucker, and no one in her immediate family was working at one of the Fletcher/ Williams plantations. The return of her family to Sweet Briar would come much later, in 2006, after a chance online encounter between me and one of Lavinia and James Fletcher's sixth-generation ancestors.

Other families moved away from Amherst but remained in central Virginia, settling in nearby counties such as Bedford and Nelson. Many of these individuals were reuniting with family members from whom they had been forcibly separated during slavery. A large contingent of freedmen and women settled in the City of Lynchburg, a dozen or so miles south of Sweet Briar, or Nelson, the adjacent county to the north. One of these was Moses Rose, a man inherited by Elizabeth Mosby in 1860. Initially, he and his wife, Malinda "Balinda" Allen, tried their hand at farming small shares of land in Amherst County. But they could not afford a home until they moved to Nelson County in the late nineteenth century. They settled in Piney River, about fifteen miles north of Sweet Briar. Those who did remain in Amherst County spread out across its four districts: Amherst, Elon, Pedlar (then called Peddler), and Temperance. Sweet Briar and Mt. San Angelo were in the first district; Lucian lived in Pedlar; and Sidney's farm, Tusculum, was in Temperance. Most of the freed families settled in either Amherst or Pedlar. The largest village in Pedlar was Coolwell.

Aside from who lived where, the census taker also recorded education and literacy levels. In the mid-nineteenth century, "public" schools as we know them today did not exist. The idea to give every child, white or black, an opportunity to go to school did not develop in Virginia until the last quarter of the nineteenth century. At the end of the Civil War, wealthy children were tutored privately, and while some communities financed schools, most poor children were valued more as laborers than scholars. Children as young as two and three were assigned chores in many families; by six or seven, they were working all day alongside their older siblings and parents and were considered too integral to the household economics to be spared from these jobs.

In the 1870s and 1880s, a political reform movement to provide schooling to a wider swath of society, including freedmen and freedwomen, slowly gained traction. And while many white politicians argued that the content of this effort should focus on industrial education, black and some white Southerners worked during the last quarter of the nineteenth-century to "transform the content and purpose of instruction in black education."[6] African Americans exercised their new-found political rights to participate in the political process. While many of these privileges would be diluted two decades later after the beginning of the Jim Crow era, Southern families took advantage of their initial enfranchisement to support social changes. One of their strongest desires was to create schools for their children and educational opportunities for themselves.

Martha Taylor, the woman who had written to Elijah asking to be bought in 1854, was one of these postbellum, adult scholars. Despite her fateful letter, she is listed in the 1880 Census as unable to read or write (as is her husband, Henry). Perhaps back in 1854 Martha had asked someone to write to Elijah on her behalf. Martha's children are both listed as "able to read," but her twelve-year-old son, Moses, "cannot write." Neither child attended school in 1879, perhaps because of a heavy workload. In late January 1883, Martha started school alongside her children. Martha wrote in a letter, "We like our teacher very well." Eventually, Moses learned to write, but in the 1900 Census, Martha is still listed as illiterate. This was not entirely true, because she wrote a handful of letters to Daisy and Indiana between 1880 and 1895. The penmanship and sentence structure in those notes demonstrate that she struggled with their composition.[7] She, like many of her adult contemporaries, may have found it difficult to continue with regular classes alongside her familial and job responsibilities.

The Taylors and their rural contemporaries may have been taught by thirty-year-old Lucinda Smith, whom the census taker identified as "mulatto," along with her one-year-old child, William. Although the state-sponsored doctrine of "separate but equal" was still decades in the future, Amherst County sponsored white schools at more than double the rate of black schools between 1870 and 1907, resulting in 103 segregated school rooms for white schools and just twenty-seven school rooms for African and Native American children.[8]

The postbellum black teachers in rural Virginian communities often had only moderately more education than their oldest students; for example, many elementary schoolteachers had only a high school education.[9] In Amherst, one such aspiring teacher, Silas Berry, tried out several different professions before a friend asked him, "Why don't you teach school?" Berry, having completed just three years of high school, walked to the home of the superintendent of schools to apply in person. Berry was seated before a chair in front of a "bright log fire" and peppered with a series of mathematical and rhetorical questions. At the end of the informal examination, he was handed a certificate with the number four on it. Not knowing what that meant or how to proceed, he went to the county seat on the next court day and, by happenstance, "ran across an old gentleman and he asked me 'was I a school teacher'"? Replying in the affirmative, the twenty-five-year-old Berry was offered a job teaching at Pleasant Grove School. And from there, he began a three-decade-long career as a teacher, where his accomplishments included an introduction to his future wife, Lelia.[10]

A week after he completed his survey of Coolwell, J. C. Hearn rode up to the fence that surrounded the gardens and houses of Sweet Briar Plantation. His arrival at the verdant hilltop that day was probably greeted by the barking of hunting dogs, the clucking of concerned chickens, and probably some hollering, as the servants or maybe three-year-old Daisy called to Miss Indie or Mr. Williams that a visitor had arrived. Indiana was newly married, and this union had produced a daughter. Hearn recorded the girl's name as Maria G. Williams—an amalgam of her maternal grandmother, Maria Antoinette Crawford, and her paternal grandmother, Harriet Georgianna Williams—but everyone called her Daisy. She was conceived about a year after her parents wed and was to be their only child.

Hearn's data collection would have been influenced by the person who opened the door to him on 18 August 1870. We know Hearn could not have stayed long—perhaps fifteen minutes or so—because he visited forty-three dwellings that same day and recorded information about 243 people. Certainly, he would have needed to dismount and set out his papers and writing implements to write down the answers to the twenty federally mandated questions he had to ask of every person in the "household." He was on horseback, riding from one farm to the

next, so although these homes were all within the same general neighborhood, he would have had to visit more than three houses an hour
(assuming a twelve-hour day). One of the implications of this relatively
rapid survey was that Hearn did not have time to fact-check everything
the interviewee told him. This sometimes introduced errors into the
final document. Depending on whether he was in a rush that warm
summer day, Hearn was probably welcomed inside by fourteen-year-
old Rhoda Miller or the more senior "domestic," thirty-five-year-old
Phoebe Ruffin, for a cup of tea. Phoebe was married to Granville Ruffin,
who lived next door. Phoebe and her husband had spent most of their
lives enslaved at Sweet Briar. We don't have any documents that preserve their thoughts and concerns at working for their former owner,
but we can imagine it was a complicated mixture of emotions. Relief
at finding a job in the economically depressed Reconstruction South?
Distrust or disgust at working for the woman who had enslaved them?

Even after freedom, the Ruffin family was not living together under
one roof. Phoebe spent most of her time at the "big house," working
for Indiana and her family. Her husband lived nearby, but in a separate
home with four of their children, including a one-year-old infant who
would have required regular feedings. The Ruffins had been enslaved
first by Elijah and then Elizabeth. Granville is listed as the eleventh slave
selected by Elizabeth, valued by the slave owners at $1,500—the high-
est of any of the individuals owned by Elijah at his death. In the next
line, it reads "Phebe [*sic*] his wife" with a perceived value of $1,050.[11]
These relatively high values show that, in their thirties, Granville and
Phoebe were in good health and in their prime. Granville was among
the men hired out by Elijah to provide additional income. After the war,
Granville worked for Sidney Fletcher at Tusculum before moving back
to Sweet Briar. Several of Granville and Phoebe's children were born
enslaved, including Armistead (born 1862) and, most likely, Henderson
(born 1865). After emancipation, they stayed together as a couple, and
the rest of their children were born free: Susan (born 1866), Catherine
(born August 1867), Emma W. (born 1869), and Moses (born 1870), who
died soon thereafter at age two.

Aside from the main house, almost all the homes at Sweet Briar
housed African American families. To fully understand the domestic
landscape of this mini-community, it helps to review the instructions
the enumerator was given. Hearn was instructed to define a "dwelling
house" as any "house standing alone, or separated by walls from other
houses in a block." In a rural community, there were no "blocks." Instead, former slave cabins were often treated as separate "dwellings."
On the Sweet Briar farm, the family mansion was Dwelling no. 355.

House no. 356 belonged to a white man named Robert Ewers. This was one of the few times the Sweet Briar farm manager was not a man of color. Robert was thirty years old and lived with his wife, Mary, and their two small children. Robert most likely lived in the cottage adjacent to Sweet Briar House, which was traditionally called the "overseer's cottage." The next two dwellings, nos. 357 and 358, would have been the small wooden cabin that survives today and another nearby structure that is no longer standing — in other words, a "house in the yard." African American families rented space in these dwellings. Henry Heiskell (born 1842) and his wife, Susan (born 1853) lived in the former, while Samuel Garland (born 1845); his wife, Lucinda; (born 1840); and their three children lived in the latter.

The next three dwellings are listed with African American "heads of households," all individuals who worked for Indiana, continuing a multi-decade relationship that began during slavery. Dwelling no. 361 included three siblings who had been enslaved by Elijah: Givens[12] (born 1844), Moses (born 1840), and Charles (born 1854). Each selected the surname Rose, probably indicating a link to an early white settler of Amherst, Rev. Robert Rose (1703–1751). Although he was an Episcopalian minister and his tombstone claims "he was a friend to the whole human Race and upon that principle a strenuous Assertor and Defender of Liberty," he enslaved people.[13] To this day in Amherst, Rose is a common surname that reflects the significant slave ownership, as well as influence, of the reverend and his large family. At Sweet Briar, several enslaved families selected the surname Rose, which may point to connections with the eighteenth-century families enslaved by Rev. Rose and his children.

In the case of Indiana's 1870 neighbors, Givens traced his ancestry through a man who called himself Sampson Rose and a woman named Chaney Davies. Both "Sampson" and "Chaney" appear on Elijah's 1860 estate settlement, suggesting that the Fletchers owned multiple generations of Givens's family. One of Givens's relatives, Silas Rose, lived a few doors away, working as a farmhand for a white neighbor, Robert Brown, who was, according to the 1870 Census, a fifty-five-year-old lawyer who had five black servants living with him and his family. Silas's brothers, Paulus and Calvin Rose, had been enslaved by Indiana. After the war, Givens rented a home on land owned by William and Elizabeth Mosby, and Paulus was hired by the couple to farm at Hamlet Hall.[14]

That summer day, in 1870, Hearn inadvertently created a sociological data set that revealed geo-spatial familial ties between neighbors and a chronological connection to slaveholders and enslaved families.

Immediately after the war ended, the Sweet Briar community retained a roughly even split between the number of black and white residents (131 to 112). But this would change as employment opportunities grew scarcer and many African American families migrated to Southern cities or Northern towns.

Ten years after Hearn's visit, on 25 June, S. B. Walker stopped by Sweet Briar to collect information for the 1880 Census. Daisy made a note in her diary that day. She practiced her French, did her math homework, and rode on a hay wagon with "Helen" (Ellen Jordan), a young black woman born the year the Civil War ended. In addition to her busy day, she noted, "the census man came and asked a great many questions."[15] Whoever answered the census taker's questions gave Daisy's age as thirteen and both Indiana's and James Henry's as forty-nine. In actuality, James Henry was only forty-five years old. Perhaps the respondent considered it shocking that Indiana was older than her husband.

James Henry listed his occupation as "minister," but he did not have his own congregation. Amid officiating for black brides and grooms and donating money to the local black church in Coolwell, he was also frequently ill, suffering from an undiagnosed malady that, based on his symptoms, we would probably identify today as antitrypsin deficiency. Indiana continued to supervise plantation operations but spent most of her time in New York City, managing the family's rental properties. During one visit to Sweet Briar, Indiana complained to James Henry, who had remained in New York, that her afternoons were "dull and uninteresting, one might live here a thousand or two years (if they could) and it would always be the same."[16]

While Indiana and James Henry enjoyed their urban lifestyle, Daisy was sent back to Sweet Briar every summer to avoid the heat and urban malaise and sickness. During those months, her parents alternated visiting, and, in between, Daisy was raised primarily by African American maids and farmhands. Only occasionally did her nearby uncle Sidney, whom she called "Sing," or her aunt Elizabeth, "Lilybell," assist in this task. Instead, the African American domestics and laborers served as the primary nursemaids, companions, and role models for Daisy during these summers. The Sweet Briar College yearbook spun these relationships as follows: "The old darkies in the quarters loved her and many were the blessings that fell from their lips for 'Lil Miss Daisy.'"[17] But one wonders what other emotions they held for Elijah Fletcher's granddaughter.

While she was separated from her parents, Daisy kept herself busy with a multitude of real and imagined chores that ranged from picking strawberries to supervising the work of others. One of the most striking aspects of everyday life at Sweet Briar in 1880 is how much the white family still relied on African American labor. Like many of their neighbors, they hired black laborers to help with the annual planting and harvests, but they also had black maids, farm managers, and babysitters. The "yard" behind Sweet Briar House probably looked similar to antebellum times, with six cabins that housed African American families. One of the nearest black residents were two teenagers, Ellen "Helen" Jordan (fifteen), and Edward Saunders (fourteen). Edward's parents, Thomas and Anne, lived a couple doors away, while Ellen's family, including her parents, Charles and Mary Jordan, lived farther away and she occasionally went home to spend the night with them. Neither Ellen nor Edward had attended school recently, suggesting that their domestic duties at Sweet Briar precluded it. In sharp contrast, Daisy had recently returned from her spring semester at an elite private school in New York City.

One of the freed slaves on whom Indiana relied most heavily to care for Daisy had initially moved away from Sweet Briar. In 1870, Martha Taylor and three of her five children—Lorena (twelve), Mary (six), and Moses Beverly (ten months)—lived in downtown Amherst, near the courthouse, about a mile or two away where Martha worked as a farmhand. It has proved very difficult to determine where her husband, Henry Taylor, lived immediately after the war. He was not living with his family. The closest match for a man of the correct name and age in the area is a firefighter living as a boarder in a Lovingston household in Nelson County, about fifteen miles north of Sweet Briar.[18]

Sometime over the next decade, Martha returned to the site of her enslavement to care for Indiana's daughter. Daisy wrote, "Martha is here all the time, [and only] goes home twice a week."[19] It is no wonder, then, that Martha made little progress on her efforts at literacy. By 1880, the Taylors had moved into a home just three doors away from the Williams family, probably one of the former slave cabins in the yard. That year, forty-seven-year-old Martha and her forty-nine-year-old husband, Henry, were raising their two adolescents, Mary (fifteen) and Moses (twelve). It isn't clear where their older daughter, twenty-two-year-old Lorena, was; she has proved elusive in the 1880 Census. At first, I assumed she had died, but in the 1910 Census, Martha said she had three living children and two deceased. The latter were probably infants who died in the late 1850s or early 1860s, while only three children are listed in the 1870 Census: Lorena, Mary, and Moses.

Mary and Moses worked at Sweet Briar alongside their mother. Mary helped Daisy collect strawberries to make a cake, picked huckleberries for the family, and accompanied Daisy to visit her aunt at Mt. San Angelo.[20] Moses was a farmhand, with tasks like hay raking, and he assisted his mother in procuring food for the family. One time, after weeks of searching, he obtained a pig from one of the Sweet Briar tenants and delivered it to Daisy.[21] Martha's husband, Henry, may have been hired to do odd jobs, but most of his paid work appears to have come from elsewhere. So, while Daisy regularly mentioned Martha, Moses, and Mary as they worked at Sweet Briar, her references to Henry were less frequent. One summer evening, she explained, "Henry Taylor works in town, [and] comes home Saturday night."[22] So, even years after slavery ended, this family still had to spend a lot of time apart to make ends meet.

Daisy did not mention one of Martha's primary tasks—watching Daisy—but outlined Martha's regular duties, including washing, ironing, quilting, and acquiring materials for sewing projects. When Daisy left Sweet Briar each fall for her sojourn in New York, she entrusted Martha with her precious birds. While going to school in New York, Daisy frequently inquired about her birds in letters to Martha. In response, Martha kept Daisy updated on local gossip and the health of her animals. In January 1883, Martha reported that although Watch (a dog) and Frisk (a cat) had both died while under the care of Daisy's aunt, the canary bird "is well and is most always singing." But as Daisy grew older, her letters to Martha decreased in frequency. In the same letter, Martha thanked Daisy for sending a "pretty little picture" but bemoaned the lack of regular letters from Daisy.

During this time, Martha's family was struggling with economic and health issues. Despite her employment during the spring and summer when Daisy was in residence, the Taylors were almost destitute during the rest of the year. One year, Martha struggled to afford the seed to feed Daisy's birds. In the end, she borrowed some seed from Elizabeth but begged Daisy to "send some seeds or Money," as she had only enough to last "a week longer." Clearly, the seasonal nature of Martha's employment was a huge hardship for her and her family. Martha wrapped up her letter, complaining, "Work is very scarce . . . times is very hard and dry here."[23] Many of Martha's African American contemporaries were struggling to adjust after the departure of the Freedman's Bureau a decade earlier and the continued economic challenges presented by broken contracts, evictions, and a weak market economy.[24]

Accordingly, other formerly enslaved families in Amherst were struggling during these years. Daisy observed several of her family's African American servants going hungry, like a washerwoman named Ida who Daisy felt looked "very thin and poor."[25] This may have been

Ida Hawkins, a widow with at least four children who was born three decades earlier, in 1850. In another case, a man who had spent more than half his life enslaved by Elijah Fletcher suffered a personal tragedy. On 24 May 1883, Daisy wrote: "One of old Uncle Daniels [sic] children died yesterday and Martha has gone to the funeral."[26] This was Daniel Bibby, who was born in the early nineteenth century and had more than a dozen children with two or more wives. In 1883, he was seventy-five years old but had recently had several children with his much younger, second wife, Jane. Their last child, Nathan, was born in 1873. The death that Daisy mentioned may have been Nathan (ten years old that year) or his older brother Eddie (thirteen years old). Jane was also dead by then, leaving him a widower twice over. But Jane's elderly mother, Sallie Fletcher, was still alive and lived with Daniel Sr.

Much of the day-to-day farm management was under the control of Logan Anderson, who was part Monacan and part African American (Figure 6.2). He lived in a small, wood-paneled cabin located a handful of yards behind Sweet Briar House.[27] Sometime around 1870, Logan married a woman named Amelia, and they had five children between 1873 and 1882. Both Logan (1849) and Amelia (1854) were born before 1865 and had been, most likely, enslaved on an Amherst plantation. After Daisy was born, Logan was the primary farm overseer. He was the one who greeted the family at the train when they returned each summer.[28] In addition to Logan's oversight, dozens of African Americans worked in and outside the "big house." A man Daisy only identified as Nelson (most likely Nelson Tinsley) worked as a laborer for a daily wage of twenty-five cents. Several individuals, including Ed Saunders, Henry Carey, and Martha Taylor, helped plant and weed a vegetable

Figure 6.2. Logan Anderson at Sweet Briar, circa 1905. Sweet Briar College Library Archives.

garden. Daisy micromanaged this group, but one can imagine they each had years of farm experience, as well as their own household gardens, and did not require direction from a thirteen-year-old.

The record that most frequently mentions Logan Anderson and his family members is Daisy's diary. In her 1880 diary, when Daisy was twelve going on thirteen, she mentioned Logan 82 times, as well as 78 times in her 1882 entries and letters (for a total of 160). To put that in perspective, she mentioned Martha 181 times (from the same sources), and her mother roughly twice as often (402 times). Daisy's frequent mention of Logan, as both a companion and a farm manager at Sweet Briar, points to his integral role in managing people and the farm. Per her usual pattern, Daisy spent the spring of 1882 in New York with her parents. Weeks before her return to Sweet Briar, her mother bought a pocketbook for Logan, and her father wrote to Logan, asking him to "buy some chickens to fatten" in advance of their return. On 3 April, Daisy and her ailing father took the train down to Sweet Briar. And, as usual, Logan was there to meet them at the station.[29]

While in residence on the farm, Daisy documented the everyday minutia of agricultural life, from churning butter to selling products. She detailed Logan fixing butter churns, delivering items to the house, coordinating other servants, pruning overgrowth at the Monument Hill graveyard, wrangling bulls, repairing broken windowpanes, fixing tools, cutting hay, hauling oats, digging potatoes, getting honey, clearing timber, straightening out incorrect deliveries, milking cows, cutting ice from a nearby pond in the winter, and managing the household. In other words, he was a mechanic, porter, butler, gardener, cattleman, rat catcher, handyman, chauffer / carriage driver, farmer, arborist, concierge, and household manager. Although Daisy never says it explicitly, it's clear from her 1882–1883 entries that Logan was also entrusted with watching her when neither her parents nor Martha were around.[30]

During the winter of 1882, Daisy and her parents accused Logan of doing something "shameful." The only perspective we have is Daisy's, when she mentions to her mother the next spring that it had something to do with money:

> Logan seems rather ashamed of his doings last winter, he says Uncle Sing told him not to write, as we were coming home, Papa gave him a lecture about that letter he wrote, he said he was very sorry he had sent it, he has not asked for the money to pay for what he said he spent, and I believe he just wanted it for himself.[31]

Logan may have asked for some household spending money that he later spent on himself (or his family). Another of Daisy's cryptic comments mentioned Logan's reticence about talking about "the dogs," suggesting that part of the problem may be related to the death of two of Daisy's pets.[32]

It is tempting to read Daisy's daily account of life at Sweet Briar as an accurate window into the everyday life of Native and African American families who worked for her parents. But she overlooked fundamental social and economic factors. One glaring absence is the consideration of Logan as a husband and father. We learn from the 1880 Census that Logan lived next door to the Williamses and that he and his wife, Amelia, had four children. Yet, Daisy never mentioned his family, except once, on Christmas Day in 1880: "Mamma and I fixed some nice things for Logan's children we gave three of them dolls and cake and candy Logan got a lot of mistletoe."[33] His family lived nearby, and Daisy saw him almost every day yet rarely accounted for his role as a parent or spouse, instead treating him as a servant.

Logan and Amelia had at least nine children, four of whom were living during Daisy's short life. Amelia died sometime between 1894 (the birth of their last child) and 1897, when Logan remarried a woman named Pamelina (who had sixteen of her own children, nine of whom were still living in 1900). She died before 1910; in that census year, Logan lived with his mother, Jessica, who was over ninety years old. Logan left Sweet Briar after his wife and mother died and was listed in the 1920 Bethesda, Maryland, census as working for a white woman, Sallie Rucker, who was originally from Amherst. Unfortunately, the document trail goes cold after 1920. He does not appear to be in the 1930 Census. If he had lived, he would have been eighty; he most likely died in Maryland.

Another perspective on Logan Anderson's life and contributions to Sweet Briar comes from an interview conducted with him by a Sweet Briar College student in the class of 1917. The anonymous alumna describes him in the yearbook article as "'Uncle' Logan, an old negro, who worked many years for the Williamses and was greatly loved by Daisy." Logan recalled how Daisy joined him on horseback twice a month to collect rent from her parents' tenants. Her father even "had a pocket made in her saddle to hold the money." The author concludes that Daisy "loved to be with Logan, and enjoyed playing with his children and helping his daughter to milk the cows." To the contrary, Daisy rarely mentioned Logan's children in her daily diary entries, casting doubt on the accuracy of the amount of time Daisy spent with the Andersons. Logan described his outings with "Miss Daisy" in a less emotional vein, relating how she "on Bounce, her pony, had ridden with him to Kentucky Pasture, where he went to salt the cattle. She would spend the day gathering wild flowers, which she would take home and plant in the garden." Logan was apparently assigned to watch Daisy while her parents were absent.

Logan is one of Daisy's few contemporaries who described the precocious child in a realistic vein. Instead of sentimental descriptions of the innocent cherub girl, Logan described a spoiled child who was used to getting "her way in almost everything": "I allus use' to try to pacify her and Mrs. Williams. Mr. Williams dun tole me when he 'gaged [hired] me: 'Now Logan, you do jest what they want, I don't ker what.'" Logan recalled that one day he was hard at work supervising farmhands during the harvest when Daisy wandered by and demanded he help her collect wildflowers. The workers were abruptly dismissed, and Logan accompanied her to get the flowers.[34] Daisy took these outings for granted, describing them as idyllic traverses through the countryside. She presumed the power relations around her as natural and her right: "Warm and clear. I took a long ride with Logan and came back by Aunt Lilybells [*sic*]. It is real warm the cherries and strawberries are beginning to go."[35]

"Another time," according to the 1917 yearbook article, "Mr. Williams scolded [him] sharply for making the ice pond so shallow. He thought it should be at least six feet deep, but when he found that Daisy had ordered it three feet deep no more words were said about it." Imagine trying to manage the diversity of tasks that Daisy herself outlined, all the time being at her beck and call. The author says Logan was proud of his skill in managing the Sweet Briar cattle herd: "Logan said, with great pride, that none of the cattle had ever been lost in the mountains." He did admit, however, he once lost six sheep, after which "Miss Daisy cried and cried." As a testament to his close relationship with the Williamses, Logan shared a story from a night in the 1890s, after Daisy's and her father's death, when he was still working for Indiana: "Mrs. Williams asked Logan to go with her to the big pine tree which is situated on the hill across the lake. She carried two tin boxes with her, and she and Logan carefully buried them. No one has ever seen those boxes from that day to this." Was the tale true? Is there gold buried in a Sweet Briar field? Maybe. Logan closed his interview by urging the author, "Chile, you come to see me sum Sunday when I ain't got nothin' to do and I'll set all day and tell you 'bout Miss Daisy and the Williamses so you kin write a great big book 'bout 'em. There's a heap to tell."[36] That book was never written, and neither was the even more valuable book that would have been a full account in their own words of Logan and his African American neighbors, who have been left out of the narrative for more than a century.

The 1880 Census carried an informative column that the 1870 Census lacked: "kinship." Reading the earlier census records, these postwar neighborhoods at first appeared surprisingly ordinary: many nuclear families with both parents alive and living in one household, a sharp contrast to the conditions for many enslaved families. But when I started tracing genealogies using tips from modern-day informants, I started noticing a pattern in the census "kinship" column. About one in ten black households contained "adopted" and "step" children. Unlike today's blended families, this phenomenon has more to do with a community-wide effort to care for children left behind from deaths (not divorce) and separations (from antebellum sales). Moreover, older couples (in their sixties and seventies) sometimes appear to have "adopted" the children of distant relatives or neighbors to enable the parents to find jobs in distant places like West Virginia or Pennsylvania. For example, Frederick (seventy-five) and Malinda (sixty-six) Rose were elderly by nineteenth-century standards, but in their 1880 home, next door to Indiana, they cared for two adopted children: eleven-year-old Anthony and seventeen-year-old Sarah. Sarah was born during the Civil War, while Anthony was born a few years after it had ended.

Similarly, James and Nancy Williams lived near Elizabeth. James was in his sixties when he and Nancy adopted a boy named Henry, who had been born several years after the Civil War, suggesting that his parents may have been forced to leave the area to find employment. We have a more complete autobiography from a man, Silas Berry, who was born in 1858 but "knew scarcely anything of [his] real mother," who did not leave her birthplace of Rappahannock County after the war. Instead, he was raised in Amherst County by a stepmother he called Mammy Kittie, whose real name was Catherine.[37] Farther from Sweet Briar House were dozens of black tenants who rented land from Indiana and James Henry Williams. Daisy mentioned three of these tenants by name: Ida (perhaps the same "very thin and poor" washerwoman from her diary), Edmonia, and Meally. From Daisy's diary entries, we learn that these women were working for Indiana to pay off their monthly rent. Although I have not been able to definitively link them to families enslaved at Sweet Briar, they and/or their relatives likely had ties to the area. Some observers consider the institution of sharecropping as a form of "neo-slavery," given the lack of financial stability and opportunities that it afforded black families.[38]

As an only child, Daisy naturally played with children her age in her neighborhood. In the 1860s and 1870s, the antebellum plantation networks were still the predominant residential pattern. Daisy would have been surrounded by the African American servants hired by her parents and nearby black neighbors who had once been enslaved by the Fletcher/Williams families. Daisy's parents apparently asked some of these children to serve in a dual capacity as friend and minder. One was Signora, a black girl born just a year or two before Daisy who grew up at Sweet Briar. Daisy and Signora roamed the Sweet Briar grounds, fishing and picking flowers. Across the road at Mt. San Angelo, Daisy's aunt Elizabeth also hired African Americans as domestics and farm laborers. In 1880, Phoebe Ruffin, who had been working in Indiana's home, began working for Elizabeth. In the preceding decade, Phoebe and her husband, Granville, had had four more children, the last when she was about forty-four years old. Years after freedom, they decided to name two of their children after their former owners: Elizabeth "Lizzie" Ruffin (born 1872) and India Ruffin (born 1875). Their last daughter, Mariah, was born in May 1879; while it is a common name, Indiana's mother was named Maria, and Daisy's real name was Maria Georgianna.

While Phoebe worked at Mt San Angelo, she and Granville did not give up their house at Sweet Briar. Phoebe may have worked at Mt. San Angelo during the week, possibly with infant Mariah in tow. Her separation from her family seems like quite a sacrifice, presumably required because jobs were in short supply. Meanwhile, the Ruffin children had to prioritize a wage-earning occupation over their schooling. Neither of their two elder daughters, Susan (eighteen) and Emma (fourteen), could read or write. Instead, the eldest worked as a housekeeper, and the younger at home. And none of their four younger children, aged three to ten, attended school in 1880. The institution of slavery cast its educational and financial shadow over the first generation of children born free.

The limited evidence that survives suggests that Sidney ran his plantation differently than his sisters did theirs. Post-slavery, he gave land and money to several men and women he once owned. For example, he gave Cornelia Broady Garland nine acres of land.[39] In 1880, Sidney's household included several African Americans born between 1810 and 1878, highlighting the longstanding connections between the two groups.[40] One was twenty-four-year-old Harriet Edwards. She and her brother Andrew worked as domestics and field hands at Tusculum. An older man, Thomas Turner, about ten years older than sixty-nine-year-old Sidney, also lived at Tusculum. Given Thomas's age, this arrangement was probably one of compassion rather than employment. Thomas may have grown up at Sweet Briar alongside Sidney.

At first, this multiracial, postbellum household did not strike me as unusual. My first hint at the secret the family had kept under wraps for more than a century was a tiny bit of gossip about Sidney's funeral.

One of the two current Sweet Briar professors of dance is Ella Magruder, née Hansen, born in Amherst to a woman who was descended from Val McGinnis. In the late nineteenth century, Val had been Sidney Fletcher's friend and neighbor. A few years ago, Ella told me a story that her own mother had passed down: Val was the only white person to attend Sidney's funeral in 1898. Well, I surmised, perhaps Sidney didn't have many friends. Dozens of African Americans attended, Ella continued, but Sidney's white contemporaries boycotted the services. In my naivete, I still didn't understand the circumstances that would lead a wealthy and, I thought, prominent member of the community to be boycotted by his white neighbors. Ella lowered her voice: "He had a mistress." Oh, I thought, now I see. But, wait, he hadn't been married, so who cared if he'd had an affair? Ella continued in hushed tones: "She was black." My first thought was, did his father know? Ella didn't know any of the details or the woman's name. But she knew the stories. They had been passed down for generations. Such is the power of the spoken word, even when it is never written down.

I had to hunt a bit to piece together Sidney's family. In Virginia, anti-miscegenation laws remained on the books until 1967. More than one hundred years after the abolition of slavery, Virginian legislators still insisted that interracial marriages were illegal. I knew what I was looking for: a woman to whom Sidney gave significant gifts or property but whom he could not openly or legally list as his wife. Armed with this theory, I started finding clues. I found the first piece of evidence in Sidney's legal documents. He could not marry Harriet Edwards because of her skin color, but no law prevented him from giving her land. On 22 December 1883, Sidney gave money and land to Harriet and her two children, Leslie and Ernest Edwards.[41] In his 1898 will, Sidney mentions an earlier agreement between him and Harriet, dated 26 June 1883, whereby she was expected to "perform her part of a certain Agreement." If she did, Sidney would give the boys $500 (each?). He also gave the threesome a tract of land that adjoined the lands of Davison, McGinnis (Val's property), and Fletcher, which amounted to seventy acres. The remaining legalese specifies that the three of them would hold the property equally until Harriet's death, at which point the two boys would share the full seventy acres. On the accompanying hand-drawn plat where the land was surveyed for the court, it looked like Sidney may have recently purchased this land from Val McGinnis. Why would he be buying land for a single mother and her two children?[42]

But this alone was not convincing evidence. Sidney left some money to two other African American laborers who worked at Tusculum in his will, so maybe he was just generous or felt guilty about once owning slaves. I researched Harriet further. She was born in 1855; her parents were Washington and Malinda Edwards. As a teenager, she worked as a domestic servant in the McGinnis household.[43] Although I have not yet been able to locate Sidney's household in the 1870 Census, a letter from Sidney to his sister Indiana shed light on the members of his household during this time. In the summer of 1875, when he was fifty-four years old and Harriet was twenty, they entertained his eight-year-old niece, Daisy.

Daisy was making a doll, and he told Indiana, "Harriet devotes her entire time in making dolls dresses and fixing things for Daisy [*sic*] pleasure." When I first read this letter, I thought Harriet was yet another African American woman pressed into babysitting the precocious Daisy. But then I started looking for additional references to Harriet. I was surprised to find that the Williams family seems to have accepted her. They sent her gifts from New York during Daisy's stay with Sidney; Daisy once wrote to her parents, "Harriet is much obliged for the neck ties you sent her." Daisy seems fond of Harriet: "harriet [*sic*] gave me a pretty dolls iron to keep all the time and she made me a nice tight leather belt and I like it very much. Hearriet [*sic*] is so kind [to] me that I Would like you pleas [*sic*] to send her a dress."[44]

Daisy's letters often mentioned Harriet making her a doll or doll's clothes. For example, in July 1875, Daisy wrote to her parents and described how Harriet "made my doll a pretty pink dress for the Indian rubber doll and a white apron."[45] Harriet apparently regularly cared for Daisy, and they clearly spent a lot of time together. That same summer, Daisy had a bad cough—Sidney's letters implied that she'd had it for quite some time; she called it "hoping coug" (perhaps whooping cough)—and Harriet made her "some vinegar and sugar and butter and made it warm for me to drink but it did not taste good so I did not drink it."[46] Daisy's letters often mentioned that the three of them— Sidney, Harriet, and Daisy—had gone fishing:

> Me and Uncle Sing and Harriet Went fishing yesterday evening I caugh 3 fish and a fish got hold of our bate and was so heavy that she broke the pole and uncle sing caugh hold of it and pulled as hard as He could but the fish got away then went some bate on the hook and we caugh another big fish and we could not get him out so the fish pulled so hard that he broke the string and got the hook in his mouth and Could not get it out.[47]

Three years later, Harriet gave birth to a boy she named Leslie and, a year later, a second son, Ernest. Unfortunately, Harriet died a few years later in 1895, leaving behind her seven- and eight-year-old sons. They did not live much longer; Leslie died in 1891 at age fourteen, while

Ernest lived only five years more, dying at eighteen. By 1898, Sidney, his common-law wife, and their two heirs were all dead.

In a surprising end to this story, Harriet's brother Andrew married a woman named Leila, and they had two children, Rufus and Clarence. Rufus operated a garage in Amherst, married, but never had children. Clarence married a woman named Harriet, and they had three children: Pauline, Clarence "Bud" Jr., and Thomas. Bud became a medical doctor and moved to Washington, DC, but he returned to Amherst and, in 1987, purchased Tusculum. Soon thereafter, he was exposed in a drug scandal and defaulted on his mortgage. Bud died in disgrace sometime in the late twentieth century and is buried at the old Amherst racetrack in the front yard of the home of a Sweet Briar professor. But, however briefly, Tusculum was owned by a descendant of one of the people once enslaved there.

Notes

1. 1870 US Federal Census, Amherst County, Virginia: Roll M593_1633, Page 399A, Image 330529, Family History Library Film 553132.
2. S. Berry, *Memories of Rev. R. D. Merchant*, 33.
3. S. Berry, *Memories of Rev. R. D. Merchant*, 18.
4. Kerr-Ritche, *Freedpeople in the Tobacco South*, 239.
5. Kerr-Ritche, *Freedpeople in the Tobacco South*, 64–65.
6. Anderson, *The Education of Blacks in the South*, 27–31, 32 (quote).
7. For example, Martha's letter to Indiana, 31 January 1895, Archives.
8. Virginia Board of Education, *Virginia School Report*, 78.
9. Anderson, *The Education of Blacks in the South*, 111–12.
10. S. Berry, *Memories of Rev. R. D. Merchant*, 19–20.
11. Division and allotment of slaves among Sidney Fletcher, Mrs. Elizabeth F. Mosby, and Mrs. Indiana Fletcher, 20 June 1864, Will Book 16, 525–529, Amherst County Courthouse.
12. His name is variously spelled Given or Givens in the historic documents.
13. Inscription on his gravestone at St. John's Church, Richmond, Virginia.
14. Mosby Account Book, 1870s, loose papers, Amherst County Courthouse. See 1871 entry, "Paulus Rose [employed] @ $110," n.p.; 1872 entry, "Given's house rent," n.p.; and 1873 entry, "Given Rose [was] hired by the year," n.p.
15. Unpublished diary belonging to Daisy Williams, 25 June 1880 entry, Archives.
16. Undated letter from Indiana [F. Williams] to Henry [Williams], Saturday, ca. 1879, Archives.
17. *Briar-Patch 1911*, edited by the Senior Class of Sweet Briar College (Sweet Briar, VA: Sweet Briar College, 1911), 7.
18. 1870 US Federal Census, Amherst County, Dwelling 309, Family 302, p. 41; 1870 US Federal Census, Lovingston Township in the County of Nelson,

Dwelling 796, Family 827, p. 107, "Taylor, Henry," twenty-eight-year-old "fireman."

19. "Daisy's Letters," 8 May 1893, in Williams, *Daisy Williams*, 89.
20. Letter from Daisy Williams to "Papa," 24 May 1879, Archives; "Daisy's Diary," 4 July 1882, in Williams, *Daisy Williams*, 49.
21. "Daisy's Letters," 4 May 1883, 82; 15 May 1883, 98; 21 May 1883, 104.
22. "Daisy's Letters," 1 June 1883, 115.
23. Letter from Martha Taylor to Daisy Williams, 24 January 1883, Archives.
24. Morgan, *Emancipation in Virginia's Tobacco Belt*, 225–26.
25. "Daisy's Letters," 8 May 1883, 88.
26. "Daisy's Letters," 24 May 1883, 107.
27. "Foreword," in Williams, *Daisy Williams*, 5.
28. "Daisy's Letters," 2 May 1883, 79.
29. Unpublished diary belonging to Daisy Williams, 23 March 1880, Archives.
30. See "Daisy's Diary," 30 April 1882, 34; 7 May 1882, 35; 14 May 1882, 36.
31. "Daisy's Letters," 10 May 1883, 91.
32. "Daisy's Letters," 2 May 1883, 79.
33. Unpublished diary belonging to Daisy Williams, 25 December 1880, Archives.
34. "Thirty Years Ago," *Briar-Patch 1917*, published by the Junior Class of Sweet Briar College (Sweet Briar, VA: Sweet Briar College), 14, 16.
35. "Daisy's Diary," 18 June 1882, 46.
36. "Thirty Years Ago," 16–17.
37. S. Berry, *Memories of R.D. Merchant*, 23.
38. Blackmon, *Slavery by Another Name*.
39. Divorce case, *Cornelia Broady v. Henry Garland*, 1888, Amherst County Courthouse.
40. 1880 US Federal Census: Sidney Fletcher's home was Dwelling 309, Family 309, p. 37, in the Temperance District within Amherst County. The members of his household included the following African Americans: Thomas Turner, Harriet Edwards, Andrew Edwards, Lesley Edwards, and Earnest Edwards.
41. 1883 Deed Book, 22 December 1883, p. 36, Amherst County Courthouse.
42. 1883 Deed Book, 3 January 1898; Sidney Fletcher's Will, Will Book 23, pp. 443–444.
43. 1870 US Federal Census: Val McGinnis, fifty-nine-year-old white merchant; Harriet, age fifteen, lived in his household, along with Mary Saunders and David Edwards (two other African Americans).
44. Other Young Daisy Letters, 1, Archives.
45. Letter from Daisy Williams, 22 July 1875, Archives.
46. Other Young Daisy Letters, 2, Archives.
47. Letter from Daisy Williams to Indiana and Henry Williams, 6 August 1875, Archives.

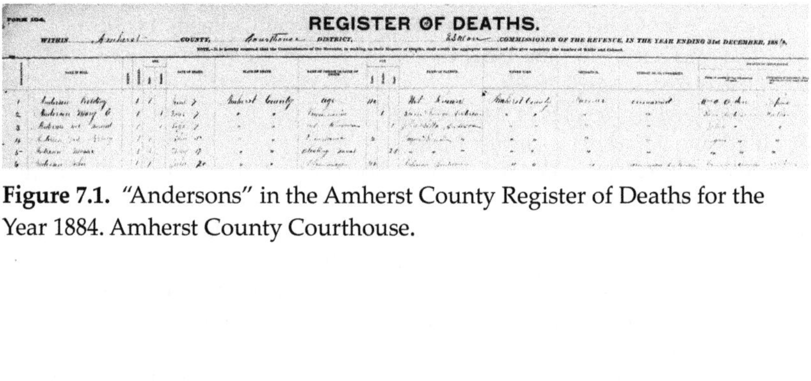
FORM 104.

REGISTER OF DEATHS.

WITHIN COUNTY, DISTRICT, COMMISSIONER OF THE REVENUE, IN THE YEAR ENDING 31st DECEMBER, 188

Figure 7.1. "Andersons" in the Amherst County Register of Deaths for the Year 1884. Amherst County Courthouse.

7

Mourning the Dead, 1884–1900

In 1884, six members of the extended Anderson family of Amherst, Virginia, died. Their deaths were duly recorded by local Commissioner of the Revenue E. S. Ware (Figure 7.1). This was decades before Virginia mandated individual death certificates; instead, each individual was given one line in the register. The commissioner attempted to answer as many details as possible: the date, place, and cause of death; the age, gender, and race of the deceased; and any known biographical information such as place of birth, occupation, spouse and/or parents, and the name of the informant. Two of the deaths recorded are those of Logan Anderson's children, both boys. Somewhat surprisingly, the older was named James Henry, almost certainly a nod to Indiana's husband. Daisy referenced his birth in a diary entry dated 8 February 1882: "[Logan's] little boy is three days old."[1] She didn't mention him by name, indicating that the Andersons likely selected her father's name later.

A year later, in May, Daisy reported, "Logan's family are flourishing as ever of course."[2] She may have been referring to its ever-growing size; between 1873 and 1884, Permelia "Amelia" and Logan had at least six children. Sadly, two-year-old James died in April 1884 of pneumonia. Because he was born after the 1880 Census, and long before the 1890 Census, this death record is one of the only pieces of documentary evidence for his life. Just a little over a month later, on 17 May 1884, Logan and Permelia lost their newborn son, Massie, from a "bleeding naval" at twenty-one days of age. No records remain to tell us how they coped with the double tragedy of losing two sons just weeks apart. But we do know they had at least five more children before Permelia died in the 1890s, at forty-five or so. Indiana and James Henry Williams also suffered the loss of a child, in 1884, but their tragedy left them childless.

Despite her coddled upbringing, Daisy was unwell for much of her life. As a young child, she complained of toothaches, and she had many teeth pulled as a teenager. She suffered from headaches and overall weakness. No one knew she suffered from a rare disease, antitrypsin deficiency, inherited from her father.[3] On 1 May 1883, Daisy and her father left New York and traveled to Sweet Briar for a multi-month sojourn in an effort for both of them to recover from a series of illnesses. The day after they arrived, the fifteen-year-old Daisy observed, "Papa stood the trip surprisingly well although he was very tired when we got home."[4] During their last summer together, the two patients variously cared for each other and were attended to by their servants, many of whom had been enslaved at Sweet Briar just decades earlier. In Indiana's absence, Martha Taylor ran the household, working every day of the week except Sunday. In contrast to antebellum times, she lived a couple miles away in Coolwell, so she walked several miles to and from Sweet Briar. At the end of a long day, Elizabeth Mosby would ask—and, one hopes, pay—Martha to stop by Mt. San Angelo to help with chores. A handful of girls helped Martha, including her own daughter Mary, a washerwoman named Ida, a cook named Sarah, and two farm tenants, Edmonia and Meally. Logan ran the farming operations and supervised a dozen or more "hands" in the fields and a few gardeners, like Henry Carey and Ed Saunders.

On most days during that long summer, Daisy wrote to her mother, Indiana, who had remained in New York to take care of the family's business matters while she and her father convalesced. Daisy's heartfelt pleas for her mother to come for a visit must have been hard to ignore. By the middle of the summer, Daisy wrote optimistically to her mother that although Aunt Lil (Elizabeth) and Uncle Sing (Sidney) "say I ought to stop studying German, that it will bring on a serious illness, and that I do not look well," Daisy observed, to the contrary, "I do not think so."[5] In the fall, she and her father returned to New York. She turned sixteen and began the fall semester at her private school. But she contracted pneumonia, and her illness took a turn for the worse in January 1884. Within just a few weeks, she succumbed to the hereditary illness that caused her lungs to fill with liquid and, effectively, smothered her. Her parents were devastated.

On the brittle January day of the funeral, grass crunched like tiny bones beneath the hooves of Daisy's beloved pony, Bounce, followed by a funerary procession of friends and family, heads downturned in mourning. Adhering to the military tradition of the "riderless horse" at funerals, Bounce led her grieving parents, her aunt and uncle, a handful of young friends, and dozens of servants in a march, silent but for the horse's hooves and hot breath, to the family cemetery. Had her health proved more resilient, Daisy probably would have inherited the plantation of her real estate magnate and plantation owner grandfather, Elijah Fletcher; instead, she lives eternally as the cherished figure at the heart of Sweet Briar College. For more than a century, Sweet Briar histories have discussed this sad day in detail. In fact, Daisy's funeral is symbolically reenacted each year, as hundreds of students recreate the trek to her grave on Monument Hill, flowers in hand, each fall on Founders Day. The narrative of her tragic death and her parents' later decision to create a college in her honor usually neglects to include any mention of the role of African Americans in every aspect of this story.

Although Daisy died in her family's apartment at 260 Fourth Avenue in New York City, her body was brought to Sweet Briar on the train soon thereafter. The Sweet Briar hired staff "met the train at McIvors [Depot] with a spring wagon pulled by two horses. The road was muddy and it took a long time to get to the graveyard, but there were many people there to say goodbye to Miss Daisy."[6] Her coffin was handled by other members of the household staff, including Sam Dawson, an African American carpenter who owned a house on Sweet Briar lands in the 1880s. He moved away after Daisy's death and lived next to the extended families of Martha Taylor and Signora Hollins, Daisy's former playmate, thereby continuing relationships formed during the antebellum period until his death in the 1920s. At Daisy's funeral, Sam and Signora served as pallbearers, carrying the coffin up the long, steep hill to the family cemetery.

Daisy's funeral probably would have included an equal number of white and black mourners. A marble headstone was carved to resemble a rock in homage to a common biblical metaphor that the Christian Creator is "rock of refuge."[7] For its Victorian audience, this symbol probably also evoked a reference to the eighteenth-century hymn "Rock of Ages."[8] Standing on top of the roughly hewn boulder was a boyish cherub with a bittersweet smile, holding a cross. In his hand, he holds a petal plucked from a floral wreath hanging off the cross; the boy is posed in the act of dropping the lone flower, symbolizing a life cut short. A shroud, also carved from marble, is draped over a door that symbolizes the entrance to heaven. The Monument Hill memorial was just one element of Indiana's mortuary rituals to honor Daisy.[9]

Indiana also directed her African American servants to carry out numerous mourning rituals. She ordered Signora and Sam to conduct an elaborate, daily ritual at the gravesite: they would fix a breakfast for "Miss Daisy," take it up the hill to the family graveyard, wait half an hour at the grave (presumable to give Daisy time to "eat"), and then return to Sweet Briar House. In an odd twist to these orders, Indiana did not want to see the two servants when they returned. When Signora was asked many years later what happened to the food, she admitted, "Me and Sam ate it." Signora also was instructed to walk Bounce, Daisy's pony, up to the grave to visit his former mistress every day between 10 a.m. and noon. The last of these postmortem rites was to carry "the papers that come in the morning's mail" up to Daisy's grave on a tray and leave it there until the next day. Whether these were letters of condolence or regular mail is unclear. Indiana continued ordering these somewhat unusual daily rituals for six months.[10] When she stopped, she also let Signora go, sending her north to Massachusetts. Was this simply a monetary decision, to fire an unneeded employee, or was the continued presence of her deceased daughter's playmate too painful?

In the end, Daisy's beloved pony got more attention in remembrances of the funeral than the individuals who carried her body to the grave. Signora later recounted that one of Daisy's riding outfits was laid across the empty saddle, while mourners led Bounce up to the graveyard.[11] After Daisy's death, her pony received more privileges than some of the hired help: he was allowed to stuff himself with corn as he roamed and even destroyed fields. Indiana had ordered that he be allowed to roam freely, regardless of the inconvenience to his handlers or the negative impact to the crops.[12] Bounce was still alive in 1906, when the college was founded. The first president, Mary Benedict, observed him "roam[ing] stiffly around the place. He didn't sleep well—I've seen him late at night in the moonlight stalking about."[13] The posthumous status of Daisy's pony stood in sharp contrast to the minimal historical commemoration afforded to the paid help that cold January day. Major players in this drama not only were afforded less respect than an animal but also had been overlooked in this historical narrative again.

In the years after Daisy's death, Indiana remained at Sweet Briar, while her husband managed their rental properties in the city. Both parents grieved deeply after the loss of their child. Living apart from 1884 to 1887, they shared some of their grief through letters. In one rather artful turn of verse, James Henry used the metaphor of a daisy, the flower, to convey the double-edged sword of mourning and joyfulness they once had with Daisy in their life: "The sweet, modest simple pretty Daisy, all complete from root to flower, and stem and leaves entire, lets the story too of a bright-episode of happy years, when the music of three hearts in unison made the light-of life dance along our path." Reading these lines reminds me that he was once a professional minister. He continues, "The period of the Golden-Rod has come, we are smitten with a rod indeed, mayhap it is a golden one that afflicts us with its chastisements now, and it may be no doubt it is a merciful hand, while it is descending so painfully upon our poor naked hearts, for some mysterious ulterior good."[14] We do not have Indiana's response, so it isn't clear whether these words were any comfort to her.

The grief of any parent who has lost a child is understandable. Indiana may have felt especially guilty and bereft because of the time she spent apart from Daisy, when she managed her business affairs in New York. She had, in fact, made some unusual decisions for a nineteenth-century mother: Indiana spent months apart from her daughter for several years (if not longer). Indiana and James Henry left Daisy at Sweet Briar for one to three months at a time each year, while they managed their properties in New York. One year, 1882, Indiana did not even accompany the thirteen-year-old Daisy back to Virginia; instead, her brother Sidney was sent on the train to pick the child up and take her back to Sweet Briar, where Martha Taylor and other black servants cared for her. I cannot help but wonder if part of Indiana's paralyzing grief after her daughter's death was a sense of guilt. In the spring of 1883, while Indiana remained in New York for business, Daisy wrote, "How I wish we could be together this Sunday . . . but I suppose we are doing our duty, and will always feel better for having done so."[15]

In the decade after Daisy's death, Indiana greatly reduced her household staff. By the fall of 1900, she was down to just two people. She made no effort to find new positions for the employees who once cared for Daisy. Despite the later categorization of several servants as beloved "mammies," Indiana did not maintain economic or social relationships with the people who once cared for Daisy, including those most beloved to Daisy: Martha and Signora. Micki McElya suggests one reason why twentieth-century authors misjudged these relationships:

> The myth of the faithful slave lingers because so many white Americans have wished to live in a world in which African Americans are not angry over past and present injustices, a world in which white people were and are not complicit, in which the injustices themselves—of slavery, Jim Crow, and ongoing structural racism—seem not to exist at all. The mammy figure affirmed their wishes.[16]

Signora was sent to Massachusetts to work for a white family led by a woman who may have been a distant relative of one of Indiana's aunts. The 1900 Amherst, Massachusetts Census lists a seventy-one-year-old white widow, Mary Williams, living with her forty-five-year-old stepdaughter, a boarder from Turkey, and three "servants." These three female housekeepers were all from Amherst, Virginia: Signora Hollins (twenty-nine), Alice Hollins (twenty-six), and Amanda Jordan (eighteen). Signora and Alice were both married, living hundreds of miles north of their husbands, an unfortunate geography necessitated by the sparse jobs in the post-Reconstruction South.[17] Many of these Amherst transplants were probably remitting some of their earnings back to relatives in Virginia.[18]

Signora worked for Mary Williams from 1897 to 1908, spending almost half her married life apart from her husband, Tobias Hollins.[19] Tobias supported his extended family, another common pattern for late nineteenth-century black families in the South: assisting the fractured generations that were torn apart by the sale of human beings during slavery. Three years after Signora went north, Tobias remained in Virginia, living with two of his nephews (perhaps his brother or sister had died) and his sister-in-law, Mary Smith.[20] Signora was lucky. She managed to return to Sweet Briar in 1909 and get a job at the newly founded college (Figure 7.2). Martha Taylor was not so lucky. By the time Indiana died, Martha had served the Fletcher family and their close relatives, including the Penns, for seven decades. This hardscrabble existence, even after slavery's end, often left her with insufficient funds to care for her own family. After relying on Martha for innumerable domestic tasks, Indiana let Martha go, pushing her aside at the age of sixty. Unlike two other former servants, Martha received nothing in Indiana's will.

Figure 7.2. Signora Smith Hollins, circa 1935. Sweet Briar College Library Archives.

Five years after Daisy's death, tragedy struck again for Indiana. At 10 a.m. on Thursday, 25 April 1889, James Henry Williams died in the family's New York apartment. The attending physician listed his cause of death as cirrhosis of the liver, but a contributing factor would have been the lifelong ailment he had passed to his daughter, antitrypsin deficiency. He lived to be fifty-eight years old. His body, like his daughter's, was brought to Sweet Briar Plantation for burial on Monument Hill. On Sunday, just days after his death, he was laid out in the Sweet Briar House parlor. Members of the First Baptist Church of Coolwell walked over to pay their last respects.[21] One audience member estimated that "50 negroes" attended his funeral, an unusually diverse group for Jim Crow Virginia.[22] After his death, Indiana retreated from social life even further. Another five years passed before she ordered a family marker to accompany Daisy's small headstone; perhaps it took her that long to accept the loss of both her daughter and husband. She sold their properties in New York so that she would not have to travel and invested in railroad stocks instead (the source of much of her cash wealth at her death).

She rarely left home or admitted visitors. The small number of visitors to Sweet Briar House in the years after Daisy and her father died would have witnessed a strange sight. Indiana, once a world traveler and sophisticated New Yorker, had barricaded herself in the house, surrounded by an eccentric collection of goods and furniture. Lucian's children accused her of an "insane aversion" to them after Indiana installed bars to protect herself from unwanted visitors and told the Amherst liveryman, Charles R. Tinsley, not to accept fares from her nieces and nephews. Lucian's children persisted; in 1898, two of his daughters asked Indiana if they could host their weddings at Sweet Briar, but she refused to speak to them.[23] In the last decade or so of her life, Indiana spent most of her time with African and Native American servants, eschewing the company of most of her white neighbors and relatives. Contemporary witnesses concluded that no "white person" resided with her during her last years.

She also began collecting linens and furniture in the 1880s for the school she hoped to open after her death. By the time she died, in 1900, she had amassed a huge collection of supplies. The inventory of Sweet Briar House filled dozens of pages with lists of sheets, pillowcases (fifty-one in one room alone), bolts of cloth, mattresses, jars, vases, framed pictures, and hundreds of books. These seemingly random collections of household items were listed alongside personal belongings such as "Picture of Daisy Williams, in bronze frame, for Mrs. Harriet Leeds [James Henry's sister, Daisy's aunt], of New York" for a total of $1. Indiana's behavior soon became fodder for local gossip. She had maintained her daughter's room as it was when Daisy died and prevented anyone from playing her piano or touching her harp. Her friends and neighbors debated what constituted a fixation or obsession versus standard grieving. By 1900, Indiana had amassed dozens of trunks filled with not only items that could conceivably benefit a future school, such as sixty-five sets of cutlery, but also dozens of dress patterns and hordes of dry goods, the latter allegedly to feed to her dead daughter.[24] Several of her neighbors concluded that she was "morbid" and "eccentric."[25]

As Indiana became increasingly withdrawn and let most of her staff go, several of her former slaves had fallen on hard times. A decade after Daisy's death, Martha wrote to Indiana (in New York) and thanked her for the $1.25 that "I was glad to get I was very much Oblige to you for it because I felt that I was in a very hard Place at that time." She had just finished moving, her son got married but she couldn't attend because of a heavy snowfall, and her husband was "very bad off" with a malady that sounded, initially, like gout. She mentioned another former slave, Margaret Galvin, and said she "keeps poorly but is not confined to Bed."[26] Martha's husband died within a few years of this letter. In the 1880 Census, the enumerator had asked how many months in the previous year an individual had been out of work, but the Amherst census taker had substituted a checkmark for a more precise accounting. Henry Taylor, age forty-nine, had a check by his name. Three years later, in 1883, Martha wrote in spindly handwriting that Henry "has been sick most every day since he came home."[27]

While Martha's description of Henry's foot sounds like a form of gout, I remembered a letter from 1854 between Elijah Fletcher and the slave owner Abraham Fost. Elijah had hired out several of his enslaved men to Fost, who wrote, "Henry is better of his lameness and will soon be able to work, his ancle [*sic*] was more severely injured, than the [doctor] first supposed, but all is right so far as the bones are concerned & [he] will eventually be a sound man."[28] This injury may have been much more serious than Fost made it out to be—understandable, since he would have been responsible for the men's health and productivity while they were under his command. After she was widowed, Martha moved in with her son Moses, who lived nearby in McIvors. Her daughter Mary and her grandson Daniel Lewis Bibby also lived there. Daniel would be one of Martha's only direct kin to survive into the second half of the twentieth century.

In 1890, Elizabeth Fletcher Mosby was the first of Elijah and Maria Antoinette's children to die. In the years leading up to her death, Elizabeth and her sister, Indiana, had had a strained relationship. Daisy, no doubt influenced by her mother's opinion, described her aging aunt as "stately and stiff as ever." On another occasion, Daisy brought her aunt some candy and complained, "She did not say 'thank you' of course."[29] Elizabeth may have been suffering from dementia. Daisy complained to Indiana that Elizabeth often repeated herself and claimed to have taken trips that never materialized or to have cooked food made by others. For example, Elizabeth claimed she visited New York City "every year," despite evidence to the contrary.[30] Elizabeth also questioned the Williamses' servants, including Martha Taylor, about what her sister and niece were doing, fueling Daisy's suspicions.

By the time she died, Elizabeth had been a widow for more than a decade and relied on African American servants to care for her and her large estate at Mt. San Angelo. Unlike Indiana and Sidney, she did not recognize any of these individuals by name or give any formal financial gifts in her last testament. Instead, in her will, dated 27 May 1890, Elizabeth left an array of household items to a wide assortment of white acquaintances and relatives: pearls, a gold watch, a silver cake basket, and silver salt cellars to her Lynchburg friend Elizabeth Ambler Gish; a silver urn, cream pitcher, and sugar bowl to Laura Ambler Rhodes. While Indiana and Sidney gave a handful of "favored" African American servants money in their wills, Elizabeth gave Edward Carr, a white farm laborer who lived next to her, one hundred acres and $150. She gave the largest lump sum, $5,000, to a distant cousin, the Civil War veteran Leigh R. Paige.

To her estranged brother, Lucian, she gave an annuity of $200, presumably as an act of charity to support him in his old age. She gave her sister "the engraving in the parlor 'The Posting Day,'" a clock, and "photos and other souvenirs of my departed niece Daisy Williams." She gave her estate to Sidney, with instructions for him to give it to the Sisters of the Holy Cross in Lynchburg after his death. In a strange conclusion to these instructions, she added that when the Sisters ceased to use the property, it should revert to Sidney's heirs.[31] This is particularly interesting, because Sidney had no legally recognized heirs. Elizabeth may have been recognizing Earnest and Lesley (sometimes recorded as Leally), the mixed-race children he had with Harriet Edwards. Or perhaps she was making a much more oblique reference to more distant relatives she expected Sidney to list as his heirs later.

Lucian Fletcher died several years later, in 1895. In the years leading up to his death, Sidney and Elizabeth tried to help their wayward brother by giving him money and land. Sidney also extended monetary gifts to Lucian's white children.[32] Lucian's black wife, Mary Woodfolk, had predeceased him, but she had told their children that their father had died in the 1860s while on a trip to California. Her side of the family may have been unaware of his passing. No evidence suggests that his estranged white wife, France Everett, mourned his death, but she did take advantage of his status as a Civil War veteran to apply for a pension in 1928. Some of their children may have mourned Lucian's passing, but, in the end, his brother, Sidney, came forward to pay $50 for his coffin and burial on the Tusculum estate.[33] Lucian died without a will, and only Sidney, Mr. McGinnis (the clerk court), and some "colored people" were at the funeral.[34]

At age seventy-five, Sidney Fletcher found himself elderly and isolated. The same year he buried his brother, Sidney's common-law wife, Harriet, died. She was just thirty-five years old. Their older son, Lesley Edwards, had predeceased her; perhaps her grief contributed to her own early death. And then, the next year, 1896, their younger son, Earnest, died at just eighteen years old. Over the past century, Sidney's plantation had changed very little. The two Tusculum houses were sandwiched together and surrounded by various outbuildings, including a kitchen, ice house, and cabins. In later court documents, one of Sidney's neighbors testified that Sidney had lived "in adultery" with a "negro woman" and their two sons.[35]

Sidney's will was signed and sealed on 3 January 1898, just months before he, at age seventy-seven, complained of feeling unwell and, after dinner on 12 April, tried to rise but fell to the floor, dead. On 13 April, the local newspaper reported: "Sidney Fletcher Dead. He Expired Suddenly in Amherst Yesterday." Sidney, "one of the wealthiest and most prominent citizens of this county," had left Tusculum in the morning to ride to a nearby farm he owned, where "the servants noticed he talked incoherently."[36] He returned to Tusculum, ate dinner, and lay down. He had been alone only a few minutes when a "servant" entered the room and found him lying dead on the floor. In his pithy will, he gave $1,000 each to two white cousins, his silverware to another cousin, and a clock formerly owned by his grandfather to a Mr. Scott. He gave Tusculum and all its furniture, books, animals, and implements to his relative John J. Williams, along with a silk farm that, Sidney suggested, John could sell to help finance the Tusculum farm. John moved into Tusculum soon after Sidney's death. He gave the "rest residue & remainder" of his estate to his sister Indiana, the executor of his will, with two exceptions. He gave $150 each to two African American men (either of whom was probably the servant who found him dead): Patrick Galvin and Lindsey Tinsley.

Patrick had worked for several of Elijah's children. His wife, Jeanette, was the daughter of Harriet Powell, and at least one of their children,

Joicy, was born enslaved around 1862. After the family was freed in 1865, they farmed at Tusculum for several years, suggesting that Sidney had owned them. Over the next decade, they moved on to land owned by Indiana. There, Patrick rented more than 200 acres of land, of which a little more than half (136 acres) was wooded and thus unsuitable for tilling. On the rest of this land, according to the 1880 Census Agricultural Schedule, he planted crops (corn, oats, wheat, tobacco) and raised livestock (two horses, one milking cow, two other bovines, five pigs, and eighteen chickens and turkeys). Today, some if not all of these acres make up part of the Sweet Briar College campus. In the nineteenth century, Patrick and his family were working to save money, and by 1900, the seventy-six-year-old patriarch had successfully transitioned from tenant farming to owning his own land. Patrick, along with his brother Robert, lived next door to Lindsey Tinsley for many years.

Lindsey (sixty-five) had been enslaved by Robert Tinsley, another Amherst County farmer. After Robert died, in 1863, Lindsey went to work for Sidney.[37] When the Civil War ended, Lindsey was about twenty-eight years old. He was a jack-of-all-trades at Tusculum. All his children (four daughters and a son) were born after the war, between 1874 and 1886. While his children were not forcibly separated from him, his family struggled to find jobs and housing during Reconstruction. By 1910, Lindsey was widowed, and one of his daughters, twenty-four-year-old Maggie M., was still living with him. In addition, he had adopted an eight-year-old boy, Melford Pollard. While Sidney was alive, he occasionally sent Lindsey over to Sweet Briar to help his sister Indiana with groundskeeping tasks like trimming the boxwood hedges. At Sweet Briar, he stayed in the house, during the same period when Indiana refused numerous requests from Lucian's children to cross the threshold, let alone spend the night.

After Sidney's death, Indiana hired Lindsey as a groundskeeper and to keep her company on Sundays; she gave him $2 to $10 per visit. Lindsey explained that Indiana had "said that I had stayed with her brother so long and done for her brother—carried his keys and everything—that she took her a liking to me."[38] She even set aside in Sweet Briar House a room she referred to as his. Indiana appreciated these weekly visits and pledged that after her death she would provide for him and her cook—the only two "colored men" working on the estate.

Indiana's health had begun to fail soon after Daisy's death. As early as 1887, Sidney wrote to "Indy" from Tusculum while she visited New York. We do not have the letter Indiana sent to Sidney, but clearly, from his comments, Indiana had "another attack" of some kind that Sidney thought was caused by "the sedentary life you lead" and the "food you eat."[39] Indiana succumbed to grief and illness on 29 October 1900. Her body was found in her daughter's room at the foot of the bed.[40] On most days, she had kept the room locked as a perpetual shrine to her daughter. The last person to see her alive was her cook, Robert "Bob" Rucker.[41] Bob had been enslaved by a J. J. Ambler, but his grandfather had been enslaved by Elijah Fletcher. In the late nineteenth century, Bob lived in Coolwell with his family. In 1892, he started working in the yard at Sweet Briar. Later, he cooked for Indiana because she had a hard time keeping a cook employed at the post, suggesting that she was difficult to work for. She had tried Sue (Bob's sister-in-law), George (his son), and Jenny Blair, who might have been a distant descendant of Permelia Blair (enslaved at Tusculum in the eighteenth century). Bob not only cooked for Indiana but also cared for her during her "sinking spells."

The week before she died, Indiana had promised fifty-year-old Bob that he "was going to have a handsome home that would come to me like a dream." Bob worried he might not live long enough to enjoy this promised reward, but she assured him he would. Bob returned to work that Saturday and prepared to begin sowing wheat on Monday. The next day, Tuesday morning, Bob learned that Miss Indie had died the night before. He never got his house, or a sofa he was promised. In the weeks leading up to her death, Indiana had told him he could have a "sofa that used to set in the office belonging to Dr. Fletcher in his young days." This office was most likely the Garden Cottage, where Sidney allegedly offered his medical services to the enslaved community. Instead, the executors gave Bob one of James Henry's overcoats but nothing else, not even the "dreenin's" from a dishpan of soap that Bob claimed Indiana had told his wife, Rachel, she could have. Bob assumed that "after the thing [estate] was settled, [the executor, Stephen R. Harding] would have authority" to give it out, but that was not the case. Bob concluded that while Miss Indie was alive, "I never was out of money," but since her death, "I have got out [of money] now."[42]

After Indiana's death, the household would have been in a state of flux for months. Her former servants would have heard the local gossip that her will was under attack from several sources, including Lucian's children (for a share of the estate that Indiana denied them during her life), Amherst County (for unpaid taxes), and the courts (which were asked to rule on the legitimacy of the surviving wills). A month after Indiana's death, she was buried on Monument Hill alongside her husband, daughter, sister, and father. As with Daisy's funeral, several African American employees assisted in the final procession to the top of that steep hill.[43]

Controversy swirled for months over mysterious papers that were said to have been burned after her death, and whether the official will was the version stored in a Lynchburg bank or the papers found in her sitting room.[44] In the lengthy court case that ensued after Indiana's death, dozens of her neighbors, employees, and friends were called on to testify about her physical and mental state of health at the end of her life. Much of this commentary revolved around whether she had changed her will at the last minute and the validity of the one that was found after her death under somewhat mysterious circumstances. Lindsey Tinsley in particular was cross-examined at length to determine Indiana's final wishes and the legitimacy of the will found in her room.

In the process of eliciting information about those documents, lawyers from both sides tried to paint a picture of Indiana's character. After being steeped in Sweet Briar College lore, which paints a very positive portrayal of her, I was surprised to read that Indiana knew she was "often regarded as miserly, stingy and mean."[45] One of Indiana's closest friends said part of the motivation for founding Sweet Briar College was that "she hoped some day to be considered a benefactor" to counter her neighbors' opinions of her character. I couldn't help but see parallels with her father's efforts to find favor with his contemporaries while recognizing that they saw him as a miser and usurer. Indiana had spent the last decade of her life widowed and plotting to erect a more grandiose memorial in honor of her dead daughter, Daisy, and her husband, James Henry. The traditional version of this story credits Indiana with most of the intent and idea to create a college for women. In reality, her decision was influenced by two generations of men (her grandfather and father) and her own husband, all of whom supported education for women.

Despite Jesse Fletcher's poverty and hardscrabble life raising fifteen children in the Vermont frontier, he scraped together money to send Elijah to college and several of his other children to preparatory schools. He extended these opportunities to his daughters, an unusual move for a colonial-era father. Elijah, perhaps out of guilt that the money spent on his education deprived some of his other siblings of similar opportunities, sent money to his family. In fact, weeks after he left Vermont, he bemoaned, "I have been . . . so expensive as to deprive the girls of all privileges for a decent education." As soon as he started receiving paychecks at his new position in Virginia, he sent a portion back home for his sisters' education. As a father of two girls and two boys, he was determined to educate them all according to the best opportunities available. His sons attended Yale University and the College of William

& Mary, both receiving advanced degrees, in law and medicine. When it came to educating his daughters, whom he sent to convents to study six subjects, Elijah was ahead of his time: "A girl will be more respected with an education than with wealth. I think female education is too much neglected."[46]

Elijah's siblings also supported women's education, as did Indiana's husband. In his own will, James Henry not only left his property to his wife but also requested that she establish a school on the plantation lands: "It is my wish that my wife should by deed or by will, secure the ultimate appropriation of my estate, in trust for the foundation and maintenance of a school or a seminary . . . as a memorial to our daughter Daisy Williams." Given this one-hundred-year background, Indiana's decision to use her wealth and land to found a college for women is hardly surprising. She had outlived her father, uncle, husband, and each of her three siblings. Her estate represented an amalgam of their estates, and she was, most likely, trying to create a legacy she felt would honor their wishes and memories: "This bequest, devise and foundation are made in fulfillment of my own desire, and of the especial request of my late husband, . . . for the establishment of a perpetual memorial of our deceased daughter, Daisy Williams."[47] And so, in keeping with their legacies of slaveholding and segregation, she left most of her land and wealth for establishing the Sweet Briar Institute, "for the education of white girls and young women."[48]

Indiana did not specify the laborers for the new college, or any of the employees beyond the initial board of trustees. But she hardly would have been surprised, if, in 1904, she had walked down the road from her former house, watching as the brick campus buildings rose, row by row, and saw Daniel Jones and his son Sterling hard at work—two African American men she had known most of her life. She did not bequeath any of her wealth to them, or to any other African Americans except the $150 she gave to Bob Rucker and Lindsey Tinsley—small consolation for the lifetime they and their relatives had worked for Indiana and her family.

Meanwhile Indiana's friend and estate executor, Stephen R. Harding, negotiated a compromise settlement with the five children of Lucian Fletcher ($25,000) and struck a deal with Indiana's tax creditors, Amherst County and the Commonwealth of Virginia ($30,000). Aside from a few other small personal gifts, the remainder of Indiana's estate would go, as she had wished, to the new Sweet Briar Institute. After years of legal wrangling, the lawsuit was summarized with this prescient note: "The thousand pages of evidence filed with this report may some day furnish interesting reading for those making historical research, as furnishing record evidence of the incidents attending the nativity and early infancy of the proposed Institution."[49]

In the end, several men who had grown up alongside Indiana, while they were enslaved and she was their wealthy and educated mistress, were the last to see her alive, and the closest she had to relatives to assist at her funeral. The casket was made by the Lynchburg undertaker W. D. Diuguid.[50] Charles R. Tinsley transported the casket from Amherst, where it probably arrived on the train, to Monument Hill. After the service, led by Rev. A. P. Gray, Bob Rucker worked alongside Sam Dawson (who had assisted Signora Hollins with Daisy's posthumous rituals), Jack Rucker (Bob's twenty-eight-year-old son), and Moses B. Taylor (Martha's thirty-year-old son) to dig a hole, carry the coffin, and fill the grave. At the beginning of the twentieth century, it was the end of an era. All the white founders of the land that became the Sweet Briar Institute had died. But dozens of African Americans with deep, multi-generational roots at Sweet Briar remained—working the lands, taking care of the buildings, and bridging the gap between a nineteenth-century Southern plantation and a newly founded women's college.

Notes

1. "Daisy's Diary," 8 February 1882, in Williams, *Daisy Williams*, 17.
2. "Daisy's Letters," 6 May 1883, in Williams, *Daisy Williams*, 86.
3. Whitley, *Daisy Williams of Sweet Briar*, 41–42; Certificate of Death in the City of New York no. 479431, Register Book of Deaths no. 8461. The cause of death is listed as phthisis. Today, a doctor would diagnose the disease as pulmonary tuberculosis.
4. "Daisy's Letters," 2 May 1883, 81.
5. "Daisy's Letters," 1 August 1883, 123–24.
6. Whitley, *Daisy Williams of Sweet Briar*, 42.
7. "Be to me a rock of refuge, to which I may continually come; you have given the command to save me, for you are my rock and my fortress." Psalm 71: 1–3.
8. Ames, *Death in the Dining Room*, 98.
9. The boy-and-cross gravestone was vandalized in the 1970s and moved to the terrace behind the Sweet Briar College Museum. Daisy's original marble-scroll gravestone remains on Monument Hill. Personal communication, Karol Lawson, 18 August 2017.
10. Interview between Signora Hollins and two Sweet Briar faculty members, 1951. A tape is stored in the Sweet Briar College Library.
11. Whitley, *Daisy Williams of Sweet Briar*, 42.
12. Stohlman, *The Story of Sweet Briar College*, 283, 305.

13. Quoted in Stohlman, *The Story of Sweet Briar College*, 94.
14. Letter from James Henry Williams to Indiana Fletcher Williams, 12 September 1885. Perkins Library, Duke University (Durham, NC).
15. "Daisy's Letters," 6 May 1883, 85.
16. McElya, *Clinging to Mammy*, 3.
17. 1900 US Federal Census, Hampshire County, MA: Roll 653, Page 2A, Enumeration District 0615, Home 13, Dwelling 29, Family 25.
18. Kerr-Ritchie, *Freedpeople in the Tobacco South*, 243–44.
19. "Hollins, Signora Mrs. domestic, Mrs. R. G. Williams," Amherst City Directory 1897, 80; "Hollins, Signora Mrs, rem[oved] to Virginia," Amherst City Directory 1909, 44.
20. 1900 US Federal Census, Court House, Amherst, VA: Sheet 8, Enumeration District 7, Dwelling 93, Family 96.
21. S. Berry, *Memories of Rev. R. D. Merchant*, 33.
22. Depositions, 694.
23. Depositions, 270.
24. Depositions, 275.
25. Depositions, 297.
26. Letter from Martha Taylor to Indiana Williams, New York, 31 January 1895. Archives.
27. Letter to Miss Daisy Williams from Martha Taylor, 24 January 1883, Archives.
28. Letter from Abrm I. Fost to Elijah Fletcher, Pattonsburg, 18 August 1854. Transcribed by Judith Evans-Grubbs. Archives.
29. "Daisy's Letters," 4 May 1883, 82; 7 May 1883, 87.
30. "Daisy's Letters," 18 May 1883, 101.
31. Daisy Williams's will, Amherst County Will Book 22, 462.
32. Depositions, 103.
33. Burial record book, p. 237, Diuguid Database, http://diuguid.gravegarden.org/details.php?id=51309.
34. Depositions, 557.
35. Depositions, 556.
36. "Dr. Sidney Fletcher Dead," *[Lynchburg] News*, 13 April 1898, 5.
37. Depositions, 352.
38. Depositions, 61 (Tinsley, 9).
39. Letter from Sidney Fletcher to Indiana Williams, Tusculum, 24 April 1887. Perkins Library, Duke University (Durham, NC).
40. Depositions, 724.
41. Depositions, 366 (Rucker, 1).
42. Depositions, 371-74 (Rucker, 6–9).
43. "The Estate of Indiana Fletcher Williams, Deceased, in Account," 6. Courthouse files organized by Karol Lawson, Amherst County Courthouse.
44. Depositions, 255–57 (Stephen Harding, 20–22).
45. Depositions, 728 (Mrs. Payne, 14).
46. *TLEF*, letter to his father, 1 October 1810, 16.
47. Copy of the Will of Indiana Fletcher Williams, p. 4, Archives LD 7251.S92. W55. Indiana Fletcher Williams's original will was signed and sealed 3

April 1899, New York City. It was probated on 23 November 1900 at the Amherst County Courthouse.

48. Copy of the Will of Indiana Fletcher Williams, p. 3, Archives.
49. *Indiana Fletcher Williams, Executor v. Emma McCall and others,* Appendix to Report of Master Commissioner, O. L. Evans, p. 10, filed 15 November 1902, Amherst County Courthouse.
50. Financial tally by the executor in "The Estate of Indiana Fletcher Williams," 6.

Fifty Year College Employee Dies

LEWIS CHAMBERS

dolph. He worked as a janitor on lower faculty Row before beginning his job as janitor in Gray. During the summers he worked on the Sweet Briar farm.

Mrs. Rockett, who has been closely associated with Lewis, says, "He will be very hard to replace because of his interest in Sweet Briar."

Lewis is survived by his wife and a daughter Beatrice, who is the wife of Jim Rose, janitor in Randolph.

READ THE ADS CLOSELY

Figure 8.1. Sweet Briar College's obituary for Lewis Chambers (1887–1956). Sweet Briar College Library Archives.

8

Forgotten Founders, 1901–2001

After several years of construction, Sweet Briar College opened its doors in 1906. African American men, including the teenage Lewis Chambers, had done most of the work. Born in 1887, Lewis was among the post-Reconstruction, freeborn African Americans who lived through the Jim Crow era and died in the middle of the civil rights movement. According to his obituary published by the college, Lewis was first assigned work as a "water-boy" alongside older African American artisans who were handcrafting bricks from local soil for the newly founded college in the first quarter of the twentieth century. Later, he divided his time between term work as a janitor and summers as a farmhand on the Sweet Briar farm. The obituary summarized his career in the title, "Fifty Year College Employee Dies," and concluded, "He will be very hard to replace because of his interest in Sweet Briar."[1] While the contributions of these black workers and their families are not always fully appreciated, they are often praised as curators of college history, despite often appearing as passive actors in those story lines.

Understandably, the college's obituary focused on Lewis's contributions to the institution, mentioning his surviving daughter, Beatrice, in passing but leaving out his more complex family connections to the institution (Figure 8.1). Like many college employees, multiple generations of Lewis's family worked at Sweet Briar. For example, Beatrice's husband, Jim, was also a janitor. One of Lewis's nephews, Robert Turner, was a twenty-year-old "assistant janitor" at the college on the eve of World War II. Beatrice Chambers Rose (1909–1991) lived in Amherst throughout her life, marrying another local resident, James Edward Rose Sr. (1905–1973) in 1928. As a person of color growing up in the Jim Crow South, she could not attend the "whites-only" school. In separate and distinctly unequal schools, she learned to read, and had begun learning to write, by the time she was ten.[2] Later, she completed her education at Amherst Training High School.[3] Despite her family's multi-decade employment at Sweet Briar, Beatrice was not permitted to apply to, let alone attend, the college.

From the beginning, Sweet Briar deployed a romanticized version of its origins to increase its attractiveness to young, white women at the end of the Victorian era. Accordingly, the college hired a famous architect to create a dignified-looking school to which families would entrust their daughters. Ralph Adams Cram and his Boston firm, Cram, Goodhue & Ferguson, created a Palladian-inspired landscape containing red brick buildings with architectural embellishments such as arcades, plazas, and balustrades and neoclassical elements from Greek and Roman designs. The "temple to learning" metaphor was writ large—even as most of the physical construction on campus was done by people who were barred from studying there. These laborers were clearing the land; hauling dirt; making, driving, and laying truckloads of bricks; and digging a lakebed for a dam.

True to the cultural mores of the time, the first thirty-six students who began classes in 1906, as well as their woman president, were under the close watch of an all-male board of seven directors. It was fourteen years before the Nineteenth Amendment to the Constitution gave women the right to vote, so the early twentieth-century version of female education was limited in spirit and intent. The 1908 college catalog stated explicitly that the college "will offer to the young women of the south carefully formulated courses of study leading to degrees, of high grade and proper adaptation to the needs and capabilities of the female mind." Those needs, it explained, included literary, scientific, artistic, and industrial branches of knowledge. But the course offerings were less ambitious: the study of "hand-sewing"; the cleaning, pressing, storing, and packing of clothes; and the study of the hygiene of the home.[4] Sweet Briar would quickly outgrow this narrow focus on the domestic arts, but in its first decade of operation, it functioned on two levels: as a postsecondary preparatory school and as a finishing school for elite, white women. Four years later, the trustees announced that the five women in the first graduating class had received "such education in sound learning, and such physical, moral, and religious training as shall in the judgment of the Directors best fit them to be useful members of society."[5]

Sweet Briar's first administrators, trustees, and faculty shared a series of tales about the college "founders," most of them designed to attract more students. One college viewbook explained, "Sweet Briar is a maker of delightful memories, charming the fancy with the beauty of its surroundings and the romance of its southern traditions and folklore." This attracted women from several states, including Northern ones. Over the next decades, that veiled reference to "southern traditions" became clearer, as the college promoted its service staff as individuals who would cheerfully and obediently care for the students. A viewbook caption reading "Tradition, Folk-Lore, History . . . Add Their Fascination to Sweet Briar" accompanied a photograph of one of the surviving slave cabins: a "picturesque old Negro cabin."[6] Similar brochures and press releases gradually made their way around the country, appearing in national newspapers and magazines.

History gradually turned into fiction. In nearby Richmond, *The Times* reported on Indiana Fletcher Williams's initial "munificence" and enhanced the story of her father's arrival from Vermont: "Tradition says that he walked to Washington" with all his worldly possessions "tied up in a red bandanna handkerchief" and then turned toward "the land of promise, which lay for him under the blue hills of Amherst county." With no mention of enslaved laborers, the author explained how Elijah used his "large inheritance of New England thrift" to become "the wealthiest man in the county." Likewise, a college brochure praised Indiana for her "splendid gift to the cause of education, untrammeled by narrowing restrictions"—apparently, the racial restriction did not count.[7] The brochure concluded with descriptions of the Sweet Briar of "to-day" (a "tradition of southern dignity and culture") and of "to-morrow" (to "make Sweet Briar a national woman's college in the South").[8]

Sweet Briar eventually succeeded in that aim, but it did so in part by suppressing information about African American families and their contributions to the formation and maintenance of the plantation and later to the college itself. If we turn to those underappreciated founders, we find that, as throughout its history, early twentieth-century Sweet Briar was run by a predominantly black workforce. When the white directors traveled to campus for meetings, it was men like Charles R. Tinsley—whose father, Nelson, had worked so hard to retrieve him from Georgia after the Civil War—who transported the directors from the train station to Sweet Briar.[9] African Americans performed most of the cleaning, cooking, and caretaking that went along with a new institution. Then as now, groundskeepers were responsible for mowing and trimming dozens of acres of lush Virginian landscape. This year-round task contributed to Sweet Briar's early popularity with students and faculty. Advertisements across the Southeast promoted the school with its "new and magnificent" buildings and a "condition for health" that was "unsurpassed."[10]

One local resident estimated that "the majority of [domestic help were] from the First Baptist Church neighborhood" in nearby Coolwell, the African American community with long-standing connections to the Fletchers.[11] One of those early community members was Martha Taylor. When Sweet Briar opened its doors, she was seventy-five years old and had already spent most of her life working for the Fletcher family and their relatives. Her son Moses had helped clear the grounds for the building construction. Martha cooked for the students until her death around 1911. Other African Americans, as well as Native Americans, moved furniture (Logan Anderson and Smoot Pettyjohn), hauled logs (Hiram Beverly), did laundry (Lucy Dobbins), and worked the vast farmlands that were still part of the Sweet Briar campus (William Chilton). A man specified only as "[Mr.] White" worked as a blacksmith, harkening back to the antebellum period when African American men from Sweet Briar and Tusculum developed highly valued skills in this trade. Earnest Christian drove a farm wagon for the college; in 1903, he named one of his daughters Daisy, perhaps in memory of Daisy Williams, who was just four years older than he.

A visitor to campus in 1910 would have encountered African American employees working in every building and throughout the rural fields. Men worked down at the brand-new lake, helping construct pumps and dams for the newly created water supply. Other Native and African American laborers built and paved new roads, connecting the various sectors of campus. Several Monacan families, such as Winston Branham's and William Bruce's households, worked on farmland owned by the college, thereby reproducing a tenant model from the postbellum era. And the crucially important laundry was primarily run by African American women, including three women who had been born enslaved: Sofia Jordan, Sofia Wright, and Louise Richardson.

Some of these employees lived in surviving tenant cabins, scattered around the lands of the former plantation. As in past eras, the white members of the college community were mostly self-segregated in and around the college buildings. At the center of this hierarchy, literally and figuratively, was Mary K. Benedict, the first college president, who had decided to live in the imposing Italianate villa while using some of the extra rooms for faculty apartments and other administrative functions. One can infer that her primary reasons for selecting this convenient location was its proximity to the newly built college buildings and its move-in readiness, having recently been a domestic residence. But after a century of such official college use, one wonders if its twenty-first century function could be expanded to include interpretive space to commemorate the everyday lives of the enslaved workers.

I had stared at the college buildings in a photograph on more than one occasion before I looked more carefully and tried to distinguish the ages of the African American men standing on one corner, and even longer before I thought to look past and behind the brick buildings to

the tree-lined road (Figure 8.2). There, I found several wooden buildings. Taken alone, these buildings could have been almost anything,
but an early twentieth-century black employee, Nannie Christian, who
described herself as "belonging to the Fletcher generation," recalled a
row of cabins "on the road that leads past the inn." The inn was the
Boxwood Inn, today the Alumnae Relations and Development Office,
and it stands at the head of Elijah Road at the back of the original laundry and power plant complex. The surviving houses in the photo may
have been built in the postbellum era to house laborers who worked
for Indiana, but the cabin in the center shared design elements with
antebellum slave cabins. This photo was glued into an old scrapbook
and simply labeled "Laundry and Power House," but its composition
revealed so much more. The four men appear to range in ages between
twenty and forty, so they would have been born between 1870 and 1890.
These men were one of the first African American generations born free
of the chains of slavery. Their parents may have been enslaved at Sweet
Briar. Here they were, digging a foundation and shoring up the walls of
a building that would provide all the power to the college classrooms
and administrative offices. Their earlier effort, the large square pillar
that serves as a smokestack for the coal-burning furnace, still stands
today.

Figure 8.2. Sweet Briar College Power Plant in the 1910s. Note the workers
standing on the corner of the building and the nineteenth-century buildings
on the far ridge. Sweet Briar College Library Archives.

When I started studying Sweet Briar's nineteenth-century antebellum black history, I was not thinking about photographs. As an archaeologist, I am most comfortable studying material culture, the physical remainders from the past. I began to piece together information about the families who lived and worked at Sweet Briar through letters, census records, wills, death certificates, and living descendants, assuming that kinship relationships on a marriage license would be worth more than a casual snapshot. I only started looking through historic photographs in the college archives to find old buildings. My purpose in poring through photos was to locate crumbling buildings and subtle sites like wells and the foundations of wooden buildings, so at first, I missed all the clues that pointed to Sweet Briar's slave past. After a year (2001–2002) of studying the on-campus slave cemetery and antebellum African American mortuary practices, I wanted to know more about the lives of the individuals buried in the graveyard. And while most archaeologists would start sharpening their trowels, I wanted an excuse to explore the aboveground remains on Sweet Briar's historic landscape. I turned to a complementary technique: an aboveground pedestrian survey, designed to locate the palimpsests of past lives.

For example, black waitstaff and cooks are involved in the preparation and serving of almost every documented meal or picnic. From the 1910s until the mid-1980s, the wood-paneled dining hall, or Refectory, was the site of carefully set circular tables and regular campus meals. And while all the seated patrons are white and many of the waiters are Sweet Briar students who needed to support themselves while at school, there is always at least one black staff member.[12] After reviewing dozens of these photographs, white students were apparently often waiting tables, but the professional staff were black. I thus realized the value of the photographs to my attempts to document the contributions and presence of African Americans during college's first half a century. Because there is such limited mention of these employees in the documentary record, the photographs were crucial to my quest.

What did these employees think of their positions? Only occasionally did pieces in the college-endorsed publications quote employees of color expressing anything other than positive accolades. Similar to the bias found in 1930s "Slave Narratives," in which interviewers were often white, most of the replies from African and Native American employees to questions from white authors were expressions of appreciation and praise for the college. But an employee occasionally expressed a different opinion. In 1994, Mitchell Carpenter retired from Sweet Briar after thirty-one years as a housekeeper and mechanical helper. A celebratory article reporting on several retirements described him as "always willing to do anything asked of him." But through the years, when he was questioned directly about his goals, his "stock answer" was, "I would like to retire from Sweet Briar."[13]

While African Americans on campus worked in low-paying jobs, Sweet Briar students regularly reached out to off-campus community members to provide financial and educational assistance. One of the first sponsored activities of the YWCA campus chapter was to tutor Monacan students who were attending a nearby Episcopalian mission school. The Monacans could not attend the public schools; instead, the Episcopal mission at Bear Mountain provided a teacher who taught the children in a one-room log cabin schoolhouse. Meanwhile, Sweet Briar nurses sponsored health clinics and advised local residents on the importance of vaccinations. Several college social groups gave gifts to area schoolchildren. The Coolwell minister Silas Berry observed that, during "Santa Claus times," the "Sweet Briar girls never turned down a donation to our church and pastor when it was in their judgment necessary." He said the students were a "genteel set of young women; a charitable set of women, a set of women of character and morals."[14] The YWCA also provided books and offered tutoring to students in local African American schools such as the Watts School (located near Rising Sun Missionary Baptist Church) and the Coolwell School (near the Baptist church of the same name).[15]

These individual acts of charity did little to offset Jim Crow practices, including segregated and unequal schools, racial discrimination, and even lynching. Throughout the 1910s, 1920s, and 1930s, Amherst County ran a "convict camp" for prisoners just down the road from Sweet Briar. A more accurate term for this arrangement was a chain gang: a group of mostly nonwhite men sentenced for a wide variety of misdemeanors and crimes who were forced to work for the state without compensation, in a virtual continuation of slave labor. A Sweet Briar employee, John Reid Sr., and his family lived next door to this outdoor prison. In the Jim Crow South, Sweet Briar was part of a much larger and pervasive cultural racism.[16]

After the first decade, Sweet Briar branched out from its narrow domestic curriculum and began offering broader opportunities for its students. African American men were instrumental in the early riding program at Sweet Briar, a tradition that held deep nostalgia, since Elijah Fletcher himself had arrived in Amherst on horseback. When the equestrian program started in 1924, student riders relied on borrowed horses from the Amherst Livery Stable, where Charles R. Tinsley tended the horses. A year later, Sweet Briar purchased all the mounts from the Amherst stable and brought them to the campus barn. These mounts required grooms. In researching these early equines and their handlers, I came across an old photograph in the Sweet Briar Archives (Figure 8.3). It was donated in 1972 to the college archives by Mary V. Shaw, class of 1920, who had written on the back, "A stable-mate of Eugenie Morenus horse (Toby)—when most horses were rented from Amherst."

For me, the composition was so clearly an African American man and his horse that I naively assumed the man was Eugenie and the horse was Toby. Then I noticed a second set of notes on the photograph that read: "Topsy ? c 1917–20" and "Groom Sterling?" As it turned out, Eugenie Morenus was a Sweet Briar faculty member, not pictured, who owned a horse name Toby or Topsy. For Shaw, the importance of the photograph lay in its depiction of a notable horse; the black man holding the reins was irrelevant. At the time, the name Sterling meant nothing to me; only later did I realize I might have found an early photograph of Sterling Jones hard at work in the decade after the college's founding. As with many of my subsequent discoveries, the evidence was hidden in plain sight but lacked context. Sterling was one of hundreds of African Americans who had lived and worked at Sweet Briar from the very beginning, but whose stories and contributions had been overlooked.

Horses at Sweet Briar also pulled supply wagons, led transport coaches (like the Fletcher family carriage), and dragged equipment that flattened and paved roads. African American grooms and stable hands played an integral role in this work. The historic evidence of

Figure 8.3. A college groom holding a faculty member's horse, circa 1917. Sweet Briar College Library Archives.

these men comes mostly from unlabeled photographs, so we have very few names. Census records provide some clues: Landon Jones (1884–1944) drove a supply wagon on campus in the 1910s and boarded at the home of George Sales (1871–ca.1960s), who worked as the stable boss in 1920. These men and several other "farmhands" were the sons and grandsons of people Elijah enslaved on Sweet Briar Plantation. As the campus grew, African Americans continued to contribute labor and specialized skills. Much of the early work was making and laying bricks for the professionally designed buildings. Despite their esoteric, nonlocal styles, all the earth for the bricks was obtained from nearby burrow pits; some of these deep cuts into the hillside are still visible. A young Sterling and his friend Lewis Chambers carried water for the brickmakers working to apply the facade of Academic, Carson Residence Hall, and the Refectory.[17]

Several of the brickmasons may have learned the skill on antebellum plantations. One of these men was Sterling's father, Daniel, born decades earlier, in 1845. We have not located any formal record of his enslaved childhood, but we do know Daniel formalized his marriage to Jemima "Minnie" Jones on a February evening in 1871; he was twenty-six, and his bride was eighteen. Their first child had been born earlier, when marriages between enslaved people were not recognized. Since emancipation, when life was a struggle to find employment or land to farm in a rural Virginia county recovering from the Civil War, Daniel and his family had eked out a hard living. Daniel died in poverty at the foot of Bolling Hill, just a few miles away from Sweet Briar, in a community of other freed slaves. In his will, he gave a milking cow to his half-sister Laura Rose Watson on the condition that she had him decently buried. Perhaps he was comforted to know Sterling had a dependable job at Sweet Briar, one that he would retain for decades.

Alongside the building projects was another, subtler construction during those early years: the creation of a series of myths to describe and contextualize the grounds and people of a former slave owner's home. Sterling Jones himself became a favorite target for college mythmakers, his life story simplified and retold dozens of times from the 1910s to the twenty-first century, more than fifty years after his death. From a certain perspective, and leaving out several messy details, it appeared to be a fairy tale about the life of a first-generation free person of color. Because Sterling lived much of his life during the twentieth century, when the government began to record facts about African Americans as citizens rather than as property, we know several indisputable facts about his life story. He was born around 1875; he died at age eighty-four in 1959 after working at Sweet Briar periodically since he was a boy. Photographs and contemporary newspaper accounts document some of his roles at the college: laborer, janitor, and the person responsible for raising and lowering the US flag on campus. Beyond that, the story diverges between reality and wishful thinking—or even mythology.

On campus, Sterling was featured dozens of times in the Sweet Briar College newspaper, alumnae magazine, and promotional brochures. In 1922, a student drew a mock college calendar, and for 14 September, she wrote ironically, "Sterling [Jones] and Tom Rose open college."[18] For the white authors and photographers, he was used as a model of a servile, black employee. They may have intended to highlight his contributions to the college, but the result was a caricature of an African American man. For example, he was often referred to by just his first name, providing a false sense of familiarity. His family life was ripe for ridicule by a white audience. He was married three times (around 1898, 1911, and 1921). These unions produced thirteen children (oral history suggests one of his wives also had several miscarriages, but those tragedies did not make it into Sweet Briar lore). Yet, multiple college accounts claimed he had nineteen children. Even more surprising was the impractical suggestion that he and all his children lived together in the small cabin behind the "big house" on campus. For example, Ann Whitley, class of 1947, wrote: "Many children had grown up in the old slave cabin behind Sweet Briar House. . . . Sterling Jones had lived there for enough years to have had three wives and nineteen children, most of the latter having grown up in the cabin."[19]

At first, I took statements like this literally; the legend of Sterling and his nineteen on-campus children was such an oft-repeated "fact" that I did not question it. Only when I created a detailed time line of events in Sterling's life did I realize his first child was born in 1900, six years before the college opened and while he was living in a community called McIvors, several miles distant from campus near present-day Monroe. In fact, none of the federal census records placed his residence at Sweet Briar at all. In the 1900, 1910, 1930, and 1940 censuses, Sterling reported owning his own home, where he lived with his family. In 1920, he was listed as widowed and living in the home of his father-in-law, Charles Jordan. His second wife, Martha Jordan Bias (herself a widow when she married Sterling), had recently passed away, and Sterling was working as a laborer on a farm, which Sweet Briar may or may not have owned. His four living children—Bertha, Mary, Lillie Pearl, and Fannie—were being cared for by their aunt Amanda Jordan, who lived next door with her husband, Walter Turner.

This residential pattern did not match the one described by Sweet Briar historians, whose accounts suggested he was on the dole or at the very least relying heavily on the largesse of his employer. After a careful study of the extant records and handful of photographs that appear to show him standing with his family on campus, I narrowed down his time in the former slave cabin to just four years: from 1921, when he was a recent widower, to 1924, when the college repurposed the structure. During that time, he was married to Aurelia Tyler, and their first two children were born in the cabin: Louise in 1922 and Dorothy in 1924 (Figure 8.4). Years later, Dorothy recalled that she was about four

Figure 8.4. Aurelia Tyler Jones and her daughter Louise in front of the Sweet Briar slave cabin. Photograph by White Studio, New York, 1927. Sweet Briar College Library Archives.

months old when they moved out of the cabin. As for his children from previous marriages, only one is of the age she was likely to have lived with him, eleven-year-old Fannie. Accordingly, the family numbered no more than five while they lived in the diminutive structure—a far cry from the imaginative fictions of college scribes.

A century later, tracking down the facts of Sterling Jones's life has been a complex undertaking—but at the time, the details would have been readily available from the man himself. So why were the romanticized stories told in the first place? And why were they repeated for so many years? One possibility is that the myth casts Sweet Briar in the comfortable role of benevolent master. Like a kindly slaveholder who treated their property "like family," Sweet Briar is depicted as rewarding a loyal black employee with lifelong housing and care for his huge brood, in return for his devoted service.

If we treat Sterling Jones as a historic figure rather than a caricature, we can more accurately untangle the threads of his life. To do this, I pored through the college-endorsed articles about him, searching for direct quotes. In 1957, just a few years before he died, he summarized his contributions to the college: "I've done pretty much of everything here at Sweet Briar." The article couches its praise in language that reinforces the Sweet Briar mythology, as reflected in its subtitle, "Sterling Jones Is a 'Tradition' Here." The author says, "He is as much a part of Sweet Briar as the boxwoods or the Senior Stairs," thereby reducing him to a category that contains inanimate objects and nostalgic rituals.[20] Sweet Briar College is very proud of its long-standing "traditions," which range from singing contests to costumed interludes and from friendly competitions to lantern bearing rituals. But to place Sterling in the category of a "tradition" is to devalue his identity as a person.

In 1924, the college reappropriated the cabin for official use. It was transformed numerous times over the years, first as a classroom; then as a tearoom, the offices of the alumnae association, a chapel; and finally as a Farm Tool Museum. All these uses obscured its original function as a dwelling for enslaved laborers who worked on Sweet Briar Plantation.[21] Decades later, on Sterling's eighty-third birthday, the college threw a party celebrating him as a "long time Sweet Briar employee."[22] It was held in Academic, another building fraught with meaning, since it was filled with classrooms that excluded his daughters and female relatives; the college was still for white women only, as Indiana had wished.

Just before Sterling and his family briefly moved into the cabin, it had been used in a publicity campaign as an informational postcard to promote the new college. In the picture, a carefully manicured boxwood hedge obscures more than half the structure. The limbs of a verdant tree hang over the roof, and the euphemistic caption reads, "Old Servants' Quarters." A brochure at the time, which also included Sweet Briar students dressed up in Indiana's gowns, showed a similar photograph with the caption, "One of the picturesque old negro cabins."[23] This reminded me of other contemporary postcards that combined a romanticized photograph with a description that appears to promise Sweet Briar students the use of servile labor. Indeed, one of these postcards was the catalyst for this book. It featured a lone figure partially obscured by an ornamental hedge in front of the president's home, the antebellum big house. After years of research, I finally came up with a lead on who the man in the postcard was: Bowman Knuckles, who worked for the college for decades.[24] I first identified him by name in another photograph from the 1950s, where he is identified only as the "gardener" and can be seen watering flowers alongside an alumna who worked as the college's landscape architect.

In the photographs, he is clearly a slight man, possibly under five feet tall; this fits with the man (or boy) in the postcard, who appears dwarfed by the hedge. In the 1920 Census, he gave his full name, James B. Knuckles, and listed his age as twenty-one, born around 1889. He died in 1971, having worked for decades as a gardener at Sweet Briar. Trying to figure out the person in the hand-colored postcard was just the beginning of my efforts to reveal other aspects of Sweet Briar's hidden or overlooked history. One fascinating aspect of Bowman Knuckles's documentary trail is that he maintained his identity as an Indian despite the efforts of racist administrators and eugenicists who tried to erase any mention of native heritage. Although the 1910 Census lists Bowman as "mulatto," he listed "Indian" on his 1917 draft card and again in the 1920 Census, just four years before the passage of the Virginia's Racial Integrity Act.

Walter Plecker (1861–1947), the infamous founder of Virginia's Bureau of Vital Statistics, spearheaded this discriminatory statute, which demanded great genealogical detail to classify individuals as either "white" or "colored," based on the presence of even one "colored" great-great-grandparent. It also erased the distinctions between black and Native Americans, classifying them all as "colored." During Plecker's thirty-four years in office, he altered the birth certificates of countless black and Native American Virginians in his quest to separate "the races" into just two categories, white and colored, forcing Virginia Indians to classify themselves as "colored" on official documents like birth and marriage certificates. This bureaucratic genocide caused countless native families to leave the state to retain their preferred ethnic identity in official records. Plecker was so efficient and ruthless in his quest to destroy the records of Native American families that he boasted, "Hitler's genealogical study of the Jews is not more complete."[25]

Remarkably, the influence of this one racist is still actively affecting Native American communities in Amherst County and beyond. His erasure of Native American ancestry on official documents such as birth and death certificates has made it difficult for Virginian Indian tribes to receive federal recognition, because those applications require proof of continuous existence since 1900. Plecker effectively wiped out at least two generations of Native American genealogical records. The Monacan tribe did not win official recognition from the Virginian General Assembly until 1989.[26] Federal recognition did not arrive until almost two decades later, when a member of the US House of Representatives, Virginian Republican Robert Wittman, introduced the Thomasina E. Jordan Indian Tribes of Virginia Federal Recognition Act. The Monacan Indian Nation was one of six Virginian tribes that won federal recognition on 29 January 2018, when the president signed the bill into law.[27] In the Piedmont region of Virginia, an exceptionally derogatory term arose that referred to individuals with a bloodline from multiple racial categories (white, black, and Indian). "Free issues," or sometimes simply "issues," is still used in some quarters and still has the power to wound with its underlying assumption of a marginalized group.[28]

Plecker's disastrous campaign has complicated research efforts to locate the employment records of Virginian Indians who worked at Sweet Briar. At Sweet Briar, Bowman Knuckles is one of the few who managed to reassert his native identity over the decades. In contrast, Winston Barham, who at more than sixty years old was one of the oldest college employees when the school opened, was listed in the 1910 Census as "mulatto." He had been born in 1851 and lived in the home of his son-in-law, William H. Bruce, and another relation, Roy Johns. In Amherst County, Branham (a slight variant on Winston's name), Johns, and Bruce are all surnames associated with individuals of Monacan descent, the nearby Indian tribe whose ancestral homeland centers on Bear Mountain.

One of the most remarkable sources of ethnographic data I uncovered was a paternalistic article that appeared in the spring 1935 issue of *The Alumnae News* titled "Our Colored Folks." Its description in the table of contents recognizes the longevity of black contributions to Sweet Briar: "Miss Long deals with the negroes who have been here from the beginning of the college or for a very long time."[29] The English professor M. Dee Long interviewed almost two dozen African American employees and included photographs, taken with an ethnographic eye for details. Sterling Jones and Signora Hollins are featured prominently. On another page, nine separate snapshots provide a visual record of the occupations available to African Americans at Sweet Briar in the early twentieth century: the maids (Clara Jordan and Mattie Rose), a washerwoman (Alice Rucker), the chauffeur (Massie Patterson), the postman (Chris Thomas), a laundry worker (Lewis Chambers), and a cook (Nannie Christian). And, for good measure, there is an accordion player, George Sales, described as a longtime employee who, before the college's founding, lived in one of the rows of cabins "that ran from the gardens down towards the lake." The author failed to include his official college occupation but says he "has always had a good ear for melody and knack for picking up tunes." After she lists the instruments he could play, she concludes, "From plantation days down he has helped to furnish dance music for many a party at Sweet Briar."[30] Whether Long intended such a reference is unclear, but to the modern ears, this description invokes the racist image of a minstrel show.

The tone of the article reflects the cultural values of many whites from that period. Alice Rucker, the washerwoman, was nominated as "class mammy" by the class of 1925. Apparently, she served as a "Dear Abby" figure, listening to student complaints and offering advice; she called the students in that class "my girls" and received Christmas greetings and pictures of their babies after they graduated. Her efforts were described as follows: "Nor is it unheard of for one in time of trouble, confident of Alice's goodness and favor with Heaven, to write asking for her prayers."[31] On the face of it, this sounds like a compliment: Alice was "in good standing with her maker" and a "prayerful woman." But the description also casts Alice in the one-dimensional role of "healer" or supplicant who prayed on behalf of white girls. When I researched Alice's life further, I learned she was married to a blacksmith; they bought a home in Amherst in the 1920s, where they raised their son, Chester. Alice received only two years of formal education, and Chester quit school after seventh grade. He worked as a shoe repairman, while Alice spent most of her life as a washerwoman.[32] College narrators claimed they adored these women, but they did not view them as equal members of the community.

In the article, Long explains that, during the 1927–1928 school year, the college developed a fundraising slogan, "Every person has a part": "All of the colored folks in the employment of the college came together and made a contribution that indicated a loyal, generous spirit." One of the older workers, whom Long refers to as Aunt Jane Jones, described her modest contribution: "If I can't keep up with the bell-cow, I can gallop with the herd." Another unnamed black employee summed up their participation best: "Of course we want a part, for having been here from the beginning, we are, as you might say, 'the colored founders' of Sweet Briar."[33] It would take another sixty-five years before the contributions and role of African Americans at Sweet Briar were given significant attention, rather than being treated as a mere sliver or curiosity of college history.

In the fall of 1955, the college celebrated its fiftieth anniversary. As part of the festivities, administrators handed out service awards to employees for their twenty-fifth and fiftieth work anniversaries. Two African American men were in the latter category: Lewis Chambers and Sterling Jones. These men had worked at Sweet Briar for half a century and one, if not both, had begun their careers working for Indiana in the 1880s. Two years later, Sterling retired from his life's work. He soon developed Alzheimer's disease. Knowing he tended to wander from home, family members took turns staying with him. On the cold winter morning of 4 January 1959, it was the turn of his grandniece Mary Jones, who was eight months pregnant. When she needed to go to the bathroom, she stepped out to use the outhouse, as Sterling's home did not have indoor plumbing. When she returned, he was gone.

A search party commenced, but the family was unable to find him. He was found buried under the snow three days later, on 7 January, near the train tracks on the way to the college. He had frozen to death. When they found him, he was not wearing a coat or hat, but he nevertheless may have been trying to walk to work at Sweet Briar, as he had done for several decades. The coroner concluded that he died while "lost in woods in extreme cold weather."[34] For more than fifty years, Sterling Jones had woken up, eaten breakfast, and set off on foot to walk to Sweet Briar College, where he worked as a janitor. It was a trek he had made, perhaps, sixteen thousand times over the course of his lifetime. On this day, his last apparent attempt at that trek cost him his life.

When Sterling passed, none of his children could have attended Sweet Briar College. It was still locked into the original provisions of Indiana Williams's will, which specified that the school was for "white girls and young women." Four years before her death, and amid her penning multiple versions of her will, the US Supreme Court handed down the *Plessy v. Ferguson* decision upholding "separate but equal" education. And just two years after her death, Virginia ratified a constitution that specified "white and colored children shall not be taught in the same school."[35] This constitution was not replaced until 1971.[36]

One year after the US Supreme Court's *Brown v. Board of Education* decision resulted in the order to racially integrate US public school classrooms, the Sweet Briar administrators decided to study the possibility of desegregating the college. This effort moved slowly. In 1957, the college hosted an interracial vesper service, but photographs of the event show a mostly segregated audience, with white students in the front rows. As Virginian Senator Byrd promoted his racist policy of "Massive Resistance" to public school desegregation, opinions on campus slowly began to change. In 1960, Sweet Briar students hosted a series of lectures about the civil rights movement and wrote letters to the editor in local papers urging the college to accept students of color. White students from nearby Lynchburg colleges joined forces with black residents to protest the segregated seating at local lunch counters. A handful of Sweet Briar students wrote letters of support for the protestors and picketed a drug store.[37] In actuality, Sweet Briar had been accepting one or two nonwhite students every year since 1940. These students were from Japan, China, India, and Turkey, and no one had objected to their attendance.[38] Accepting African Americans, however, was another matter.

By 1963, Sweet Briar faculty were investigating legal options to seek relief from the will's terms and integrate the student body. The faculty were concerned that the racially restrictive admission policy would decrease the college's ability to retain first-rate teachers and students of the highest caliber and that the college would have trouble obtaining financial support from foundations, private donors, and federal sources. They even worried Sweet Briar would lose its accreditation and membership in national organizations. On 2 November 1963, the Board of Directors and the Board of Overseers of Sweet Briar College adopted a resolution that recognized its obligation to the founder's will but said it also must meet the obligations of "past, present, and future students of Sweet Briar."[39]

Thus, they directed the Executive Committee to "take whatever legal action may be necessary and appropriate to secure a judicial determination as to whether we may, consistently with the charitable purposes of Indiana Fletcher Williams, admit qualified persons to Sweet Briar College, regardless of race." The faculty concurred with this decision and in March 1964 concluded, "'Sound learning' cannot flourish in an atmosphere which denies the reality of the world today."[40] Empowered by the Civil Rights Act of 1964, which barred federal aid to secondary schools that did not accept students regardless of race, the college began to pursue legal action in the Amherst Circuit Court. On 5 September 1964, Virginia's segregationist attorney general urged the court to uphold the "plain and unambiguous" college charter. The regional judge, C. G. Quesenbery, sided with the attorney general in a 1965 opinion.

In the meantime, the college tried to file an "assurance of compliance" connected to Title VI of the Civil Rights Act so that its federal funding would not be terminated. But the funding was cut, as the college's documentation of the ongoing court case was deemed to fall short of actual compliance. On 25 April 1966, Sweet Briar College appealed to the US District Court for the Western District of Virginia and obtained a temporary restraining order that enabled it to bypass the racial restrictions of Indiana's will. One month later, given the injunction, the Sweet Briar Board of Trustees was advised it could begin to admit students of color. In August 1966, the college announced the admission of its first African American student.

After several months of wrangling between the US District Court (in Charlottesville) and the attorney general of Virginia and the Commonwealth's attorney for Amherst County, the Supreme Court of the United States remanded the case back to the Western District to make a final decision. On 17 July 1967, that three-judge court issued a permanent injunction that enjoined the attorney general of Virginia and the Commonwealth's attorney of Amherst County from ever enforcing the racial restriction intended by "white" in Indiana Fletcher Williams's will. This decision provided a legal endorsement of the board's earlier, 28 May 1966 decision to admit students "on standards of academic qualification and character, without regard to race, creed or color."[41]

The legal battles were over, but the necessary cultural and social changes were just beginning. While many alumnae applauded the college's efforts, and some current students even risked alienating their parents by participating in pro-integration efforts, other members of the community were dismayed. Several dozen alumnae wrote letters critical of the very notion of integration, threatening board members who pursued the efforts at integration. Others skirted around the issue of integration and instead focused their complaints on breaking Indiana's "intent." For example, one alumna wrote that she was "increasingly distressed and dismayed because a college purporting to exist by, and to teach by, the highest standards of principle and morality, should so completely and deliberately abandon those principles as to violate a last will and testament for the sake of Federal government money."[42] In 1965, a college board member resigned after twenty-four years because she felt the decision violated the trust Indiana had handed down to them. Other authors expressed their beliefs more openly, using vitriolic and racist language to express their displeasure.[43]

The opposition to integrating the college was not confined to campus. One Lynchburg resident wrote to the college that he was "sorry to read in the papers that you and so many of the faculty members or [*sic*] a lot of Negro lovers that College or any other School that takes in Negroes or [*sic*] a degraded School and a disgrace to any city of state any where."[44] A man from Albemarle County feared that Sweet Briar's decision to integrate its classrooms would "turn the country into a mulatto, degenerate nation."[45] In the face of such racist and derogatory sentiments, it is obvious that the fight to integrate the college was just one step on a long road to equality.

While the lawyers argued their case, the on-campus climate was a surreal blend of *Gone with the Wind* and *Uncle Tom's Cabin*. In May 1960, the annual May Day celebration took "Way Back When" as its theme. As it turns out, "back when" was envisioned as a minstrel show, with the May Queen and her "court" dressed in hoop skirts being entertained by students in blackface.[46] Even more telling, perhaps, was a gathering in the on-campus chapel. The National Association for the Advancement of Colored People had been invited to the college chapel for a prayer meeting—a refreshing opportunity for interracial worship. Yet, the audience was segregated, with the front rows occupied by white people. Although most of the audience members were black, the front pews were apparently reserved for white Sweet Briar students, replicating several hundred years of mostly segregated worship in Virginia.[47]

As the college was slowly integrating its classrooms, segregation of the staff persisted. Only whites were hired as college administrators, while a large percentage of the groundskeepers and housekeepers were African American. A large proportion of the hourly staff members were of African and Native American descent and lacked the professional opportunities of their white peers. Between 1906 and 1960, more than 350 African Americans worked at Sweet Briar. Several dozen of these individuals worked for more than thirty years, yet none were promoted beyond that of an hourly wage earner with minimum managerial responsibilities. If you add up those hours, it translates to thousands of years of combined service. They comprise at least one hundred families, with a wide array of duties and responsibilities. An employment list that included one hundred local families would have touched many of the 4,500 African Americans living in Amherst in 1960 in some way.

During the second half of the twentieth century, the pages of the college yearbook and alumnae magazine slowly changed from the stark distinction between white students versus black workers. While there were still black chauffeurs, cooks, and maids, black students and their families were slowly added to those pages. Even more gradually, the black staff members were able to send their own children to Sweet Briar. Barbara Rose Page, a descendant of Givens Rose, graduated in 1983, just four years before her daughter Janet Page, class of 1987. Shirley Reid, who did not go to college, had a daughter graduate from the Sweet Briar class of 1991.

Notes

1. Fenrick, "Fifty Year College Employee Dies," 4.
2. 1920 US Federal Census Amherst County: Roll T625_1879, Page 3B, Enumeration District 11, Image 35.
3. Family Tree belonging to "arose4u," Ancestry.com, accessed 2 January 2019, https://www.ancestry.com/family-tree/person/tree/114599530/person/240129717105/facts.
4. *Sweet Briar Catalogue* (Sweet Briar, VA: Sweet Briar College, 1908), 13 (quote), 64–65.
5. Von Briesen and Vickery, *Sweet Briar College*, 5–6.
6. *Sweet Briar To-Day and To-Morrow*, 1, 3.
7. "A Great and Noble Gift by a Great and Noble Woman," *The Times* (Richmond), 10 March 1901, 16.
8. *Sweet Briar To-Day and To-Morrow*, 13.
9. Financial tally by Indiana's executor in "The Estate of Indiana Fletcher Williams, Deceased, in Account," 44–46.
10. "Sweet Briar College for Women," *Baltimore Sun*, 27 August 1909, 4.
11. S. Berry, *Memories of R. D. Merchant*, 33.
12. 1956 photograph of "Refectory Waitress." Archives.
13. "In the Spotlight: Au Revoir, but Not Farewell!" *Sweet Briar Alumnae Magazine* 64, no. 4 (1994): 11.
14. S. Berry, *Memories of R. D. Merchant*, 34.
15. Amherst County Heritage Book Committee, *Amherst County Virginia*.
16. 1910 US Federal Census, Elon District, Amherst County, Virginia, Roll T623_1621, pp. 11B, 12A, and 12B, Family History Library Film 1375634.
17. Whitley, "1946–1956," 37.
18. "Calendar," *The Briar Patch 1922*, published by the Junior Class of Sweet Briar College (Sweet Briar, VA: Sweet Briar College, 1922), 224.
19. Whitley, "1946–1956," 37.
20. "Sterling Jones is a 'Tradition' Here," *Sweet Briar News*, 13 November 1957, 2.
21. Rainville, *Roots, Restoration, Remembrance*, 12–16.
22. "Happy Birthday," *Sweet Briar News*, 5 November 1958, 4.
23. *Sweet Briar To-Day and To-Morrow*, 7.
24. In the 1910 US Federal Census, he is listed as "gardener," and under "industry," he filled in "college gardener."

25. Rountree, *Pocahontas, Powhatan, Opechancanough*, 12–16, 234n116.
26. "Extending State Recognition to the Monacan Indian Tribe of Amherst County," House Joint Resolution no. 390, 24 January 1989, http://virginiain dianarchive.org/items/show/66.
27. Thomasina E. Jordan Indian Tribes of Virginia Federal Recognition Act of 2017, Public Law no. 115-121, https://www.congress.gov/bill/115th-con gress/house-bill/984/all-info.
28. Seaman, "Amherst County: A Workshop for the Study of Social Change," xx.
29. *The Alumnae News* [Sweet Briar College] 4, no. 3 (1935): 1.
30. Long, "Our Colored Folks," 11 (photographs), 9.
31. Long, "Our Colored Folks," 12.
32. Olinger and Wilkins, *Amherst, Virginia*, 43, 62; The 1930 US Federal Census, Amherst Courthouse District, 5B, lines 78–80.
33. Long, "Our Colored Folks," 8.
34. Certificate of death, Sterling Jones Sr., signed 12 January 1959, Amherst County Courthouse.
35. 1902 Constitution of Virginia, Article IX, Section 140.
36. Lassiter and Lewis, *The Moderates' Dilemma*, 102.
37. "Sweet Briar Students Oppose Discrimination," *Lynchburg News*, 1 May 1960, 2; "Lunch Counters' Action Wins Praise," *Lynchburg News*, 20 November 1960, sec. D, 2. Thanks to Dr. Karol Lawson for this source.
38. Supreme Court Decision 1966, 8. A list of countries of origin for Sweet Briar students, including the Bahamas, China, Honduras, India, Japan, Korea, Lebanon, Morocco, Pakistan, Peru, South Africa, Vietnam, among others, *Bulletin of Sweet Briar*, November 1966, 4.
39. *The Sweet Briar College Case*, 5.
40. *The Sweet Briar College Case*, 6.
41. *The Sweet Briar College Case*, 7–10, Appendix E: Final Order, 18.
42. Letter from Lorton Virginia to "Mrs. Henry C. Pannell, President," 5 December 1966. Archives. Even though her husband had died in 1946, four years before she was appointed president, the writer addressed the note to "Mrs. Henry C. Pannell."
43. Letters loosely compiled into "1967 Court Case" folders in the Archives. For more information on the case itself, see *Sweet Briar Institute v. Robert Button, et al.*, 387 U.S. 423 (1966).
44. Letter from John D. Donady to "Miss Pannell," Lynchburg, 2 June 1966, Archives.
45. Letter from E. M. Gilmer of Albemarle County to "Sir," 1 November 1964, Archives.
46. Karol Lawson's time line, *Lynchburg News*, 1 May 1960, B4.
47. Photograph of NAACP meeting, Sweet Briar College, 21 March 1960, Archives.

Figure 9.1. A plaque honoring the individuals buried in the cemetery for enslaved families on the Sweet Briar College campus. Photograph by Cassie Foster, Sweet Briar College, 21 September 2018.

9

COMMEMORATING FOUNDERS

I began this book by suggesting that the narratives about African and Native Americans at Sweet Briar had been overlooked and undervalued for many decades. To retain the meaning of old sites and stories, we must create new rituals that remind us of their meaning and importance. The anthropological archaeologist Paul Shackel concurs, "Traditions, meanings, and memories are invented, and they become legitimate through repetition or a process of formalization and ritualization characterized by reference to the past."[1] These new rituals might fall under Eric Hobsbawm's concept of "invented traditions," whereby a relatively new tradition is assigned a false sense of longevity to legitimize it. Regardless of the "authenticity" of a tradition, all these rituals change over time, and perhaps now is the time to effect a transformation at Sweet Briar and beyond. In Figure 9.1, a floral bouquet lies on top of the boulder marking the location of the on-campus slave cemetery; it was placed there by Rev. Jasper Fletcher, the four-generational "great" grandson of an enslaved couple at Sweetbrier Plantation. The inscription reads: "Sweet Briar Plantation Burial Grounds: Sacred Resting Place of Unknown Founders Who Labored to Build What Has Become Sweet Briar College. We Are in Their Debt." This commemorative plaque was erected in 2003 when the college held its first commemorative ceremony at the burial ground. In this last chapter, I review the wide variety of rituals the college community has created and participated in over the past two decades in the hope that these efforts will inspire other institutions of higher learning to change their top-down founding narratives to fully acknowledge the contributions of generations of "invisible founders."

Sweet Briar College prides itself on the fact that a woman, Indiana Fletcher Williams, founded and financed the institution. Over the past century, various rituals and memorials have arisen to honor that gift, the most significant being the annual procession to the family graveyard where Indiana and her daughter, Daisy, are buried. On Founders' Day every October, students, faculty, and staff walk to the base of a towering granite memorial, adorned with a life-sized statue of an angel, and lay daisies on the footstones below. The view of the college buildings from that hallowed hilltop reveals a carefully curated view-shed that requires the regular trimming of visible trees. In contrast, the view toward another, shorter hilltop is more opaque and goes un-noticed by most visitors. On this more modest topographic rise lies a very different cemetery: the sacred spot where enslaved families buried their dead. The stark contrast between the two burial grounds—one carefully manicured, in plain sight, integrated into a century of ritual behavior, and the other, lost to memory for decades, overgrown, and infrequently visited—serves as a metaphor for the long-unacknowl-edged people of color who have lived and worked at Sweet Briar for two centuries.

Slavery is probably far from the minds of most visitors to the Mon-ument Hill cemetery, where Indiana, Daisy, and some of their kin are buried. Its marble and granite markers stand on top of a high and scenic hill, with a commanding view of both the college below and the foothills of the Blue Ridge Mountains to the west. One side of the six-hundred-foot-high hill is carefully pruned, and the trees that stand downhill from the site are regularly trimmed so that the memorial can be seen from be-low. This maintenance plan is not simply because of the initiative of the groundskeepers; in one of the few codicils to Indiana's will, she required that the graveyard "shall be perpetually kept in good order."[2]

In addition to the Fletchers and Williamses, two other white, ante-bellum families are buried here: the Woodruffs and Basses. Both sets of graves, husbands and wives, predate Elijah Fletcher's death. They were not related to Elijah by blood or marriage but were the previous own-ers of the land in and around the cemetery. As wealthy, white men and women who owned large parcels of rural land in the early nineteenth century, their economic livelihood would have been based, in part, on enslaved labor. We do not yet know where the enslaved workers who labored on this land before it was called Sweetbrier were buried. And while we may never know with certainty where these individuals were buried, a small burial ground located in a field about a quarter of a mile away from the college, alongside an old fence line, is one possibility. Enslaved individuals may also be buried in unmarked graves located just outside the stone boundary that surrounds the whites-only Mon-ument Hill graveyard. On other Southern plantations, those types of graves were often marked by nothing more than a subtle depression, often obscured later by well-meaning groundskeepers.[3]

The Monument Hill graveyard is the focus of one of the most iconic and celebratory traditions at Sweet Briar. The apostrophe in Founders' Day has not always been included, so it is unclear whether earlier iterations of the event were meant to honor a sole founder, Indiana, or multiple members of her family. Its origins date to the mandate in Indiana's will that care and attention be spent on her family's graveyard as a condition of her founding gift.

The first documented Founders' Day was in 1909, only three years after the college's founding, when the original cohort of graduating students asked for permission to wear their caps and gowns for a procession from campus to Monument Hill. To this day, seniors don their graduation gowns for the first time on this occasion and walk to the graveyard, where they place the eponymous flower on Daisy Williams's memorial. The students danced until 2 a.m. on that first night in 1909.[4] President Mary K. Benedict spoke at the ceremony, reminding her audience that a century earlier, Elijah Fletcher had received his degree from the University of Vermont. The first Sweet Briar diplomas were modeled after the one Elijah had earned in 1809.[5]

In 1917, a first-year student wrote a short story from Daisy's point of view, as if she were observing this ceremony for the first time. In the fanciful tale, a squirrel informs Daisy it is spring, and Daisy crawls into a thick boxwood to find a playhouse she had constructed as a child, decades earlier. She hears laughter as she hides in the bushes and observes as "girls clad in white walked arm in arm over the green sward." She watches them enter a structure—likely the current Academic building—where they celebrate the ten-year anniversary of the college's opening. Daisy catches the words "Founder's Day" in the wind and then deciphers the lyrics of a song:

> Sweet Briar, Sweet Briar, flower fair,
> The rose that on your crest you wear,
> Shall never fade, but always bear
> Thy beauty, oh, Sweet Briar.[6]

Here, Daisy's ghost becomes an external source of validation for the new school's celebratory ritual. At this early date, the modifier for "Founder" is singular, clearly referring to Indiana. In later years, other college administrators were recognized for their contributions on the festive day. In 1928, for instance, Founders' Day exercises framed a memorial service to honor former President Emilie Watts McVea, who had died during the preceding summer.[7] Despite many references to the construction and administration of the college, African American founders were regularly overlooked during these celebrations. In 1934, a speaker observed

> Founders' Day is the one occasion of the academic year when we are invited to acknowledge the creation of a physical institution and the

spiritual motives which such creation symbolizes. . . . It is appropriate for us to remember on Founders' Day not only the Williams family as the original founders of Sweet Briar, but also others who in the early years so built themselves and their work into the college that they too may be spoken of as its founders.[8]

The speaker's only "outstanding" example of such founders was N. C. Manson, the college's first legal counsel.

Alumnae and community members were invited to return to campus for the festivities during subsequent Founders' Days. The fall 1936 issue of *The Alumnae News* encouraged its readers to "come back and reminisce . . . the woods will be glorious and the mountains will be taking on deep purple tones."[9] Multiple ceremonies were held on Founders' Day: scholarship presentations, announcements of distinguished alumna awards, dramatic performances, vesper services, and encomiums to past presidents, culminating in a Founders' Dance. In 2010, when selected as the keynote speaker at the annual Founders' Day ceremony—now held in the fall rather than at graduation—I broke with tradition and organized my comments around Sweet Briar's unknown laborers. "Just as we trace the generations of Elijah Fletcher descendants who left their mark on the landscape and formation of the college," I noted, "we can research the African American families whose labor ensured the success of the plantation and college." The next day, I gave a longer version of my lecture about African American heritage at the college boathouse. Afterward, the audience and I walked to the graveyard where enslaved people were buried for a commemorative ceremony designed by the student group Unity in collaboration with the college chaplain.

In 2014, a new Founders' Day ritual was introduced. That morning, a small group of students and administrators brought flowers to the slave cemetery, thereby creating a parallel procession to the afternoon walk to Monument Hill. After a century of focus on a handful of white founders, this new tradition helped recognize the African and Native Americans who have worked to build and sustain Sweet Briar. In 2015 and 2016, alumnae continued the ritual, leading morning processions to the site. In the fall of 2016, students in a Sweet Briar psychology class drafted a petition to "acknowledge and celebrate" the "enslaved population of Sweet Briar Plantation that made the institution possible." As part of this effort, they circulated a petition to request a ceremony for these "invisible founders" during Founders' Day.[10] And, finally, on 21 September 2018, these commemorative services came full circle. That year, the Black Student Alliance planned a commemorative ceremony, echoing elements of the original 2003 event, which included singing,

Bible and poetry readings, and the participation of descendants (Figure 9.2). The 2018 ritual may have solidified the new pattern: to hold a sunrise procession and service at the burial ground of the enslaved during Founders' Day weekend. There is reason to hope there will be continued interest in this contemplative event, thereby encouraging the Sweet Briar community to remember and honor the contributions of all college founders.

Sweet Briar was one of the first institutions of higher education in the United States to publicly recognize the contributions of an enslaved community. On a sunny afternoon in April 2003, Sweet Briar College President Betsy Muhlenfeld welcomed a crowd of several dozen college and community members to this sacred site to "claim our past . . . to acknowledge and embrace many of the unknown people who labored as slaves on the Sweet Briar Plantation." She recognized that, until recently, this type of commemorative event would not have happened because slavery was "something to be hidden." She pledged: "We will no longer pretend that this place that is Sweet Briar College has always been a refined institution of higher learning. We will value deeply the facts of the matter—the importance of place, and of the origins of this college in a plantation worked by slave labor." She concluded her com-

Figure 9.2. Olivia Byrd, class of 2019, reads a Bible verse at the 2018 memorial service for the enslaved founders. Three descendants look on: Rev. Jasper Fletcher, Camica Fletcher, and Edith B. Jackson-Cabbell. Photograph by Cassie Foster, Sweet Briar College.

ments with a plea invoking the past: "Though they did not choose so
to labor, we pray that [those who lie buried here] would value what
the plantation has become, and stand as Co-Founders."[11] The statement
mirrors the sentiment of the Sweet Briar employee who, in 1935, referred to African Americans as "the colored founders" of Sweet Briar.

The ceremony was the culmination of my first two years of work
at Sweet Briar, as well as the contributions of community members
who had preserved the oral histories of African and Native American
families for generations. More than a decade earlier, a member of the
class of 1988 had documented another historic cemetery on campus.
A history student working on her senior project, Shela Silverman had
heard from a local resident that there was a forgotten slave cemetery
on campus. When she visited the site, Silverman observed it was being
used as a jumping course by the equestrian program. She witnessed
"a horse jump nailed to two trees, which, when jumped over, was directly over one of the four remaining granite markers that had been
used to mark the grave sites."[12] Disturbed by the irreverent use of the
site, she wrote to President Nenah Fry and the college chaplain. Eventually, word reached the head of the riding program, Paul Cronin, who
promptly removed the jumps, telling her there was another site with
notably spaced stones. Nothing was done at the time, but just before
Cronin retired in 2001, he invited two college officials—the dean of co-
curricular life, Valdrie Walker, and the college horticulturalist, Donna
Meeks—to visit the site with him.

As a newly hired professor at Sweet Briar that same year, I was in-
trigued by the existence of an antebellum burial ground. I had studied
New Hampshire cemeteries but knew nothing about the burial practices of enslaved families.[13] Accordingly, I partnered with archaeologists at James Madison University and the University of Virginia to
complete a map of the burial ground. Next, I designed a sign to help
visitors understand the mortuary landscape. Meanwhile, Dean Walker
worked with faculty, college trustees, and community members to plan
a spring "rededication." She reached out to descendants of the antebellum plantation community to solicit their comments about dedicat-
ing an on-campus slave cemetery, calling families with the last name
Fletcher in the local phone book. One of them was Rev. Jasper "Eddie"
Fletcher; many years later, my documentary research would lead me
to one of his ancestors, Lavinia Fletcher, an enslaved woman at Sweet
Briar. After Dean Walker had connected with one of the descendant
families, I printed brochures to guide visitors and the Sweet Briar
grounds staff volunteered dozens of hours to clear the overgrown site
for a ceremony in the spring of 2003.

As Dean Walker and I finalized the plans for an event to remember the enslaved workers, we weren't sure who would turn up or how it would be received by on- and off-campus constituents. We were relieved to see a large crowd on a Thursday evening in April 2003. Rev. Fletcher welcomed the group and shared that he had spent many decades sharing stories about his family history. Yet, even though he lived only six miles away, he had never visited campus before that day. On that spring day, Sweet Briar was years away from integrating the multiple strands of its history into an established ritual, but it was a beginning. After the ceremony, the guests were invited to a reception at the college museum, where two students had curated exhibitions about Elijah Fletcher and Daisy Williams. It was too early in our research to provide a more appropriate display related to the histories of the enslaved families.

That spring, I began a series of interviews with Rev. Fletcher that eventually led us to explore several other local cemeteries, connect with his extended family (and learn from their research), and work with another researcher, Bob Vernon, who helped uncover the documentary trail between an enslaved woman born in 1835 and the African American "Fletchers." Although the identities of those buried in the Sweet Briar graveyard remain unknown, I have tested several methods for studying these unmarked graves. One common archaeological approach to studying cemeteries is to prepare an aboveground survey to establish the perimeter of burials, drawing a map of the depressions and any surviving markers—and, perhaps, excavating some of the graves to establish the socioeconomic identities of the deceased. Centuries of excavations in burial grounds have demonstrated that we can learn a great deal from skeletal remains. In the case of antebellum burials of enslaved individuals, we can assess physical attributes from a careful study of human remains, namely their levels of stress, nutrition, disease, and diet.[14]

But these results come at a significant ethical cost: disturbing the bodies of men, women, and children, usually without the permission of direct descendants. Over fifteen years, I have led descendants from more than a dozen separate enslaved families at Sweet Briar on tours of the plantation burial ground. No one has disagreed with my initial decision to let these souls rest in peace. This may change in the future as private DNA testing increases in popularity.[15] Fifteen years ago, the argument for digging up skeletons to sample DNA to identify the mortuary population fell into the category of wishful thinking. True-crime accounts of identifying individuals from their DNA works only because there is a population available for comparison, such as a sample from a toothbrush provided by a known family member or, in the case of criminal investigations, state and national databases. Sampling DNA from individuals in the Sweet Briar burial ground would be useful only if dozens of potential descendants stepped forward to offer comparative samples.

The passage of time since the cemetery's rediscovery has led to advances in other techniques. In 2008, I worked with a graduate student at the University of Tennessee to use ground-penetrating radar (GPR) and gradiometry to see if there are additional unmarked burials at the site and how closely the surviving markers corresponded to belowground features. The GPR machine works by transmitting an electromagnetic signal (a high-frequency radar pulse) from a surface antenna into the ground. The machine measures the time between the transmission of the pulse and its reflection back from changes in the composition of the sediment. Any change in the consistency of the soil transmits back as a reflection. Accordingly, the holes dug for a grave, the pits left behind by fallen trees, or any other disturbances in the ground appear as a cluster of anomalies. But after walking the surface of the multi-acre site with the stroller-like carriage that held the recording device, we received minimal new information because of extensive non-mortuary disturbances from fallen trees and gopher holes, as well as from rock outcroppings just below the surface. Next, we tried gradiometry, using a machine to measure slight variations in the strength and direction of the earth's magnetic field. Here again, there was background "noise" — in this, case iron-rich soils — that interfered with clear results. The final verdict was "inconclusive results: can neither confirm nor refute existence of burials."[16]

The final archaeological method, other than excavation, would be to scrape the ground surface, digging down just a few inches to reveal any changes in the color or texture of the soil. This technique has been employed with a high degree of success in many US cemeteries. Once the topsoil is removed, graves are revealed by stains in the dirt that take the characteristic form of a roughly shaped oval or rectangle. For example, archaeologists used a small backhoe to carefully remove the topsoil associated with a long-lost graveyard used by a pre-twentieth-century community of free African American families in Albemarle County, Virginia. After clearing about three thousand square feet, the investigators exposed the outlines of at least fifty grave shafts.[17] A similar technique could be tried at Sweet Briar, although the uneven and rocky ground would make it difficult.

At Sweet Briar, in place of these archaeological techniques, I chose to map all visible aboveground depressions and markers, paying particularly close attention to the most convincing patterns, which included paired head and footstones. I then designed a brochure and a small on-site exhibition in the form of a twenty-six-by-twenty-six-inch interpretive panel to ensure that all visitors were informed about our findings. In all my ethnographic interviews with nearby residents and descendants, I asked a standard question: Has anyone in your family ever talked about a relative being buried at Sweet Briar? This was followed by inquiries into receipts from past mortuary rituals, such as funeral home bills, or a mention of pallbearers or bell ringers at a funeral. During years of asking these questions, I have found only one promising lead: an old photograph.

The 1930s black-and-white photograph features a college employee named Charlotte Wright and appears in the article about black workers at Sweet Briar College (chapter 8). Additional images featured eight other African American employees—men and women at work in clearly identifiable locales around campus. When I studied the portrait carefully, I realized Charlotte was dressed in mourning, wearing a black wimple and standing outdoors, far from any college buildings. Since the picture lacks a caption, I cannot prove the hypothesis that it shows Charlotte in the personal task of mourning her husband, but some tantalizing clues support it. Charlotte was about seventy-five years old in the photograph and had just lost her husband John Wright. In the accompanying article, the author reports that even though Charlotte had "more husbands than Chaucer's Wyf of Bathe," she was only able "to bury and wear mournin'" for one of them.[18] Was Charlotte photographed in mourning at the Sweet Briar slave cemetery, or elsewhere? Circumstantial evidence for the former is that all the other photographs in the article were taken on campus. The unnamed photographer was most likely the faculty author herself, or a student. Either way, it is highly unlikely that a white woman would have traveled away from Sweet Briar in 1935 to snap a picture of Charlotte Wright in a local graveyard. We may never have conclusive proof, but I believe this is an example of a named individual buried at the campus cemetery: John Wright. John and his brother, Joe Wright, both worked for Sweet Briar for decades. John was born around 1861, and he and his family were probably enslaved in Amherst County. He may very well be buried at Sweet Briar next to his parents.

It is difficult to determine exactly when this cemetery's location was lost to modern memory. In the 1950s, photographs show the site as a hayfield clearly demarcated by a ring of trees, just above a large lake that was popular with swimmers and boaters. But sometime in the intervening decades, the college stopped growing hay on that hilltop, and the site was quickly overgrown with trees and bushes. In 2008, five years after the cemetery was rededicated, the African American Fletcher descendants celebrated one of their family reunions. For the first time, they were able to include a commemorative ceremony for their ancestors at the cemetery. Rev. Jasper Fletcher led a traditional Christian prayer. Another relative—Washington, DC, resident Tracey Carter—led an impromptu libation ceremony. Inspired by her understanding of West African rituals, she encouraged everyone to take any liquids they had with them (water, even soda pop) and pour it onto the earth while calling out the names of ancestors, a means of reconsecrating the ground. She concluded: "It's the perfect place for a prayer of libation . . . We're on the gravesite of our ancestors."[19]

Through such rituals, deeply meaningful to the living, we hope the dead will never again be forgotten. While contemporary mortuary rituals at Sweet Briar may feature more prominently than at many other schools, a focus on understanding institutional connections to slavery has become increasingly common at American colleges and universities. Over the past two decades, more and more of these institutions of higher education have begun to address their role in the slave trade.

Most Northern universities were founded after slavery was abolished in the region but profited from it nonetheless. The founders of Brown University in Rhode Island, and several of the trustees and early donors of Dartmouth College in New Hampshire, earned money from the slave trade. The oldest institution of higher learning in the United States, Harvard University, founded in 1636, used enslaved labor to construct campus projects, attend to the daily needs of students and faculty, and provide funding from off-campus plantations owned by Harvard alumni. In 1781, years after slavery was outlawed in Massachusetts, Harvard Law School received its inaugural bequest at the death of a wealthy man, Isaac Royall Jr., whose family made its fortune in the slave trade and from a Caribbean sugar plantation.[20] In each of these instances, students, faculty, and staff have interrogated the archival records and conducted oral histories to retrieve the historical connections between their institutions of higher education and the system of slavery.[21] One of the first schools to recognize and study the connection between the institution and slavery was Yale University.

Yale's three hundredth anniversary in 2001 was marked by the revelations of three doctoral candidates in the Department of History. These junior scholars revealed that the institution had relied on money earned by slave traders for its first scholarships, endowed professorships, and even its library.[22] One author, a philosophy student, argued,

"Universities are first and foremost supposed to stand up for the truth." Accordingly, he and his colleagues suggested Yale set an example by frankly confronting its reliance on this tainted money and its continued celebration of many of those traders through the honorific naming of campus buildings, including eight of the ten residential colleges named for slave owners.[23] Watching the Yale story unfold during the year I arrived at Sweet Briar, I reflected that, for universities and colleges in the South, the legacy of slavery is even more direct. Many Southern campuses were built with forced labor by people enslaved on site or by slaves hired out from nearby plantation owners as blacksmiths, millers, and construction laborers. Even schools founded decades after slavery officially ended, like Sweet Briar, had financial and demographic origins in slavery.

In the years that followed, a dozen colleges and universities assessed their own roles in the institution of slavery. The anthropologist Mark Auslander carefully reviewed the financial and oral-historical evidence and concluded that Emory College was "deeply embedded in the structures and contradictions of a slavery-based society."[24] At Brown University, President Ruth Simmons appointed a Steering Committee on Slavery and Justice (SCSJ) to study her institution's multi-century relationship to the transatlantic slave trade and domestic slavery. The group quickly came to understand that some of Brown's founders and benefactors had used funds derived from the slave trade to benefit the university.[25] Over the past decade, the SCSJ has become a significant research center for the interdisciplinary study of slavery and its contemporary impacts.[26] While other Northern schools may have thought they had minimal or no connections to slavery, Craig Wilder's 2013 book, *Ebony and Ivy: Race, Slavery, and the Troubled History of America's Universities*, laid out multiple paths of complicity for institutions located north of the Mason Dixon line. After years of hunting down stray references in university archives, Wilder concluded that many of the nation's earliest colleges, along with churches and the state, were "the third pillar of a civilization based on bondage."[27]

In Virginia, several institutions came to a similar conclusion. In 2009, the College of William & Mary established a formal committee to research the seventeenth-century institution's connection to slavery and racial discrimination. The Board of Visitors, acknowledging that the college had "owned and exploited slave labor," endorsed the Lemon Project. Named after an enslaved man, the project is "a multifaceted and dynamic attempt to rectify wrongs perpetrated against African Americans by William & Mary through action or inaction."[28] Initially spearheaded by professors Jodi Allen and Terry Meyers, the Lemon

Project remains one of the most active centers in Virginia focused on studying, teaching, and commemorating the lives of enslaved laborers.

Other Virginia schools have addressed their troubled histories by gathering stories, by restoring antebellum buildings, and through other means. At the men's Hampden-Sydney College, a Sweet Briar alumna and former student of mine, Elizabeth Baker, created a blog called *The Untold Story*, contributing numerous essays and photographs about African Americans who once worked for the college or its antebellum predecessors. The blog format enabled Baker to share information with descendants, solicit feedback, and receive information from family historians. A hundred miles away, on Virginia Tech's campus, a log building associated with an old plantation still stands alongside a scenic lake. The cabin predates the 1872 acquisition of the property by the school. In 2015, Professor Elizabeth Fine submitted a proposal to the Virginia Foundation for the Humanities to assemble a team of consultants and members of the local African American community to create an exhibition about the structure to highlight the rich African American history of the area.[29] I joined colleagues from nearby historic sites (Carla Whitfield, the superintendent of the Booker T. Washington National Monument) and institutions (Lauranett Lee, then the curator of African American history at the Virginia Historical Society) to discuss creating a dynamic exhibition in the space.

Many other Virginia colleges and universities have commissioned studies, conducted archaeological work, or mounted online resources to document and disseminate their institutions' investment in slavery, while others have tried reaching out to their communities. In 2013, the president of the University of Virginia, Theresa Sullivan, appointed a task force to explore the university's "historical relationship with slavery and enslaved people." In an effort to include community members in research and events planning, she formed the President's Commission on Slavery and the University (PCSU). I served on a local community advisory board for that effort until 2018, when the first stage of research and outreach culminated in a report and a series of recommendations.[30] One of our first tasks was to plan a commemorative event to honor the individuals buried in a recently rediscovered graveyard. In October 2012, a construction crew began work on a planned expansion of the historic University of Virginia Cemetery and Columbarium. They were surprised to learn there were graves outside a stone wall that university officials thought marked the outer perimeter of the cemetery. Instead, archaeologists confirmed sixty-seven additional grave shafts.[31] After additional archival research was conducted, the team concluded that the graves belonged to African Americans who once worked for the university, many of whom were most likely enslaved. One October night in 2014, more than 150 people lit candles and walked through the cemetery, joining to pour libations over the graves and observe a moment of silence. Before the graveyard procession, the crowd gathered under a makeshift tent to listen to speakers, hear a poem written for the occasion by Brenda Marie Osbey, and receive a eulogy by a local pastor.

University of Virginia faculty members continue to research and publish information about slavery at "Thomas Jefferson's University." They have hosted a "cornerstone institute" for high school students wanting to learn more about this history, and named two new buildings in honor of formerly enslaved workers: Skipwith Hall (named after Peyton Skipwith, an enslaved stonemason) and Gibbons House (after William and Isabella Gibbons, enslaved by two University of Virginia professors).[32] In 2017, the university announced approval of a design for a memorial to enslaved laborers referred to as the Freedom Ring. This is the capstone to work begun by undergraduates more than a decade ago, when they held a design competition and raised money from on-campus social groups. The newly designed memorial to enslaved laborers will replace an earlier one: in 2010, the university placed a small, discreet marker at the base of the Rotunda, a World Heritage site with complicated design restrictions, that read, "In honor of the several hundred women and men, both free and enslaved, whose labor between 1817 and 1826 helped to realize Thomas Jefferson's design for the University of Virginia." This modest, one-by-four-foot slate slab failed to satisfy the students, and the PCSU eventually espoused their goal to create a more significant memorial.[33] In August 2018, the university set aside $2.5 million from its Strategic Investment Fund to match private donations in order to construct a newly designed Memorial to Enslaved Laborers. This design, which incorporates input from students, the University of Virginia community, and the broader Charlottesville community, features a raised wall that encircles an area roughly equivalent to the famed University of Virginia Rotunda. An inner wall will include the names of enslaved individuals that have come to light after years of research. The memorial's construction began in January 2019.[34]

Ongoing debates on many campuses focus on when and how to rename structures that honor former slaveholders. In some cases, community members feel they have been consulted only as a courtesy, without having an opportunity to craft and implement ideas. Sweet Briar, along with other institutions of higher education, continues to seek the best balance between community outreach and institutional

188 • *Invisible Founders*

values. At Sweet Briar, one building was renamed after the longtime African American employee Dorothy Jones Sales (1924–2004). The building had served as a bookstore for years but in 2005 was converted into an academic building to be used by the education department, and named after Dorothy. She was one of Sterling Jones's children and a college employee for more than fifty years. After her first marriage to Basil Jordan ended in divorce, she married George W. Sales. Unfortunately, her married name has led to some confusion, since the shortened name, Sales Building, sounds like a business department.[35] The symbolism behind the act of renaming seems to have faded as, in the thirteen years since her death, fewer and fewer faculty and staff remember her, let alone her long-dead relative. It is, of course, unrealistic to expect students to know the names and stories of all past staff members.

After more than fifteen years of reclaiming and commemoration at Sweet Briar, there is much to celebrate. As on other campuses, our early efforts to address the subject of slavery fell into three broad categories: research, community outreach, and one-time memorializations or installations of a statue or marker. However, even after hundreds of hours of research, tens of thousands of dollars spent on memorialization, and countless time spent in discussion on and off campus, the impact of these efforts will fade if the community fails to remember its dead. A statue erected for all the right reasons will lose its impact if its symbolism is forgotten. This scenario can be seen on every college campus when students, faculty, and staff walk past old monuments or forget the origins of institutional names.

In addition to honorific building titles, Sweet Briar has instituted several annual awards named after important members of the college community. These gifts, and the accompanying ceremonies and press coverage, provide an opportunity to explain name origins and recognize individual contributions. For example, the Shirley Reid Award for Excellence is named after a librarian who worked for more than fifty years at Sweet Briar and whose grandparents were enslaved by Elijah Fletcher. Her surname dates back to a white man named John Read who bought land in Amherst County in the early eighteenth century. In 1764, he gave 115 acres along the James River to his son Alexander.[36] The first use of the surname by African American families may date to this time. By the late 1800s, dozens of African American families in Amherst County used this family name. In 1954, just as the Kansas School Board won its case against the federal government in the *Brown v. Board of Education* decision, Shirley Pendleton Reid joined Sweet Briar College as a housekeeper in the library.

I first met Shirley the way many Sweet Briar students and faculty did: at the interlibrary loan desk. By the time I arrived in 2001, she was already a legend. She had worked for the college for nearly five decades and was exceptionally good at tracking down hard-to-find titles. One day in 2004, a colleague, the classics professor Judy Evans-Grubbs, knowing of my research interests, told me she had just found out Shirley was a direct descendent of "Jimbo" and "Nicey." Because of my active efforts to locate descendants of the enslaved community, I immediately recognized these names from Elijah Fletcher's 1852 will. I assumed Shirley was a distant descendant, many generations removed. Years later, as I returned to reconstructing the family trees of the enslaved community and their descendants for this book, I found a "Shirley" in the records easily enough. She was born in 1937, so she was listed in the recently released 1940 Census (the bureau withholds details of census interviews for seventy years to protect the privacy of the living). She was the youngest of eleven children born to James and Elizabeth Pendleton.

Her father, James, was born in 1887, just two decades after the end of the Civil War, amid Virginia's divisive period of Reconstruction and black disenfranchisement. His parents were James (Jimbo) and Nicey. Shirley was not a distant descendant of enslaved individuals; Jimbo and Nicey were her own grandparents. She was only two generations removed from a man and woman who had been held in bondage at the very site where she worked. When I tell people that a percentage of today's Sweet Briar staff members are descended from members of its enslaved community, I am met with disbelief. But after a few moments, my listeners usually nod their collective heads and reply something along the lines of, "Well, yes, that makes sense, doesn't it?" But when I begin to outline the very few generations—just two or three, in some cases—that connect some of the housekeepers, physical plant workers, groundskeepers, and other employees to that seemingly distant past, they are floored. Shirley Reid passed away in 2017, just a few years after she retired, after fifty-three years as a Sweet Briar employee.

Across the highway from Sweet Briar, on land owned by the college, the Virginia Center for the Creative Arts (VCCA) recently began a funding campaign to support the Robert Johnson Fellowship. The VCCA was originally housed in the historic Mt. San Angelo before the building burned down in the 1970s. Today, recently built dormitories and dining areas have been constructed on the site of the ruin, but the tradition of African American families working on the land continues. Robert Johnson's great-great-great-grandfather was Septimus Johnson. This unusual first name appears in the list of Indiana's share of her father's human property in association with those of two other children—Milly and Amanda—and a woman named Mary who, based on her proximity on the list, is probably their mother. In 1869, when Septimus married Susan Edwards, he listed his parents as Henry and Mary Johnson. Robert was therefore the fourth generation of Johnsons to work at Sweet Briar or its affiliated plantations. On the fellowship fund-raising page, organizer Alonzo Davis wrote that Robert "left no facet of the VCCA untouched by his special blend of charm, wit, and grace." He also listed some of his talents: "caregiver, chef, host, driver, and poker player extraordinaire."[37] Johnson died in 2006 and even now, eleven years later, his friends and colleagues hope to preserve his memory.

In this chapter, I am encouraging community members to find new ways to commemorate the lives of extraordinary individuals. I specifically want to discuss nontraditional means for remembering the dead and their contributions. In addition to the standard options—writing newspaper articles, making speeches at college events, or compiling research into books—Sweet Briar's history has been featured in more creative means of communication, including a play, family histories, ghost stories, and a children's book.

In 2012, the local Endstation Theatre Company joined Sweet Briar and the VCCA to host a competition to encourage playwrights to use local history as inspiration. Tearrance Chisholm won and decided to write about the college's complex past. On one of his first visits, I gave him a tour of the campus slave cemetery. Over the next year, I met with him several times, touring the college archives and sharing some of the archival information and stories of individuals I had uncovered over the years. Using those pieces of information, this gifted playwright crafted a clever, original, and eloquent script based on a fictional character: the first black tenured professor at Sweet Briar. On 5 August 2014, Chisholm directed *In Sweet Remembrance* on the stage of the eight-hundred-seat college auditorium. The responses to this fictional story based on Sweet Briar's complicated racial past demonstrated that this history still resonates with the community.

Chisholm's play did not tread lightly through Sweet Briar's difficult past. It imagined a black scientist, Diana Singer, who had no interest in her own family roots, only the scientific method. But she increasingly experiences hard-to-explain mirages, memories, and visitations from the African American employees from Sweet Briar's past. Following the model of Charles Dickens's *A Christmas Carol*, Diana is visited by the ghosts of Martha Taylor and others, who challenge her beliefs about herself, her present, and her values. The production featured difficult scenes like one chronologically juxtaposing an antebellum slave auction with a contemporary "slave for a day" fund-raising event held by a fictionalized Sweet Briar student club. When the only African American member of the club protests the event, she is ostracized by her peers and goes to the new faculty member for support. To the student's disappointment, Diana tells her she is overreacting. Surprising twists like this made the two-hour play very emotional. In the script, Chisholm wrote, "It's as if the walls, the floors, the very earth [at Sweet Briar] have memory."

Just as riveting was the campus reaction to the full production of the play. While an earlier practice read-through in the spring had not been particularly controversial, the two-hour onstage performance elicited strong responses. The play was not an attempt to belittle or insult Sweet Briar, Chisholm explained: "My goals for the piece were to initiate a dialogue that would begin to unearth some of the issues concerning minority students and staffing. I hoped the play would be a bridge into addressing the amount of diversity on campus."[38] The result was a complex study of what it means to be African American in the academy today and how our past is always with us, whether we choose to acknowledge it or not.

Because of the actors' schedules, the play was held at the very beginning of the school year as one of the welcoming activities for the 2014 incoming students. As with any freshman class, first-year students are the least vested in Sweet Briar traditions and had little background for comprehending the sophisticated messages Chisholm hoped to convey. The play left the seventeen- and eighteen-year-olds in the audience, having undergone several days of introductory activities, college paperwork, and a performance that lasted until 10 p.m. on a Wednesday, bewildered. Some of the black students wondered if they had just signed up for four years of racial tension, while some of the white students couldn't understand why they had to watch a play about African Americans at Sweet Briar.

Then, provocative signs appeared on dorm water fountains, reading "Colored" and "White Only." Most people assumed this was a racist action, akin to writing the N-word on a bathroom stall. I had my doubts. Having taught elements of civil rights history for more than a decade to college students who were born two or three decades after Martin Luther King Jr. was killed, I suspected most white students were not aware of historically accurate Jim Crow terminology. But the story didn't end there. Several weeks before the play opened, a white police officer had killed an unarmed black teenager in Ferguson, Missouri. The murder of Michael Brown (1996–2014) provoked protests throughout the country. On 3 September, a month after the play debuted, two unidentified men called Sweet Briar and demanded "justice." They asked, "Who is the white girl that did this? [placed the sign on the water fountain]" and ended the brief call with "Ferguson and not this. Hands up! Don't shoot!" and "We're coming up there. We want justice." For the first time in its history, Sweet Briar activated an emergency system and went into lockdown for almost an hour. I was teaching class that day. When I first heard the alarm, I checked my phone for a weather update, expecting that a cataclysmic disturbance like a tornado or a hurricane was bearing down on us. Instead, for several dozen tense minutes, I stayed by the door, telling my students to huddle far away in a corner. I had no idea how to prevent someone from coming through the locked door, but felt I had to take some measures, however inadequate, to protect my class.

My initial instinct about the identity of the sign maker proved correct. After days of campus and community backlash, an African American woman came forward and admitted she had created the signs in an effort to promote discussion. This student argued she was well within her First Amendment rights to post the signs to continue the thought-provoking discussion stimulated by the play. The anonymous phone callers were never identified. After a few weeks, the tension surrounding the performance and subsequent lockdown dissipated. In fact, discussion ended so completely that, at the time, I considered it likely that several more years would pass before the campus community would be willing to openly discuss the history of slavery at Sweet Briar.

In 2018–2019, the Sweet Briar student body is 27 percent nonwhite, several people of color hold senior administrative positions, and the college has just hired its first tenure-track African American faculty member. And yet, among the dozens of black employees at Sweet Briar who are direct descendants of the enslaved community, almost all are in minimum wage, hourly jobs. None are professors, administrators, or other high-ranking or highly paid members of the Sweet Briar community. We still have a great deal of work to do to address and rectify the socioeconomic inequalities enforced by decades of slavery at Sweet Briar and subsequent injustices institutionalized during the Jim Crow era.

No story about the legacy of slavery would be complete without two other protagonists: ghosts and story keepers. Tales of "haints" have provided an unusual but important vehicle for remembering aspects of the plantation era at Sweet Briar. Stories about the supernatural reveal just as much about the living as they do about the dead. Whether you believe in spirits or not, storytellers reveal their own values by attempting to make sense of the chaotic. The cultural historian Tiya Miles suggests that today's obsession with the return of the dead, or "ghost fancy," as she calls it, is "a cultural tsunami fed by . . . reality and dramatic TV series about ghosts and other undead creatures (vampires, zombies, demons); local paranormal hobbyist groups; books; websites; social media spaces; and a plethora of ghost tours."[39]

More than a third of Americans say they believe in ghosts. This figure was likely higher in the last quarter of the nineteenth century, as spiritualism began to increase in popularity and newspapers contained regular accounts of ethereal sightings. One scholar, Peter Underwood, attempted to classify these apparitions into more specific, functional categories: elementals, poltergeists, historical ghosts, mental imprint manifestations, death-survival ghosts, apparitions, time slips, ghosts of the living, and haunted inanimate objects.[40] Why such diversity? Why not just believe that the souls of the dead return to teach us, warn us, or simply visit us? As the psychology professor Christopher French explains: "What we have is people trying to make sense of something that, to them, seems inexplicable. . . . So you get the misinterpretation of noises or visual effects that do have a normal explanation, but not one that people can think of. People assume that if they cannot explain something in natural terms, then it must be something paranormal."[41]

At Sweet Briar, events that seemed inexplicable to the community included Daisy's death, the fate of some of Indiana's family fortune after she died, and the identity of a skeleton found buried under an old hearth in Sweet Briar House. Many of the college's ghost stories date to the 1910s and 1920s, a period of instability as the new institution struggled to invent itself and attract a large base of students. During these uncertain years, students reported seeing the ghosts of Indiana and Daisy, not as frightening apparitions but rather as benevolent spirits who watched over the college. For some descendants of the enslaved, the stories took a different turn. One black messenger named Earnest who worked at the college in the 1910s was "heard often to murmer [sic] as he entered the walk [up to Sweet Briar house] 'Miss Indy, if you do nothin' to me, I'll do nothin' to you.'"[42] This reminded me of admonitions I heard frequently when studying historic African American cemeteries. Informants would tell me about a family graveyard and offer to take me. But when we arrived on site, they would caution me about crossing the boundary from profane to sacred ground. Miles recalls her great-grandmother's warning, "Never cross water," which Miles interprets to mean, "There is a line between the spirit realm and our realm. It is fluid. Beware."[43]

These stories might seem benign or even trivial, but Miles's detailed study of "ghost tours" at Southern plantations and museums reveals that ghost stories sometimes represent biographies of enslaved African Americans that were used by "a commercial industry that seemed to be piggybacking on black culture through the vehicle of the ghost tour."[44] In the case of Sweet Briar's ghosts, there has been little economic profit from these stories, but the emphasis on the white ghosts of those who founded and continue to care for the college from the grave reinforces the invisibility of people of color.

In reclaiming the once-hidden history of black family relationships at Sweet Briar, several descendants have written their own accounts. Some, like the librarian Shirley Reid, have compiled family genealogies and collections of family tales they have shared with their own relatives. Shirley carefully documented her connection to Jimbo and Nicey and presented the manuscript to her family members.

A fictionalized account was written by an alumna and descendant of the enslaved community, Barbara Rose Page. One of her ancestors was Givens Rose, the former confederate soldier who lived to be 102 years old. Barbara graduated from Sweet Briar College in 1983, at the age of forty-one, and lives about ten miles away from the college in Piney River (Nelson County). After retiring, she turned to writing. One of her first publications, based on her memories of her grandfather and aunts, was the children's book *Annie's Trip to Grandma's*, illustrated by another Sweet Briar graduate, Karla Murray. In the book, Barbara's great-uncle Jasper Rose (1882–1973)[45] takes his four daughters (Annie, Helen, Mary, and Julia) to visit his mother (Barbara's great-grandmother), Malinda Cashwell. Jasper's brother, Arthur Rose, was Barbara's grandfather. Arthur, in turn, married Josephine Bowling and had a son named Samuel C. Rose, who married Theresa "Tessie" Morse and raised a daughter, Barbara. Confused? Only a handful of relatives would know the precise connection between the author and the main character, Jasper, to follow the story.

But all of us can benefit from the insight this slim volume provides into black lives in the early 1900s. Barbara relates aspects of daily farm life, which is probably foreign to many of her grandchildren, nieces, and nephews. This rural black family planted corn; raised chickens, roosters, and pigs; and made their own woven chairs. Some of the men in the Rose family were skilled blacksmiths. When matching the genealogical information provided in the book with my own research, I realized the "granddaddy" in the story had a real-life counterpart in Moses Rose, a man enslaved at Sweet Briar. He was born around 1840 and probably learned his smithing skills while enslaved on the plantation. Working backward in time, it appeared very likely that Moses's parents, Daniel (1812–1881) and Pamelia (ca. 1825–1930) Rose were owned by Indiana's sister, Elizabeth. Daniel's parents were Moses (born ca. 1795) and Mary (born ca. 1800) Rose. While these are common first names, one of the children enslaved at Tusculum in the early 1800s was named Moses; his father was Ned, who would have been born around 1770, making him a contemporary of Rev. Robert Rose, one of the early white settlers in Amherst. Barbara Rose Page may be the sixth or seventh generation of African American "Roses" who trace their local roots back to the mid-eighteenth century. Fittingly, Barbara dedicated her book in part "to my grandchildren and to all children who love to read stories."[46] This method of recording family history in a format suitable for younger generations to enjoy and remember helps ensure that future generations will grow up hearing these stories.

Another story being preserved is that of Martha Penn Taylor, who played such a pivotal role in the Fletcher family for generations, living long enough to work for the college as a cook. One of her descendants, Audrey Lopez, wrote to me in 2012: "I recently began researching my family tree when I discovered several of your websites featuring Martha Penn Taylor. I was happy to find that she is my great great great grandmother." We began to share notes and continue adding missing pieces of the puzzle to Martha's story. Audrey is drafting a family history, which she plans to present to her family.

Among the African American story makers of Sweet Briar, Signora Smith Hollins stands out for her intriguing and prolific tales. Born around 1866, she lived to be one of the last people who knew Daisy Williams. A critical look at her life history through multiple lenses illustrates many of the themes of this book. The college-focused version of her life centers on Signora as a conduit to information about Daisy. Stories from her neighbors, still circulating today, suggest that she dabbled in black magic. And then there is her own carefully constructed autobiography, curated over decades. The best-known version of her life was written by Sweet Briar authors. As a longtime college employee and an interesting personality, she was often interviewed by students and faculty members. M. Dee Long's 1935 article singled her out as "first among 'the colored founders' of Sweet Briar."[47]

In a practice reminiscent of slave owners who erected gravestones or saved photographs for a small number of "faithful slaves," Signora, along with Sterling Jones, was often honored in paternalistic or racist terms. In 1936, for instance, the head of the music department wrote an essay about the "Early Days at Sweet Briar." Remembering the college's first years, Helen Young wrote of the "delectable delicacies as beaten biscuit, batter bread, Virginia ham, etc. prepared by Signora, the cook, of happy memory."[48] Presumably, the author meant her own, pleasant memories, because Signora lost her husband right around that time. In the same year, the Cleveland Alumnae Club designed a "Daisy and Signora" doll to raise money, based on the once popular "double doll," a cloth toy depicting a white girl on one end and—if the doll is turned upside down and inside out—a black girl on the other. "Daisy" wore a print dress, while "Signora" was clothed in a darker dress, her hair covered by a bandana (Figure 9.3).[49]

Throughout the college's early years, a handful of black employees were chosen to participate in cornerstone-laying ceremonies for new buildings. In 1932, when the Daisy Williams Gymnasium was built, a cluster of students gathered around an imposing figure in front of the elaborate brick arched windows and the half-built white pilasters. Signora Hollins stood in front of the unfinished entrance wearing her black derby hat and an elegant pleated coat, carrying her trusted cane. Accounts from that day describe her comments, which took the form of a eulogy for the long-departed Daisy.

When Signora died in 1954, the college posted an obituary entitled "Daisy Williams' Negro Playmate Succumbs at 88." An elderly wom-

Figure 9.3. A "Daisy and Signora" doll made by Sweet Briar alumnae to raise money for the college in 1936. *The Alumnae News* [Sweet Briar College] 6, no. 2 (1936): 13. Sweet Briar College Library Archives.

an's obituary doesn't often focus on her childhood playmate, but the college prioritized Signora's role as "the last of those who knew and loved the little girl in whose memory Sweet Briar was founded." The rest of the short biography surmised that Indiana sent Signora away after Daisy's death because she couldn't stand the sight of a living child her daughter's age, briefly sketching her career as a housekeeper and refectory worker "for a time."[50] In other words, Signora's most notable accomplishments revolved around her connection to Daisy Williams. For decades, Signora's only role in college histories was to serve as a mouthpiece for yet more "founding myths" about Daisy and her mother.

But after years of taking these tales at face value, I realized something didn't add up. Extensive genealogical research provided further information about Signora's parents. Her mother, Phoebe Cousins, was a free woman of color from nearby Fluvanna County. Her biological father was an enslaved man, Joshua Smith, who did not live with the family. Signora claimed her aunt Rosa had cooked for Indiana, which was where and when she met Daisy. This might be true, but her claims do not match other pieces of documentary evidence such as census records. In 1870, the census recorded a young Signora, along with her brother, Frederic, in her mother's household in Harris Creek, several miles away from Sweet Briar. They lived with a white woman named Caroline Roberts, for whom Phoebe worked as a domestic servant. Ten years later, Frederic and Signora were living with their stepfather, Samuel Euille, in Elon, which is also located far from Sweet Briar.

The census, of course, provides only a small window into the everyday lives of Amherst residents. Signora described how she fished, swam, and picked flowers with Daisy when they were children.[51] Based on Signora's chronological framing of these events, they should have occurred in the 1870s. Perhaps it was between 1870 and 1880 that Signora joined her aunt Rosa at Sweet Briar, or only during the summers when Daisy was home from New York City. Yet, Daisy never mentioned Signora or Aunt Rosa in her diaries or letters, even though we have years' worth of daily diary entries and the occasional letter to Martha Taylor asking for and relating local gossip. Signora's version of events implies she was either playing with or taking care of Daisy until the sickly girl's death in 1884. Yet, she does not figure in Daisy's 1880–1881 diaries or in the diaries and letters that covered May 1882 through December 1883.

Signora's tales of life at Sweet Briar in the 1880s take a fascinating turn after Daisy's death. She relates how Indiana asked her and another servant to carry food and mail to Daisy's grave. No sources corroborate this story beyond Signora's own memories. Returning to documentary records, we learn that, five years after Daisy's death, Signora married a man named Tobias Hollins. While Signora claims Indiana sent her away to the North sometime after Daisy's death, the first record of Signora in the North is much later, in the 1897 city directory for Amherst, Massachusetts. There, Signora is listed as a "domestic" for a Mrs. R. G. Williams. Interestingly, although she was far from home, Signora worked alongside another African American woman from Amherst, Virginia: Alice Hollins, a relative of her husband's.

Between 1909 and her death in 1954, Signora was well-known as someone who could "talk by the hour of the olden days." This included various tellings of her own story: how Signora struggled to save money after she was sent to Massachusetts. After more than a decade away, she left her position as a maid to rejoin her husband and accepted offer of a job to cook at Sweet Briar College. In that role she was famous for her "delectable delicacies [such] as beaten biscuit, batter bread, [and] Virginia ham." During this time she and her husband owned a farm in Amherst. After her husband died in 1914, she moved in with her brother, Frederic Smith. After his death in 1946, she lived out her days in a small shack in Coolwell, just down the hill from Crab Apple Lane. She died of esophageal cancer in the summer of 1954.[52] Two years later, she could be seen in a promotional movie designed to attract students to Sweet Briar.[53] The footage had been taken during the last year of her life.

After her death, the college burnished Signora's memory because of her connection to Daisy, glossing over her father's enslavement and the financial exigencies that required her to live and work apart from her husband for many years. It also kept a lid on the other stories about Signora, tales that are hard to pin down today because even now, half a century after her death, few of her former neighbors feel comfortable talking about her. As one college employee and Crab Apple Lane resident explained to me, "When I was a kid, I was afraid of her." As a child, this neighbor would visit Signora's house only when accompanied by a sibling, recalling the disturbing presence of snakes inside the home. She remembered Signora "putting a snake on you" and keeping them as pets. Other Coolwell residents claimed she "crawled on her belly like a snake." My informant added that "Miss Sig" ate red clay, especially after it rained. When I asked her why, she thought it had to do with a "heart condition," but it sounds like a symptom of schizophrenia or obsessive-compulsive disorder, two mental health conditions associated with pica, a condition that causes the sufferer to eat unusual substances lacking nutritional value.

Signora was one of Sweet Briar's first ethnographers. Not only had she known Daisy and "Miss Indie," but she was strategic about which stories to share with her white audience, helping shape a century's worth of memories about this mother/daughter pair. Many of her stories revolved around ghosts. In this sense, Signora's tales mirror a larger narrative theme that was common throughout the South. In one ethnographic calculation, more than 50 percent of formerly enslaved Southerners who were interviewed by the researchers in the Slave Narratives from the Federal Writers' Project reported believing in and/or seeing a "haunt."[54] Signora's "ghost stories" reveal her superstitions, as well as invaluable historic information. In one of her accounts, she reported that, the day before the college opened (in 1906), she came out of the faculty apartments, where she was working as a cook, and found Indiana waiting for her. Signora was well aware Indiana had been dead for six years but claimed she "thought nothing about it." Miss Indie, Signora continued, was wearing her "usual black skirt and white shirtwaist" (meaning she wasn't spectral), and the pair walked together toward campus. When they came into sight of the former slave cabin, Indiana, presumably disoriented by the new college buildings, asked "where the iron gate was to Amelia's house"—a reference to the cabin behind the main house where Amelia and Logan Anderson had once lived—and "where was Daisy's pony." Signora was unable to answer her questions. This is the only record of an iron gate standing between the "big house" and the former "slave cabin." It's hard to know how to cite that piece of information in future reports: "personal communication, Indiana Williams," or "Signora, informant"? During this same encounter, Signora said Indiana told her about money buried in three locations: "behind the well under a large flat rock at the end of the well drain," on the "other side of the boxwood hedge" near Daisy's hitching post, and "under an old pine tree that is a stump now near a large white rock on the hill across the field from the lake."[55] It isn't clear whether a search was ever mounted for the hidden treasures.

Signora saw Indiana on a second occasion, as the ghost walked through the Sweet Briar College Refectory, apparently viewing the yet-to-be opened college buildings. In both sightings, it is as if Indiana is surveying and approving of the school her money created. What a useful story for Signora to contribute! And while it isn't clear when Signora started sharing these tales, she was firmly in place as a campus storyteller and legend by 1931 when she was asked to place the cornerstone for the newly completed Daisy Williams Gymnasium. The last time Signora recalled seeing Indiana was in the fall of 1916, on the ten-year anniversary of the college's opening. Indiana continued her efforts to reveal the location of hidden money. This time, she told Signora, "Her silver was buried in a wall in Sweet Briar House—sealed up in the wall on the landing of the front staircase." Unlike the first three locations, this one appears to have been correct. In 2001, Ann Whitley, the college curator and unofficial historian, claimed, "College carpenters opened the wall: the silver was indeed there." Whitley continued, quoting Signora from an unnamed source that might be a 1953 interview: "It was wrapped up in three paper packages and they were black with dirt. The spoons looked like gold and I don't know what happened to it after that."[56] Did this really happen? Either way, Signora Hollins is enshrined in college histories as a source of expert knowledge about Daisy and Indiana. And sightings of Indiana and Daisy continue to this day, though without any further leads as to the locations of hidden treasures.

In her compelling book about the craft of writing, Elizabeth Sims reminds us of what, at the core, a hero is. A hero isn't only someone who saves a person from a burning building or a firefighter who talks a young person out of committing suicide. Instead, the Greeks and Romans defined a hero as someone whose "deeds were so extraordinary that he was elevated by the gods to a place above human level."[57] Heroes take dramatic risks, sacrifice themselves, and push themselves beyond their perceived limits. I can think of no more powerful heroes than the parents who persisted in raising their children under the horror of human ownership.

Part of my purpose in writing *Invisible Founders* is to enlarge the definition and knowledge regarding Sweet Briar's heroes. In 2001, on the centennial anniversary of the college's founding, *Sweet Briar Alumnae Magazine* published several retrospective articles.[58] Each summarized the catalysts for and methods through which the college was created. Each generation of Fletchers was described as more compelling than the last. Elijah was born in poverty and rose to riches, passing down his plantation to his children. His daughter Indiana inherited Sweet Briar and managed agricultural and business deals that few of her female contemporaries pursued. Indiana, in turn, had only one child, precocious Daisy, who returned to campus as a spirit to encourage Sweet Briar students. A tidy, multigenerational story, with male and female heroes, young and old protagonists, and a happy ending: a nationally acclaimed institution of higher education for women.

But beyond each of these well-lauded individuals are hundreds of unsung heroes. In addition to the dozens of African and Native Americans discussed in this book, hundreds more contributed to the growth and success of Sweet Briar, first as a plantation and then as a college. It is important to commemorate those lives and to remember heroes such as Martha Taylor, whose persistence kept her family intact; Signora Hollins, who defied racial boundaries to gain a modicum of respect and status in a segregated, postslavery world; Nelson Tinsley, who fought tooth and nail to reclaim his own children; and many more. Their lives, and our efforts to reconstruct their family trees almost a century later, are but a few compelling examples of the roots that stretch deep below the standard stories of Sweet Briar's founding families.

The cultural practice of remembering—as well as its powerful corollary, forgetting—is influenced by many factors, including the force of nostalgia. While most Sweet Briar alumnae and current students know elements of the Fletcher family history and contributions, few can name a single African American resident of the plantation. This is despite a ratio of, roughly, one white Fletcher descendant to twenty or more people of color during much of the plantation's operation. Telling their stories and enacting rituals to remember them, translating history into contemporary actions, is our best chance at preventing the slide into obscurity of our founders—so that they are invisible no longer.

Notes

1. Shackel, *Memory in Black and White*, 11.
2. Indiana Fletcher Williams's will, 2.
3. Rainville, *Hidden History*, 129–30.
4. "On the Campus," *The Alumnae News* [Sweet Briar College] 13, no. 2 (1938): 14.
5. *The Briar-Patch 1910*, edited by the Senior Class of Sweet Briar College (Sweet Briar, VA: Sweet Briar College, 1910), 121.
6. Rozelle, "Daisy's Vision," 145.
7. "Service Includes Several Addresses on Founders' Day," *Sweet Briar News*, 31 October 1928, 1, 4.
8. "Founders' Day," *The Alumnae Magazine* [Sweet Briar College] 4, no. 2 (1934): 13.
9. Valentine, "From the Alumnae President," 5.
10. Posted on "You went to Sweet Briar College if . . ." Facebook page, 6 December 2016.
11. "Sweet Briar Plantation Burial Ground Dedication Ceremony," *Sweet Briar Alumnae Magazine* 75, no. 1 (2003): 43.
12. Silverman, "A Description of Some Rituals at Sweet Briar College," 62.
13. Rainville, "Hanover Deathscapes."
14. Blakey, "Bioarchaeology of the African Diaspora in the Americas."
15. "DNA Testing Provides Shortcut to Trace Family History," *Morning Edition*, 6 January 2016, http://www.npr.org/2016/01/06/462114359/dna-testing-provides-short-cut-to-trace-family-history.

16. "Sweet Briar College Geophysical Survey Results." Unpublished report submitted by Palmyra A. Moore (then an ABD student at the University of Tennessee), 11 January 2007.

17. Bowles family cemetery. Thompson, *Phase II Archaeological Evaluations*, 26.

18. Lee, "Our Colored Folks," 14.

19. Ramsey, "Fletcher Family Comes Full Circle."

20. Beckert and Stevens, *Harvard and Slavery*, 7.

21. Examples of published works by groups at universities and colleges studying slavery include Harvard (Beckert and Stevens, *Harvard and Slavery*), Northern institutions (Wilder, *Ebony and Ivy*), Georgetown University (*Report of the Working Group on Slavery, Memory, and Reconciliation*), Furman (*Seeking Abraham*), Rutgers (Fuentes and White, *Scarlet and Black*), University of Virginia (Martin, von Daacke, and Faulkner, *President's Commission on Slavery and the University: Report to President Teresa A. Sullivan*), and Clemson (*The African American Experience at Fort Hill*).

22. Dugdale et al., *Yale, Slavery and Abolition*.

23. Zernike, "Slave Traders in Yale's Past Fuel Debate on Restitution."

24. Auslander, "Other Side of Paradise."

25. "Steering Committee on Slavery and Justice," Brown University, accessed 14 January 2019, http://www.brown.edu/Research/Slavery_Justice.

26. "Center for the Study of Slavery and Justice," Brown University, accessed 14 January 2019, https://www.brown.edu/initiatives/slavery-and-justice.

27. Wilder, *Ebony and Ivory*, 11.

28. "The Lemon Project: A Journey of Reconciliation," College of William & Mary, accessed 9 January 2019, http://www.wm.edu/sites/lemonproject/

29. Fine, "Developing Interpretive Plan of African American History for the Log Outbuilding."

30. University of Virginia, *President's Commission on Slavery and the University*.

31. Rivanna Archaeology Services, *Beyond the Walls*, 39.

32. Bromley, "UVA Building Named for Former Slave"; Bromley, "New U.VA. Residence Hall, Gibbons House, Named for Former Slave Couple."

33. Clemons, "Students Want Larger Slave Memorial at UVA"; Bromley, "Design of UVA Memorial to Enslaved Laborers Wins Approval."

34. Bromley, "Work on Memorial to Enslaved Laborers Gets Underway."

35. The inscription on the building is Dorothy Sales Building, but few use the complete name in conversation.

36. "Reid, Alexander," George Samuel Reid Family Roots, accessed 7 January 2019, https://imareid.com/research-files/surnames/read-reed-reede-reid/reid-alexander.

37. A. Davis, "Robert Johnson VCCA Fellowship."

38. Kershner, "Art in a Complex World."

39. Miles, *Tales from the Haunted South*, 2.

40. Cited in Clarke, *Ghosts*, 18.

41. Cited in Wen, "Why Do People Believe in Ghosts?"

42. Young, "Early Days at Sweet Briar," 7.

43. Miles, *Tales from the Haunted South*, 1.

44. Miles, *Tales from the Haunted South*, 8.

45. He is buried in the Broady Family Cemetery I visited with Jasper "Eddie" Fletcher in 2005.
46. B. Page, *Annie's Trip to Grandma's*, copyright page.
47. Long, "Our Colored Folks," 8.
48. Young, "Early Days at Sweet Briar," 7.
49. "The Cleveland Alumnae Club," *The Alumnae News* [Sweet Briar College] 6, no. 2 (1936): 13.
50. "Daisy Williams' Negro Playmate Succumbs at 88," *Sweet Briar Alumnae News*, October 1954, 8.
51. As recounted to various faculty members, including a 1951 interview between Signora Hollins and Prof. G. Noble Gilpin and Jovan De Rocco. "The Signora Stories," *Sweet Briar Alumnae Magazine* 64, no. 2, (1994): 24.
52. Signora Hollins Certificate of Death, 13 July 1954, registered 15 July 1954 by Dabney M. Settle; "Daily Williams' Negro Playmate Succumbs at 88," *Sweet Briar Alumnae News*, October 1954, 8; Long, "Our Colored Folks," 7–8; Young, "Early Days."
53. *Spirit of '56: Sweet Briar College*, historic movie about Sweet Briar College, available on YouTube, https://www.youtube.com/watch?v=jlvnBwehmTs. Signora appears at minute 8:05–8:30.
54. Escott, *Slavery Remembered*, 103.
55. Whitley, "Ghost Stories," 14.
56. Whitley, "Ghost Stories," 15.
57. Sims, *You've Got a Book in You*, 24.
58. *Sweet Briar Alumnae Magazine* 72, no. 2 (2001).

 # Bibliography

Archival Sources

Amherst County Will Books. 1800–1860. Amherst County Courthouse.
Amherst County Deed Books. 1780–1900s. Amherst County Courthouse.
Amherst County Marriage Books. 1800–1900s. Amherst County Courthouse.
Depositions of John W. Daniel and others, taken on 10 May 1902, to be entered as evidence in the case of *S. R. Harding, Administrator of I.F. Williams, deceased v. Mary F. Brammer and others*. Circuit Court for the County of Amherst. Pages are hand-numbered in red, 1–797.
Unpublished letters of Elijah Fletcher, including correspondence between him and his business colleagues, ca. 1840s–1850s. Sweet Briar College Library Archives (cited as "Archives" in the text).*

*Note: There is not yet a finding aid or accession system for the documents in the Sweet Briar College Library Archives. Thus, there is no way to cite the material other than to describe it.

Published Sources

Ackerly, Mary Denham, Lula Eastman, and Jeter Parker. *Our Kin: The Genealogies of Some of the Early Families Who Made History in the Founding and Development of Bedford County, Virginia*. Lynchburg, VA: J. P. Bell Co., 1930.
The African American Experience at Fort Hill. Clemson, SC: Clemson University, n.d. https://www.clemson.edu/about/history/properties/documents/African AmericansatFH.pdf
Ames, Kenneth L. *Death in the Dining Room and Other Tales of Victorian Culture*. Philadelphia: Temple University Press, 1992.
Amherst County Heritage Book Committee. *Amherst County Virginia Heritage Book*. Vol. 2. Marceline, MO: Walsworth Publishing Co., 2004.
Anderson, James D. *The Education of Blacks in the South, 1860–1935*. Chapel Hill: University of North Carolina Press, 1988.
Auslander, Mark. "The Other Side of Paradise: Glimpsing Slavery in the University's Utopian Landscapes." *Southern Spaces*, 13 May 2010. https://southernspaces.org/2010/other-side-paradise-glimpsing-slavery-universitys-utopian-landscapes.
Avirett, James Battle. *The Old Plantation: How We Lived in Great House and Cabin before the War*. New York: F. Tennyson Neely Co., 1901.
Balaguer, Menene Gras, ed. *Chiharu Shiota: The Hand Lines*. Barcelona: Actar Publishers, 2013.
Beckert, Sven, and Katherine Stevens. *Harvard and Slavery: Seeking a Forgotten History*. Cambridge, MA: Harvard University, 2011.

Berry, Diana Ramsey. *The Price for Their Pound of Flesh: The Value of the Enslaved, from Womb to Grave, in the Building of a Nation*. Boston: Beacon Press, 2017.

Berry, Silas. *Memories of R. D. Merchant*. Self-published for the Coolwell First Baptist Church and given to President Meta-Glass in December 1935.

Billings, Warren M. *The Old Dominion in the Seventeenth Century: A Documentary History of Virginia, 1606–1700*. Published for the Omohundro Institute of Early American History and Culture. Williamsburg, VA: University of North Carolina Press, 2007.

Blackmon, Douglas. *Slavery by Another Name: The Re-enslavement of Black Americans from the Civil War to World War II*. New York: Random House, 2008.

Blakey, Michael L. "Bioarchaeology of the African Diaspora in the Americas: Its Origins and Scope." *Annual Review of Anthropology* 30 (2001): 387–422.

Blassingame, John W., ed. *Slave Testimony: Two Centuries of Letters, Speeches, Interviews, and Autobiographies*. Baton Rouge: Louisiana State University Press, 1977.

Board of Supervisors [of Amherst County, VA]. *Facts of Interest about Amherst County, Virginia*. Presented by Jamestown Exposition Company, 1907. http://www.amherstcountymuseum.org/amherst1907.html

Bromley, Anne E. "Design of UVA Memorial to Enslaved Laborers Wins Approval." *UVA Today*, 9 June 2017. https://news.virginia.edu/content/design-uva-memorial-enslaved-laborers-wins-approval.

———. "New U.VA. Residence Hall, Gibbons House, Named for Former Slave Couple." *UVA Today*, 26 March 2015. https://news.virginia.edu/content/new-uva-residence-hall-gibbons-house-named-former-slave-couple.

———. "UVA Building Named for Former Slave and Stonemason Peyton Skipwith." *UVA Today*, 13 April 2017. https://news.virginia.edu/content/uva-building-named-former-slave-and-stonemason-peyton-skipwith.

———. "Work on Memorial to Enslaved Laborers Gets Underway." *UVA Today*, 7 January 2019. https://news.virginia.edu/content/work-memorial-enslaved-laborers-gets-underway.

Brown, Alexander. *The Cabells and Their Kin: A Memorial Volume of History, Biography, and Genealogy*. Boston: Houghton Mifflin Co., 1895.

Clarke, Roger. *Ghosts: A Natural History—500 Years of Searching for Proof*. New York: St. Martin's Griffin, 2013.

Clemons, Tracy. "Students Want Larger Slave Memorial at UVA." NBC29, 16 July 2010. http://www.nbc29.com/story/12749526/students-want-larger-slave-memorial-at-uva.

Coelho, Philip R. P., and Robert A. McGuire. "Diet versus Diseases: The Anthropometrics of Slave Children." *Journal of Economic History* 60, no. 1 (2000): 232–46.

Cohen, Benjamin R. *Notes from the Ground: Science, Soil and Society in the American Countryside*. New Haven, CT: Yale University Press, 2009.

Crawford, Chas. Travis. *The Crawford Family (North Carolina and Tennessee): With Interesting Notes on the Origin and History of the "Crawford Clan."* Privately printed by the author, 1924.

Crawfurdiana, Laurus. *Memorials of That Branch of the Crawford Family Which Comprises the Descendants of John Crawford of Virginia, 1660–1883: With Notices of the Allied Families*. New York: E. O. Jenkins, 1883.

Davis, Alonzo. "Robert Johnson VCCA Fellowship." Indiegogo, 24 August 2016. https://www.indiegogo.com/projects/robert-johnson-vcca-fellowship--2#.

Davis, Bailey Fulton. *The Deeds of Amherst County, Virginia, 1761–1807 and Albemarle County, Virginia, 1748–1763*. Easley, SC: Southern Historical Press, 1979.

Dew, Charles B. *Bond of Iron: Master and Slave at Buffalo Forge*. New York: W. W. Norton & Co., 1994.

Dugdale, Anthony, J. J. Fueser, and J. Celso de Casto Alves. *Yale, Slavery and Abolition*. New Haven, CT: Yale University Press, 2001.

Duke, Maurice, ed. *Don't Carry Me Back! Narratives by Former Virginia Slaves*. Petersburg, VA: Dietz Press, 1995.

Dunn, Richard S. *A Tale of Two Plantations: Slave Life and Labor in Jamaica and Virginia*. Cambridge, MA: Harvard University Press, 2014.

Dusinberre, William. *Strategies for Survival: Recollections of Bondage in Antebellum Virginia*. Charlottesville: University of Virginia Press, 2009.

Elijah Fletcher of Nelson County, Virginia. No date or imprint, ca. 1850s.

Ely, Melvin Patrick. *Israel on the Appomattox: A Southern Experiment in Black Freedom from the 1790s through the Civil War*. New York: Alfred A. Knopf, 2004.

Escott, Paul D. *Slavery Remembered: A Record of Twentieth-Century Slave Narratives*. Chapel Hill: University of North Carolina Press, 1979.

Esposito, Sandra F. "Clifford–New Glasgow Historic District." VDHR no. 005-5042. National Register of Historic Places, NPS nomination form 10-900, OBM no. 1024-0018, 6 August 2011.

Fenrick, Jeanne. "Fifty Year College Employee Dies." *Sweet Briar Newsletter* 29, no. 13 (1956): 4.

Fine, Elizabeth C. "Developing Interpretive Plan of African American History for the Log Outbuilding at Solitude." Grant Proposal to the Virginia Foundation for the Humanities, 2015.

Fuentes, Marisa J., and Deborah Gray White. *Scarlet and Black, Vol. 1: Slavery and Dispossession in Rutgers History*. New Brunswick, NJ: Rutgers University Press.

Genovese, Eugene D. *Roll, Jordan, Roll: The World the Slaves Made*. New York: Vintage Books, 1976.

Ginsburg, Rebecca. "Escaping through a Black Landscape." In *Cabin, Quarter, Plantation: Architecture and Landscapes of North American Slavery*, edited by Clifton Ellis and Rebecca Ginsburg, 51–66. New Haven, CT: Yale University Press, 2010.

Glymph, Thavolia. "Noncombatant Military Laborers in the Civil War," *OAH Magazine of History* 26, no. 2 (2012): 25–29.

Halloran, Vivian Nun. *Exhibiting Slavery: The Caribbean Postmodern Novel as Museum*. Charlottesville: University of Virginia Press, 2009.

Hening, William Waller. *The Statutes at Large: Being a Collection of all the Laws of Virginia from the First Session of the Legislature, in the Year 1619*. 13 volumes. New York: R. & W. & G. Bartow, 1819–1823.

Houck, Peter. *Indian Island in Amherst County*. Lynchburg, VA: Warwick House Publishers, 1993.

Hurston, Zora Neale. *Dust Tracks on a Road*. New York: Harper Perennial, 1996.

Ingber, Alix, ed. *Tradition and Change: A Sweet Briar Anthology*. Sweet Briar, VA: Sweet Briar College, 2000.

Jackson, Lawrence P. *My Father's Name: A Black Virginia Family after the Civil War*. Chicago: University of Chicago Press, 2012.

Johnson, Walter. *Soul by Soul: Life Inside the Antebellum Slave Market*. Cambridge, MA: Harvard University Press, 1999.

Jordan, Ervin L., Jr. *Black Confederates and Afro-Yankees in Civil War Virginia*. Charlottesville: University Press of Virginia, 1995.

Journal of Proceedings of the Convention of the Protestant Episcopal Church of the Diocese of Virginia Which Assembled in the Borough of Norfolk on the Nineteenth Day of May, 1831. Richmond, VA: John Warrock, 1831.

Kerr-Ritchie, Jeffrey R. *Freedpeople in the Tobacco South: Virginia, 1860–1900*. Chapel Hill: University of North Carolina Press, 1999.

Kershner, Geoffrey. "Art in a Complex World: *In Sweet Remembrance* at Sweet Briar College." Howlround Theatre Commons, 8 January 2015. https://howlround.com/art-complex-world.

Kingsbury, Susan Myra, ed. *The Records of the Virginia Company of London*. Washington, DC: Government Printing Office, 1906.

Kraus, Nancy W. "The Glebe." DHR no. 005-0010. National Register of Historic Places, NPS nomination form 10-900, OBM no. 1024-0018, 7 January 2008. https://www.dhr.virginia.gov/wp-content/uploads/2018/04/005-0010_The_Glebe_2008_NRfinal.pdf

Kulikoff, Allan. *Tobacco and Slaves: The Development of Southern Cultures in the Chesapeake, 1680–1800*. Chapel Hill: University of North Carolina Press, 2012.

Lassiter, Matthew D., and Andrew B. Lewis. *The Moderates' Dilemma: Massive Resistance to School Desegregation in Virginia*. Richmond: University of Virginia Press, 1998.

Lawson, Karol. "'I have lately bought me a Plantation': A Brief History of Farming and Land Use at Sweet Briar." Exhibition introduction and checklist, Whitley Gallery, Sweet Briar Museum, March 2013 to April 2014. http://sbc.edu/museum/wp-content/uploads/sites/94/i-have-lately-bought-me-a-plantation-exhibition.pdf.

Livingston, John. "Elijah Fletcher, of Nelson County, Virginia." In *Portraits of Eminent Americans Now Living: With Biographical and Historical Memoirs of Their Lives and Actions*, vol. 3, 15–20. New York: E. Craighead, 1854.

Long, M. Dee. "Our Colored Folks." *The Alumnae News* [Sweet Briar College] 4, no. 3 (1935): 8–14.

Martin, Marcus L., Kirt von Daacke, and Meghan S. Faulkner. *President's Commission on Slavery and the University: Report to President Teresa A. Sullivan*. Charlottesville, VA: Rector and Visitors of the University of Virginia, 2018. http://vpdiversity.virginia.edu/sites/vpdiversity.virginia.edu/files/PCSU%20Report%20FINAL_July%202018.pdf.

May, Nicholas. "Holy Rebellion: Religious Assembly Laws in Antebellum South Carolina and Virginia." *American Journal of Legal History* 49, no. 3 (2007): 237–56.

McDonald, Travis. *Tusculum, Amherst County, Virginia: Restoration Field School Investigation Report*. Forest, VA: Thomas Jefferson's Poplar Forest, 2003.

McElya, Micki. *Clinging to Mammy: The Faithful Slave in Twentieth-Century America*. Cambridge, MA: Harvard University Press, 2007.

Miles, Tiya. *Tales from the Haunted South: Dark Tourism and Memories of Slavery from the Civil War Era*. Chapel Hill: University of North Carolina, 2015.

Morgan, Edmund S. *American Slavery, American Freedom*. New York: W. W. Norton & Co., 2003.

Morgan, Lynda J. *Emancipation in Virginia's Tobacco Belt, 1850–1870*. Athens: University of Georgia Press, 1992.

Morgan, Philip D. "Slaves in Piedmont Virginia, 1720–1790." *William and Mary Quarterly* 46, no. 2 (1989): 211–51.

Morgan, Philip D., Sarah Hughes, and Michael Hucles. *Don't Grieve after Me: The Black Experience in Virginia, 1619–1986*. Hampton, VA: Hampton University Press, 1986.

Nelson, Bernard H. "Confederate Slave Impressment Legislation, 1861–1865." *Journal of Negro History* 31, no. 41 (1946): 392–410.

Nelson, Lynn A. *Pharsalia: An Environmental Biography of a Southern Plantation, 1780–1880*. Athens: University of Georgia Press, 2007.

Olinger, Mary Frances and Lee Wilkins, eds. *Amherst, Virginia: From Amherst Courthouse to Town of Amherst a Pictorial History*. Amherst, VA: Central Virginia Printing, 2010.

Page, Barbara Rose. *Annie's Trip to Grandmother's House*. Illustrated by Karla Murray. Lynchburg, VA: Warwick House Publishers, 2010.

Page, Max. "Sites of Conscience: Shockoe Bottom, Manzanar, and Mountain Meadows." *Preservation Magazine*, Fall 2015. https://savingplaces.org/stories/sites-of-conscience.

Palmer, Paul C. "Servant into Slave: The Evolution of the Legal Servitude of the Negro Laborer in Colonial Virginia." *South Atlantic Quarterly* 65 (1966): 355–70.

Percy, Alfred. *The Amherst County Story*. Madison Heights, VA: Percy Press, 1961.

Rainville, Lynn. *Hidden History: African American Cemeteries in Central Virginia*. Charlottesville: University of Virginia Press, 2014.

———. "Hanover Deathscapes: Mortuary Variability in New Hampshire Cemeteries, A.D. 1770–1920." *Ethnohistory* 43, no. 3 (1999): 541–97.

———. *Roots, Restoration, Remembrances: The Sweet Briar Slave Cabin*. Self-published booklet, 2015.

Ramsey, Suzanne. "Fletcher Family Comes Full Circle, Holds Reunion at Sweet Briar." *Sweet Briar College News*, 4 August 2008.

Report of the Working Group on Slavery, Memory, and Reconciliation to The President of Georgetown University. Washington D.C.: Georgetown University, 2016.

Richards, T. Addison. "The Rice Lands of the South." *Harper's Monthly Magazine*, 19, no. 114 (1869): 721–38.

Rivanna Archaeological Services. *Beyond the Walls: An African American Burial Ground at the University of Virginia, Vol. 1 — The Cemetery "H" Expansion Project*. VDHR no. 2012-0277. Prepared for the University of Virginia, June 2013.

Roberts, Andrea. "When Does It Become Social Justice? Thoughts on Intersectional Preservation Practice." National Trust for Historic Preservation, 19 July 2017. http://forum.savingplaces.org/blogs/special-contributor/2017/07/20/when-does-it-become-social-justice-thoughts-on-intersectional-preservation-practice.

Roediger, David R. "And Die in Dixie: Funerals, Death, and Heaven in the Slave Community 1700–1865. *Massachusetts Review* 22, no. 1 (1981): 163–83.

Rountree, Helen C. *Pocahontas, Powhatan, Opechancanough: Three Indian Lives Changed by Jamestown*. Charlottesville: University of Virginia Press, 2006.

Rozelle, Maynette. "Daisy's Vision." *The Sweet Briar Magazine* 8, no. 3 (1917): 144–45.

Schwarz, Philip J. *Twice Condemned: Slaves and the Criminal Laws of Virginia, 1705–1865*. Baton Rouge: Louisiana State University Press, 1988.

Seaman, Catherine. "Amherst County: A Workshop for the Study of Social Change." *Sweet Briar College Alumnae Magazine* (Fall 1971), 5–7.

———. *Amherst County Environmental Studies*. Lynchburg, VA: J. P. Bell Co., 1973.

———. *Tuckahoe and Cohee: The Settlers and Cultures of Amherst and Nelson Counties, 1607–1807*. Sweet Briar, VA: Sweet Briar Printing Press, 1993.

Seeking Abraham: A Report of Furman University's Office of the Provost and Task Force on Slavery and Justice. Greenville, SC: Furman Task Force on Slavery & Justice, 2018.

Shackel, Paul A. *Memory in Black and White: Race, Commemoration, and the Post-Bellum Landscape*. Lanham, MD: Altamira Press, 2003.

Shefveland, Kristalyn Marie. *Anglo-Native Virginia: Trade, Conversion, and Indian Slavery in the Old Dominion, 1646–1722*. Athens: University of Georgia Press, 2016.

Silverman, Shela. "A Description of Some Rituals at Sweet Briar College." Honors thesis, Sweet Briar College, 1988.

"Sidney Fletcher." In *Obituary Record of Graduates of Yale University: Deceased from June 1900 to June 1910—Presented at the Annual Meetings of the Alumni, 1900–1910*, 1341. New Haven, CT: Tuttle, Morehouse & Taylor Co., 1910.

Sims, Elizabeth. *You've Got a Book in You*. Cincinnati, OH: Writer's Digest Books, 2013.

Stohlman, Martha. *The Story of Sweet Briar College*. Sweet Briar, VA: Alumnae Association of Sweet Briar College, 1956.

Stoll, Steven. *Larding the Lean Earth: Soil and Society in Nineteenth-Century America*. New York: Hill & Wang, 2002.

Swanson, Drew. *A Golden Weed: Tobacco and Environment in the Piedmont South*. New Haven, CT: Yale University Press, 2014.

Swarns, Rachel L. "Meet Your Cousin, the First Lady: A Family Story, Long Hidden." *New York Times*, 17 June 2012. https://www.nytimes.com/2012/06/17/us/dna-gives-new-insights-into-michelle-obamas-roots.html."

Swarns, Rachel L., and Jodi Kantor. "In First Lady's Roots, a Complicated Path from Slavery." *New York Times*, 7 October 2009. http://www.nytimes.com/2009/10/08/us/politics/08genealogy.html.

The Sweet Briar College Case, 1963–1967. Sweet Briar, VA: Sweet Briar College, 1968.

Sweet Briar To-Day and To-Morrow. Sweet Briar, VA: Sweet Briar College, 1920. Archives LD 7251.S92.S91.

Thompson, Stephen M. *Phase II Archaeological Evaluations of Site 44AB374 and Site 44AB518, Belvedere Station Development Tract, Albemarle Country, Virginia*.

VDHR no. 2006-0394. Submitted to Stonehaus Development by Rivanna Archaeological Services, July 2006.

Thornbrough, Gayle, ed. *The Diary of Calvin Fletcher, Volume 1: 1817–1838.* Indianapolis: Indiana Historical Society, 1972.

Valentine, Elizabeth Taylor. "From the Alumnae President." *The Alumnae News* [Sweet Briar College] 6, no. 1 (1936): 5.

Vaughan, Alden T. "Blacks in Virginia: A Note on the First Decade." *William and Mary Quarterly* 29, no. 3 (1972): 469–78.

Vaughan, Alden T. "The Origins Debate: Slavery and Racism in Seventeenth-Century Virginia." *Virginia Magazine of History and Biography* 97, no. 3 (1989): 311–54.

Virginia Board of Education. *Virginia School Report: Annual Report of the Superintendent of Public Instruction of the Commonwealth of Virginia with Accompanying Documents—School Year 1918–1919 and 1919–1920.* Richmond, VA: Davis Bottom, 1921.

Vlach, John M. *Back of the Big House: The Architecture of Plantation Slavery.* Chapel Hill: University of North Carolina Press, 1993.

Von Briesen, Martha, ed. *The Letters of Elijah Fletcher.* Charlottesville: University of Virginia Press, 1965.

Von Briesen, Martha, and Dorothy S. Vickery. *Sweet Briar College: Seven Decades, 1901–1971.* Richmond, VA: Whittet & Shepperson, 1972.

Walsh, Lorena S. *From Calabar to Carter's Grove: The History of a Virginia Slave Community.* Charlottesville: University of Virginia Press, 1997.

Wen, Tiffanie. "Why Do People Believe in Ghosts?" *The Atlantic,* 5 September 2014. https://www.theatlantic.com/health/archive/2014/09/why-do-people-believe-in-ghosts/379072.

Whitley, Ann Marshall. "1946–1966." *Sweet Briar Alumnae Magazine* 46, no. 1 (1976): 33–38.

———. *Daisy Williams of Sweet Briar.* Sweet Briar, VA: Sweet Briar College Museum, 2003.

———. "Ghost Stories and Mysteries of Sweet Briar." *Sweet Briar Alumnae Magazine* 79, no. 2 (2001): 10–15.

———. *Indiana Fletcher Williams of Sweet Briar.* Sweet Briar, VA: Sweet Briar College Museum, 1992.

Wiencek, Henry. *The Hairstons: An American Family in Black and White.* New York: St. Martin's Griffin, 1999.

Wilder, Craig. *Ebony and Ivy: Race, Slavery, and the Troubled History of America's Universities.* New York: Bloomsbury Press, 2013.

Williams, Daisy. *Daisy Williams: September 1867–January 1884.* Sweet Briar, VA: Sweet Briar College, 1934.

Wright, Carroll D. *The History and Growth of the United States Census.* Washington, DC: Government Printing Office, 1900.

Young, Helen F. "Early Days at Sweet Briar." *The Alumnae News* [Sweet Briar College] 5, no. 3 (1936): 6–8.

Zernike, Kate. "Slave Traders in Yale's Past Fuel Debate on Restitution." *New York Times,* 13 August 2001. https://www.nytimes.com/2001/08/13/nyregion/slave-traders-in-yale-s-past-fuel-debate-on-restitution.html.

🌿 Index

Williams, Indiana Fletcher
  annual procession to grave of, 175
  birth and childhood of, 48, 51
  characterizations of, 95, 147
  during Civil War, 93
  death of, 146, 149
  on father's death, 86
  in founder narratives, 1, 147, 155,
    175, 200
  ghost stories involving, 193,
    199–200
  grief at loss of child and husband,
    1, 139, 141–42
  health problems of, 145–46
  inheritance from father, 73, 85,
    88–91, 115
  marriage of, 98–99, 118
  mourning rituals for daughter
    Daisy, 137–38
  museum exhibitions on, 7–8

relationship with brother Lucian,
    79, 141
  as slave owner, 90, 91, 93
  Sweet Briar Plantation as
    characterized by, 91–92, 121
Williams, James Henry, 98–99, 114,
    121, 138–39, 141, 148
Williams, John J., 144
women
  education for, 147–48
  as slave owners, 90
  voting rights for, 154
Woodfolk, Mary Elizabeth, 78–79,
    143–44
Wright, John and Charlotte, 183

Y
Yale University, 184–85
Young, Helen, 196

Lightning Source UK Ltd.
Milton Keynes UK
UKHW021250280322
400720UK00006B/393